HENRY V

HENRY V

The Life of the Warrior
King & the Battle of
Agincourt 1415

Teresa Cole

AMBERLEY

First published 2015

Amberley Publishing
The Hill, Stroud
Gloucestershire, GL5 4EP

www.amberley-books.com

Copyright © Teresa Cole, 2015

The right of Teresa Cole to be identified as
the Author of this work has been asserted in
accordance with the Copyrights, Designs and
Patents Act 1988.

ISBN 978 1 4456 3679 5 (hardback)
ISBN 978 1 4456 3695 5 (ebook)

British Library Cataloguing in Publication Data.
A catalogue record for this book is available
from the British Library.

Typesetting and Origination by Amberley
Publishing.
Printed in the UK.
Map design by Thomas Bohm at User design.

CONTENTS

CAST OF CHARACTERS

The following all played a major part in the life and fortunes of Henry V. Since many have the same first name or title the following guide may help to identify who's who. They are introduced by the name most frequently referred to in the text. More information on many of them, and on the extended family of Henry V, can be found in Appendix I.

ARUNDEL, Thomas – Archbishop of Canterbury. Chancellor to Henry IV. Worked with Henry, Prince of Wales, on the Royal Council.

ARUNDEL, Richard FitzAlan, Earl of – Brother of Thomas Arundel. One of the Lords Appellant involved in a power struggle with Richard II.

ARUNDEL, Thomas FitzAlan, Earl of – Son of Richard FitzAlan. Military commander under Henry V at Harfleur.

BEAUFORT, Henry – Legitimated son of John of Gaunt. Bishop of Lincoln, Bishop of Winchester and ultimately cardinal. Uncle to Henry V and long-term Chancellor during his reign.

BEAUFORT, John – Legitimated son of John of Gaunt. Earl of Somerset. Uncle to Henry V.

BEAUFORT, Thomas – Legitimated son of John of Gaunt. Earl of

Dorset, Duke of Exeter. Uncle to Henry V and served as Admiral of England and military commander under him in his campaigns in France.

BERNARD, Count of Armagnac – Father-in-law of Charles, Duke of Orleans, and leader of the Armagnac faction in France. Later Constable of France.

BOUCICAUT, Marshal – Originally Jean Le Maigre. Marshal of France and commander of French forces at Agincourt.

BRADMORE, John – Physician who treated the serious arrow wound of Henry, Prince of Wales, after the Battle of Shrewsbury.

CHARLES VI – King of France and later father-in-law of Henry V.

CHARLES, Duke of Orleans – Nephew of Charles VI of France. Led French forces at Agincourt and was taken prisoner.

CHICHELE, Henry – Archbishop of Canterbury following Archbishop Arundel. Chancellor of England after Bishop Henry Beaufort.

CORNWAILLE, Sir John – Military commander under Henry V.

D'ALBRET, Charles – Constable of France and leader of French forces during Agincourt campaign.

DAUPHINS Louis, John and Charles – Sons of Charles VI and successively heirs to the French throne. Dauphin Charles subsequently became Charles VII.

DE GAUCORT, Raoul – French commander at the siege of Harfleur and later a prisoner of Henry V.

DE GROSMONT, Henry – First Duke of Lancaster and originator of the wealth and power of his son-in-law John of Gaunt. Great-grandfather of Henry V.

DU CHATEL, Tanneguy – Military captain of Dauphin Charles and possible murderer of John, Duke of Burgundy.

EDMUND, Earl of March – Son of Richard II's nominated heir and possible rival for the throne. Imprisoned by Henry IV. Freed by Henry V and served him loyally as military commander.

GLENDOWER, Owen – Self-proclaimed Prince of Wales who rebelled against Henry IV and tried to establish an independent Welsh principality.

HOLLAND, Sir John – Military commander under Henry V in France and leader of sea patrols in the Channel.

HUMPHREY OF LANCASTER – Duke of Gloucester. Youngest brother of Henry V.

JAMES I OF SCOTLAND – A prisoner in England from the age of eleven. Later fought in France under Henry V.

JOHN OF GAUNT – Duke of Lancaster. Third son of Edward III. Father of Henry Bolingbroke and grandfather of Henry V.

JOHN OF LANCASTER – Duke of Bedford. Third son of Henry Bolingbroke and younger brother of Henry V.

JOHN THE FEARLESS – Duke of Burgundy. Leader of Burgundian faction in France until his death. Sometime ally of Henry V.

KATHERINE OF FRANCE – Otherwise Katherine of Valois. Daughter of Charles VI of France and wife of Henry V.

MORTIMER, Edmund – Uncle and supporter of Edmund, Earl of March. Supporter of Owen Glendower. Fought Henry, Prince of Wales, in his Welsh campaigns.

OLDCASTLE, Sir John – Lollard peer and friend of Henry V who later attempted to raise a rebellion against him.

PERCY, Henry, Earl of Northumberland – Early supporter of Henry IV who later plotted to overthrow him.

PERCY, Henry, 'Hotspur' – Son of the Earl of Northumberland. Early supporter of Henry IV and justiciar to Henry, Prince of Wales. Led a rebellion against Henry IV which ended at the Battle of Shrewsbury.

PHILIPPE OF BURGUNDY – Son of John the Fearless and later ally of Henry V in France.

POPES BENEDICT, GREGORY AND JOHN – Rival popes at the time of the Western Schism in the Catholic Church.

POPE MARTIN V – Pope elected at the Council of Constance, with the aid of the English delegation, to put an end to the Western Schism.

RICHARD II – King of England overthrown by Henry Bolingbroke. During the time of Bolingbroke's exile, he held the future Henry V hostage.

SIGISMUND – Holy Roman Emperor and supporter of Henry V's claim to the throne of France.

THOMAS OF LANCASTER – Duke of Clarence. Second son of Henry Bolingbroke and brother of Henry V.

WARWICK, Thomas de Beauchamp, Earl of – One of the Lords Appellant involved in the power struggle with Richard II.

WARWICK, Richard de Beauchamp, Earl of – Son of Thomas de Beauchamp. Close friend and military commander of Henry V.

WORCESTER, Thomas Percy, Earl of – Sometime governor of Henry, Prince of Wales. Brother of the Earl of Northumberland and joined him in rebellion against Henry IV.

UMPHRAVILLE, Sir Gilbert – Military commander in France under Henry V.

YOLANDE OF ARAGON – Mother-in-law and staunch supporter of Dauphin Charles.

I

A CHILD OF SMALL IMPORTANCE
1386–1399

An astrological treatise on his birth, claimed to have been commissioned by Henry himself during his reign, states that the future King of England was born at 11.22 precisely on the morning of 16 September 1386. On the other hand, the town where he was born confidently asserts that the correct date is 9 August 1387.

The fact is that no one knows for sure, the baby being so relatively unimportant at the time that the exact date and time were not recorded. True, he was a great-grandson of King Edward III, but that was not a unique privilege. Edward had twelve legitimate children, most of whom survived to adulthood, and all but one of the sons, at least, married and had children and grandchildren of their own.

Henry's grandfather was John of Gaunt – more correctly John of Ghent, the place of his birth, but consistently rendered the way it must have been pronounced at the time. He was the third of Edward's five sons to survive infancy, and, after the eldest, the Black Prince, probably the best known, his chequered career spanning four decades of English history.

It was the old king's policy that his sons should marry for wealth and power, and John of Gaunt certainly did that. When he took a wife, at the age of nineteen, his father-in-law was Henry de Grosmont, not only Edward's close friend, most trusted captain and one of the first to be admitted to the newly founded Order of the Garter, but a man of immense wealth, with a string of titles and castles spread across the land. He had fought for Edward in Scotland and in France, and it is estimated that the ransoming of prisoners in one campaign alone brought him the staggering sum of £50,000. Not only that, but he proved, in later life, to be a man of some learning, authoring a devotional book and being involved in the foundation of Corpus Christi College, Cambridge. As a final accolade, in 1351 Edward bestowed on him the newly created title of duke, raising him from Earl of Lancaster to Duke of Lancaster. In fact the only thing in which Henry de Grosmont may be said to have failed was in the production of an heir. He had two daughters, and it was the younger one, Blanche, that John of Gaunt married in May 1359.

Half of all that wealth would have been a sizeable inheritance, but then, barely a year after Henry's death from the plague in 1361, his other daughter died childless and the whole estate fell into the hands of his son-in-law. The title of Duke of Lancaster became extinct with the death of de Grosmont, but was later bestowed again by King Edward upon his son, so, at a stroke, John of Gaunt became Duke of Lancaster, Earl of Derby, Earl of Lincoln and Earl of Leicester, with over thirty castles to his name and estates in almost every county of England. He is seen as the founder of the House of Lancaster, and was at the time the most powerful magnate in all the land, but the wealth and property that gave him that position owed more to the exploits and acumen of Henry de Grosmont than to any achievements of his own.

It is therefore not surprising that when, after two daughters, Blanche gave him a son, the boy should have been called Henry. This Henry was born in April 1367 at Bolingbroke Castle in Lincolnshire, where his mother had also been born, and thus became known as Henry of Bolingbroke. His mother died when he was a small child, possibly from yet another visitation of the plague, and within a few years his father had married again, his new wife Constance of Castile bringing him among other things a disputed claim to the throne of that Spanish kingdom.

John of Gaunt seems to have adopted his father's policy as far as the marriage of his son is concerned, but there is a story attached to the bride selected for Henry of Bolingbroke.

Mary de Bohun was, once again, one of two sisters destined to inherit the substantial wealth of the Bohuns, an ancient family stretching back to the time of William the Conqueror. Her older sister had become the wife of Thomas of Woodstock, youngest brother of John of Gaunt and considerably his junior. It is claimed that, with an eye to the inheritance, this younger brother had put pressure on Mary, then a child of ten or eleven years, to enter a convent, but this didn't at all suit John of Gaunt. On payment of a large sum of money to the king (the sort of wooing common at the time) he obtained permission for Mary to marry his son. Then, so the story goes, she was abducted from the convent, probably not too unwillingly, and the marriage took place. The exact date is unknown, but John obtained the licence to marry in June 1380 and the latest date suggested is February 1381. At the time Mary was probably twelve and Henry fourteen or fifteen.

Having achieved his aim, and in the process causing a rift with his brother that would have lasting consequences, we are told that John did not intend the young couple to cohabit until Mary had reached the age of sixteen. Whether this was out of kindness to so young a bride or from other considerations we don't know. As Shakespeare comments about the fourteen-year-old Juliet, 'Younger than she are happy mothers made,' and so it proved in this case. Whatever his father's intentions, the first child of Henry and Mary was born at Monmouth Castle in 1382. The boy, christened Edward, lived only days, and it was not then until 1386 or 1387 that Henry of Monmouth, the future Henry V, became his father's eldest son and heir.

Like his predecessor he was born at Monmouth Castle, one of his father's favourite residences, and, although little of it now remains, it was unlikely to be the 'cold and stony' place described by one writer. The castle had been greatly improved by Henry de Grosmont, and, given the wealth and prestige of the House of Lancaster, it would surely have been filled with all the comfort and luxury available to a noble household of the time. In late summer, looking out over the windings of the rivers Wye and Monnow, it was no doubt a very pleasant place to be born.

We are told that Bolingbroke was not present in the castle when his son was born. One account suggests he was busy about the royal court, while local tradition declares that he was hunting in the nearby Forest of Dean, a likely enough pastime given that hunting was both a pleasure and a necessity in providing food for a household and garrison of some scores of people. At the time he was also in effective control of all the estates of John of Gaunt, who had departed for Castile in July 1386 in a fruitless campaign to claim the throne of that country. It is likely, then, that the twenty-year-old Henry had plenty to occupy his mind, quite apart from the birth of a son.

Very little is known about the early life of Henry of Monmouth. What we have is largely gleaned from the accounts kept by the various households in which he lived. We are told that he was a small, weak baby, and the accounts show that he had a nurse, one Joan Waryn, for whom he later made provision when he was king. As was usual for noble households of the time, he would have moved around the country from estate to estate, from castle to castle, regularly during his childhood.

Over the next few years three brothers, Thomas, John and Humphrey, were added to the family, and then two sisters, Blanche and Phillipa. It is probable that Mary de Bohun was a more constant presence in her son's life than his father, who was frequently away at court, and indeed at one point spent more than a year on a leisurely journey through Europe and a pilgrimage to the Holy Land. She would, however, have been almost constantly pregnant or recovering from childbirth during most of this time, and the first big change in young Henry's life came with the arrival of her last daughter, on 4 June 1394, for she died in childbirth. She would have been around twenty-five years of age and her eldest son was seven.

Annual pregnancies and early death in childbirth were not at all unusual at the time, and a contemporary would no doubt have said that Mary had done her duty in providing her husband with a clutch of fine, healthy sons and marriageable daughters. Still, the loss would have been felt by the boys, at least, who would have been old enough to have memories of her, and this may be one reason for the generally close, supportive relationship between the brothers that was evident during almost the whole of Henry's life.

By this time, too, his education would have been well underway. As a boy of noble birth he would have begun learning the arts of war almost from the cradle. Riding, swordsmanship, the use of a lance in the joust; these, together with hunting and hawking, had formed the bedrock of a noble education for generations. Times were changing, however. This was the high point of the ideal of chivalry, and the 'parfit gentil knight' was not only expected to have courage and honour and skill at arms, but also to appreciate the gentler arts of literature and music.

We know Henry was reading from an early age. It is quite likely that his mother taught him, or possibly a governess or a priest attached to the household. Not only English but French and Latin, too, would have been part of his curriculum, and music was also a necessary accomplishment, and one much favoured by both his parents. So we read of harp strings and grammar books being bought for the boy, along with clothes, shoes and a scabbard for his sword.

The year after his mother's death Henry suffered an illness serious enough to merit the summoning of a doctor from London to visit the boy at Leicester. Whatever the illness was he seems to have made a complete recovery, and nor is there any further mention of smallness or weakness. Indeed, he was apparently a typical product of his age, revelling in hunting and outdoor activities of all kinds. It is noted that he attended his first tournament at around ten years of age.

Fighting and book learning were, however, only a part of the education of a noble boy. For the acquisition of 'courtesy' and 'honourable learning' and knightly lore, he would be expected to enter the household of a great magnate, first as a page and later a squire, perhaps ending as a knight himself. His duties would include waiting at table, cleaning armour, running errands and assisting in arming a knight for battle or tournament, as well as learning all the niceties of courtly manners. It is likely that Henry began such service the year after his mother's death, possibly in the household of his grandfather, John of Gaunt, the mightiest of the magnates. It is equally possible, however, that he may have had some place in the king's household, even before the momentous events that were to shape his destiny.

The seeds of that destiny had been sown some time before, in fact at around the time of Henry's birth, so we must go back a little to trace the origins of the conflict that would pitch young Henry of Monmouth into the very forefront of English history.

At the time of Henry's birth the reigning monarch was King Richard II. He was a grandson of Edward III, and therefore a cousin to Henry Bolingbroke and his exact contemporary. He had become king at the age of ten, his own father having died the year before, and, being underage, a council had been appointed to administer the realm for him. There were many at the time who accused John of Gaunt of coveting the throne for himself and his son, but his behaviour seems to have been exemplary. Though he was not part of the ruling council, he still had considerable influence behind the scenes, but all his efforts seem to have been aimed at supporting rather than undermining the young monarch.

Contemporaries they may have been, but there seems little similarity in character between Richard and his cousin Henry Bolingbroke. There is no doubting the young king's courage. At the age of fourteen he had faced down an angry mob at the time of the Peasant's Revolt and by his personal leadership averted a likely massacre. As to his wisdom and steadiness of character, however, there are considerable question marks. Indeed, later in his reign his mood swings are recorded as so sudden and extravagant that, if true, he would almost certainly today be diagnosed as bipolar.

Some suggest that his success in dealing with the Peasant's Revolt may have inflated the king's opinion of himself, and it is certain that from then on there is a record of discord between himself, his governing council and his parliament. He was growing up, however, and beginning to find the restraints imposed on him irksome, and there was such a mixture of interests and ambitions within the restraining bodies that harmony was always unlikely. The personal badge he chose for himself was a white hart, usually shown with a golden chain around its neck. The chain is said by some to have been insisted on by the king to represent his resentment of these restraints on his freedom of action.

Two particular counsellors had been appointed to guide the king. One, the Earl of Arundel, he is reputed to have detested from the start. The other was Michael de la Pole, son of a wealthy wool merchant and a former retainer of John of Gaunt. He had already given twenty years of loyal service to Edward III, and soon won the young king's trust and friendship, more especially, perhaps, as he negotiated his marriage in 1382 to Anne of Bohemia. This marriage, unusually for the time, seems to have been an entirely happy one, its only failure being the lack of a child and heir for the king.

By 1386 the tensions between the king and those who sought to control him had resolved into two principle areas. First was the conduct of the war with France. This had been rumbling on intermittently for the king's entire lifetime, and from time to time drew in other adversaries such as Scotland, Flanders and Castile. Recent campaigns had been expensive and generally disastrous, and the blame for this was laid at the feet of the king's chief counsellor, de la Pole. The country, the commons and most of the lords wanted to continue the fight with increased vigour, dreaming of another Crécy or Poitiers. The king's instinct, backed by de la Pole, was for peace. For some time John of Gaunt held a measure of balance between the two parties. He favoured the continuance of the war, but particularly had his eyes on the throne of Castile, at the time an ally of France. His stock with the king fell ever lower, however, until, as a relief to both, an expedition to Castile was sanctioned in 1386, and in July of that year he left the country, not to return for another three years.

The second area of contention between Richard and his parliament was the king's extravagance and generosity to his friends. Time and again demands were made that the king should 'live of his own' (on the profits from his own estates), without taxing the people, and gifts of money, land and titles were condemned. Two particular 'favourites' of the king were singled out for criticism. One, Robert de Vere, Earl of Oxford, came from an ancient family and had been a childhood friend of the king. The other was de la Pole, now raised to the title of Earl of Suffolk. No doubt greed, jealousy and envy played their part in this tension, but the king's own actions did little to help. In the very month the commons were petitioning that he make no further gifts and submit his accounts to a parliamentary commission, he appointed de Vere Marquis of Dublin with powers over all the Irish lands subject to the king's writ, together with an enormous grant of money for their upkeep.

In the autumn of 1386 these two bones of contention came together with deadly results. Under very real threat of a French invasion, Parliament demanded the dismissal of de la Pole from his office of Chancellor. When Richard refused, a further demand was made that he come in person to Parliament to dismiss him. The instigators of this move were the king's youngest uncle, Thomas of Woodstock (ironically raised to the title of Duke of Gloucester on the same occasion de la Pole received his peerage), and Richard's hated counsellor the Earl of Arundel. Both were bitter enemies of de la Pole and jealous of his position with the king. At the same time Gloucester took the opportunity of reminding both the king and Parliament of the steps that had been taken to depose King Edward II barely sixty years before.

Richard agreed to receive a deputation from Parliament, no doubt expecting a selection of knights, lords and burgesses. Instead Gloucester came himself, along with Arundel's brother Thomas, Bishop of Ely. Again veiled threats were made that there was a precedent for deposing an unsatisfactory king, and in the light of this Richard agreed to remove his friend and Chancellor from office. De la Pole was promptly put on trial before Parliament accused of corruption and subverting the law, and, despite evidence to the contrary, was convicted and imprisoned.

Pressing home their advantage, Parliament next declared that a council should be formed to supervise the king and control his revenue and appointments for a period of one year. Such a council might have brought about much-needed reform in the administration, but since its two chief members were Gloucester and Arundel it was never likely to succeed. In defiance of this Richard immediately released de la Pole from prison, and spent the spring of 1387 touring the Midlands and the north attempting to raise support for himself. He consulted the chief judges of the day, who gave it as their opinion (whether freely or not is another matter) that, among other things, the appointment of the council was an infringement of the royal prerogative of the king, that the king alone had the right to appoint and remove ministers, and that those responsible for the recent attacks on the king and his ancient rights were traitors.

Matters came to a head in November 1387. Richard returned to London accompanied by a group of his close supporters, including de la Pole, de Vere, the Archbishop of York, Chief Justice of the King's Bench Robert Tresillian and Richard's former tutor Sir Simon Burley. He had, however, little in the way of armed support.

Gloucester and Arundel had, meanwhile, recruited others to their cause. On 14 November a formal 'appeal' or accusation of treason was made against five leading friends of the king, with the demand that they be arrested and put on trial before Parliament. Those making this accusation, the 'appellant lords' as they were then called, were Gloucester, Arundel and the Earl of Warwick. A little later they were joined by two younger men, barely into their twenties, Thomas Mowbray, Earl of Nottingham, and Henry Bolingbroke, now titled Earl of Derby.

With little option but to obey, Richard agreed to their demands but fixed the date of the parliament for 3 February 1388, thereby buying some time for the accused. De la Pole fled to the Continent, the archbishop to his diocese, and de Vere, apparently with the king's blessing, rode to Cheshire, Richard's most loyal county, to raise an army for the king.

On 20 December, however, hastening southward with some 4,000 men, de Vere found the crossing of the Thames at Radcot Bridge strongly held against him by the forces of Henry Bolingbroke, and while he hesitated Gloucester's army appeared on his other side. It was a hopeless position and, taking advantage of a foggy winter's day, de Vere managed to slip away and escape to the Continent, from which he never returned.

Richard, who had retreated to the Tower, was visited there by the Lords Appellant and, again under threat of deposition, was forced to agree to all their demands. The so-called Merciless Parliament met in February, and, despite the absence of all but one of the accused, the Appellants, led by Gloucester, recited an increased list of offences against them. All were then found guilty. The archbishop, as a clergyman, was protected from the death penalty, but the others were condemned and the sentences carried out on Nicholas Bembre, a former mayor of London, and Chief Justice Tresillian, who was found in hiding soon after the trial.

Not content with this, further offenders were purged from the king's household, including his old tutor Burley, who, to the consternation of many, including Henry Bolingbroke, was put to death in May 1388. As a final act, the parliament voted the sum of £20,000 to be divided between the five Lords Appellant in recognition of their good services, and all, both lords and commons, swore a new oath of loyalty to the king.

This might seem an extraordinary act on the part of men who had just done all they could to strip him of power and destroy his friends, but, publicly at least, throughout the whole episode they had been at pains to stress the innocence of the king. It was his friends and counsellors who had led him into error and caused the conflict, so the charges said, and these friends had now paid the price. There was no more talk of deposition. The king was the king still – but the self-appointed council continued to rule in his name.

This episode is the first time we hear of any involvement of Henry Bolingbroke in the politics of the time, and it is hard to estimate how far he sympathised with the originators of the action. He was very young, and for the first time representing the interests of the House of Lancaster without any guidance from his formidable father. We know he protested at the condemnation of Burley, and he may have done on other occasions. Certainly when Gloucester was trailing the idea of deposing the king, we might expect Henry to point out that his father came higher in the line of succession than Gloucester, being some fifteen years his senior. All in all it was an interesting lesson in the possible ways of dealing with an unsatisfactory king, but it may well be that it was with a sense of relief that Henry returned to his young family when it was all over.

The final act came abruptly on 3 May 1389. The story goes that, at a council meeting, Richard suddenly demanded of Gloucester, 'How old am I?' When the answer came that he was twenty-three, he then declared that he must, therefore, be old enough to take up his proper role in governing the country. It could have been an explosive moment, but wasn't. Lessons had been learned all round. When the council quietly resigned their duties, the king chose two elder statesmen who had served his grandfather to be Chancellor and Treasurer, and when, later that year, John of Gaunt returned, richer but crownless, from Spain, the transfer of power was complete.

Thereafter John of Gaunt became the king's most loyal supporter and the two became closer than they had ever been, particularly when, in 1396, Richard approved Gaunt's marriage to Katherine Swynford, his long-time mistress. A little later he legitimated the four children of that union, bestowing an earldom on the oldest, John Beaufort.

In the meantime the Lords Appellant had deemed it better to melt away, Warwick to his estates, Arundel to plan a crusade and Henry Bolingbroke and Gloucester to aid the Teutonic knights at the siege of Vilnius in Prussia. Bolingbroke was out of the country for much of the next four years, travelling in Europe and making a slow pilgrimage to the Holy Land, and in that time it seemed that all had been forgiven and forgotten between the king and his rebellious lords.

One small spark shows that this was not so. In 1394 Richard's beloved wife, Anne, died. Arundel came late to her funeral and, in what might have been a deliberate insult, asked leave of the king to depart before it was over as he had business to attend to. Richard's fury erupted in violence, striking the earl across the face with the verger's wand and imprisoning him in the Tower for some weeks. A further clue to the king's mental state might be that he had the palace at Sheen, where he had lived with his wife, razed to the ground soon after her death.

Nothing more came of this incident save that Arundel and Gloucester began to draw together again. It was to be another few years before Richard showed his hand against his former enemies and before then he had achieved some measure of success and even popularity. Settlements were made with France and Scotland to bring an end to expensive wars, and even in Ireland there was an improvement in relations following a personal expedition by the king.

As part of the settlement with France, Richard had married the French king's seven-year-old daughter Isabelle. This was not the most appropriate match for a king without an heir. Some romantics have suggested it was because he did not want to replace his newly dead queen, but it is likely that diplomacy played a larger part. Personal feelings very rarely came into such matters. Among those speaking loudest against the marriage, and against many other acts of the king, were Gloucester and Arundel. They were about to experience Richard's revenge.

These two, together with Warwick and other magnates, found themselves invited to a state banquet. Gloucester and Arundel stayed away, the former pleading illness, but Warwick attended, and after an apparently pleasant evening found himself imprisoned in the Tower. The next day Arundel was persuaded by his brother, now Archbishop of Canterbury, to surrender himself to the king, who, he was assured, meant him no harm. He was immediately imprisoned at Carisbroke Castle on the Isle of Wight, and for his services the archbishop was exiled for life. Gloucester was arrested by the king himself, and, on pleading for mercy, was told he would have just the same amount of mercy as he had shown to Burley. His prison was even further afield, in Calais, with Thomas Mowbray as his gaoler.

The king claimed to have discovered a new plot against himself. No evidence of such a plot has ever been found, and the game is rather given away by the fact that, when it came to a trial, he chose to play the appellants' own trick against them. Eight young men were found, including the newly legitimated John Beaufort, now Earl of Somerset, to accuse these three of treason – not a new treason but the acts of 1387/88, apparently pardoned long ago.

Gloucester never made it to his trial. A confession of treason was forced from him by Mowbray, and as soon as it was written and delivered to a judge he was murdered. Arundel was tried before Parliament at the end of September 1397. He remained defiant to the end, was found guilty and beheaded – accompanied to the block by an armed guard led by Thomas Mowbray. When his turn came Warwick broke down completely, confessed to everything put to him and escaped with his life. He was first ordered to be exiled on the Isle of Man for life, but later was returned to the Tower.

The new Lords Appellant were all rewarded with titles by the king, Mowbray becoming Duke of Norfolk. Henry Bolingbroke, too, was honoured, acquiring the title Duke of Hereford. His father, as High Steward, had both opened the trial and announced the sentences, and it seemed that the House of Lancaster was now as closely bound to the king as it could be.

Not so. Less than six months had passed before the next act in the drama. In January 1398 Henry Bolingbroke declared before Parliament that Mowbray had made treasonable statements to him and tried to draw him into a conspiracy against the king. The statements amounted to the fact that, as the last remaining Lords Appellant of 1388, they were likely to be the next victims of Richard's vengeance.

Mowbray immediately denied any wrongdoing. A committee of Parliament was appointed to investigate and to try and produce a settlement of the dispute. When this did not happen, a date was fixed for a trial by battle as was the custom at the time. On 16 September 1398 lists were prepared at Coventry. All was in readiness when abruptly Richard intervened. Instead of a trial he banished Mowbray for life. Bolingbroke, too, was exiled for ten years, though this was later reduced to six.

Why he did this remains a mystery. Some have suspected he didn't want the issue proved, that he didn't want to lose either, or possibly that he had determined to lose both. Many of his actions at this time seem eccentric, tyrannical and even against his own best interests.

One notable figure who seems to have made no protest at all was John of Gaunt. Maybe he kept quiet out of indebtedness to the king over his marriage and the legitimation of his children. It is equally possible, though, that he didn't know his own son's mind and feared he really might have had thoughts of treachery.

As his father's fortunes changed, so too did those of young Henry of Monmouth, for the first time drawn into the affairs of his elders. Wherever he might have been before, he was now placed in the king's household as a hostage for the good behaviour of his family. It was, by all accounts, a very benevolent captivity. Richard treated the boy well, encouraged him in all his endeavours, and spent far more time with him than his father ever had. In return it seems likely that a real affection sprang up between the twelve-year-old and his captor.

In the summer of the same year a crisis had arisen in Ireland. The Irish chiefs, pacified and reconciled by the king's visit just a few years before, now rose again in revolt. Worse than that, the Earl of March, Richard's Lord Lieutenant in Ireland and also the nominated heir of the childless king, was killed in battle. A new campaign was needed and preparations began almost at once.

Then in February 1399 John of Gaunt died. Many thought that Henry Bolingbroke would now be pardoned and brought home from his exile in Paris to enter into his inheritance. He had been promised he would not be disinherited and would be allowed to appoint agents to receive and manage any property that might fall due to him. Now, however, it was announced that the letters patent granting these rights had been made 'by inadvertence and without suitable advice', that they were null and void, and that consequently all the vast estates of John of Gaunt would fall instead into the hands of the king. Almost as a side issue, Henry's exile was increased to a lifetime banishment.

Seemingly oblivious to the shockwaves echoing around his nobility at this blatant theft, Richard calmly continued his preparations for the Irish campaign, and at the end of May departed for Ireland. He took with him not only a strong force of men, but also the majority of the English nobility, his treasure, Crown jewels and regalia – so much that strange rumours began to circulate in England that he had no intention of returning. Two absentees from this campaign were the Earl of Northumberland, Henry Percy, and his son, also Henry but named Hotspur by the Scots after the speed with which he charged into battle. They sent word to the king that troubles on the Scottish border prevented them from leaving their northern stronghold, and were allowed to remain at home.

Also in the king's train in Ireland was Henry of Monmouth. Although still, probably, a surety for his father's behaviour, he seems to have enjoyed himself on campaign, and was in fact knighted by the king. But while Richard vainly sought a decisive meeting with the rebels, things were moving at home.

Scarcely had the king arrived in Ireland than Henry Bolingbroke set out from Paris, accompanied by Thomas Arundel, former Archbishop of Canterbury, and his nephew the son of the late Earl of Arundel. Together with a small company they landed at Ravenspur on the Humber and made their way to Pontefract Castle, a stronghold of the House of Lancaster. Within a matter of days Northumberland and his son, along with the Earl of Westmoreland and most of the north of England, had rallied to him. He swore he had come only to claim his inheritance, but as they set out southwards, urgent messages were sent from London to Ireland, and the Duke of York, who had been left in charge in England, together with most of the king's council, fled westward.

By the time the messages reached the king in Ireland Henry was well set. Then it seemed there were not enough boats to transport Richard's army, and he was advised, foolishly or possibly treacherously, to split his force, sending half to north Wales while he accompanied the other half to the south.

When he landed at Milford Haven towards the end of July it was probably too late even then to turn back the Lancastrian tide. News that the Duke of York had submitted affected the king badly. No longer knowing who he could trust, he abandoned his force in the south, though some accounts say these had already started to disperse following treachery on the part of their leaders. Instead he struck out for his most loyal county of Cheshire in the north. That he chose the coastal route may suggest he already realised he might have to flee for his life, but in any case Henry was there ahead of him.

The Earl of Salisbury had raised a force for the king in Cheshire, but hearing rumours that Richard was already dead, he allowed these to disband and withdrew to Conway Castle, leaving Chester and all the surrounding area to be occupied by Henry's forces without even a fight. On 11 August Richard joined him at Conway.

From here we have two different accounts of what followed. According to the official Lancastrian version, Richard was visited at Conway by the Earl of Northumberland and Archbishop Arundel. After hearing what they had to say he agreed to abdicate, asking only that his life should be spared and that he should be given an honourable livelihood. He then accompanied them to Chester to meet Henry, and thence to London where he was lodged in the Tower.

The other version, from those more sympathetic to Richard, is rather different. Visited by Northumberland and the Archbishop, he was told that Henry wanted only his inheritance and that his claim should be submitted to a full Parliament. Northumberland then swore on the Holy Sacrament – the most sacred of all oaths

– that no harm should come to the king and that he would retain his full title and power. No doubt with a strong sense of déjà vu, Richard accepted, set out with them towards Chester and was immediately ambushed by Northumberland's men and taken prisoner.

Whichever version is correct, the outcome was the same. When the cousins arrived in London, Richard was escorted to the Tower, while Henry Bolingbroke took up residence in the Palace of Westminster.

AN EDUCATION IN WARFARE
1399–1408

It would be interesting to know exactly when on his journey Henry Bolingbroke decided to try for the crown. Some accounts suggest that it was Archbishop Arundel and his nephew, determined to avenge brother and father, who pushed him towards the throne. Certainly at his meeting with the northern lords in Doncaster he was still denying any such ambition, but by the time he came face to face with Richard at Chester he must have known there was no going back. They had danced this dance before, little more than a decade ago, and Henry could be sure that, whatever his position then, he had no hope of escaping this time with his head still on his shoulders as long as Richard was king.

A parliament had been summoned in Richard's name for 30 September. Again the official account says that Richard's abdication was read to them and accepted and the throne declared vacant. It also says he had been visited by Northumberland, Arundel and Bolingbroke in the Tower and signed this document cheerfully, handing his signet ring to Henry as a nomination that he should replace him as king. Other accounts, some by eyewitnesses, tell a different story – of Richard raging against his captivity, of his being promised a chance to put his case before a full parliament, and later of his gloomy recitation of the many earlier kings who had been 'exiled, slain, destroyed or ruined' by their countrymen. It is, no doubt, this account which provided Shakespeare with the inspiration for his famous 'deaths of kings' speech in the play *Richard II*.

And what of Henry of Monmouth while all this was happening? He had been left behind in Ireland at Trim Castle. It is significant that, if he was supposed to be a hostage for his father, there was never any attempt to use him as such. No threats were made, no harm ever came to him. We have, indeed, one rather fanciful record of a conversation when Richard informed the boy of his father's actions. On Henry's protesting his innocence of any involvement, Richard is supposed to have replied, 'There is one Henry that will do me much harm, but I know that you are not he.'

In early September Bolingbroke sent for his son. Instead of returning to his father, however, Henry is reported to have gone to Richard instead, and only at his insistence to have obeyed his father's command and joined him. It was, no doubt, a confusing time of divided loyalties for a thirteen-year-old.

It was by now clear to all that Bolingbroke was going to be king. The difficulty was in how to frame his claim to such an elevation. That Parliament was not entirely happy with the story of Richard's abdication may be seen in the fact that, even after that had been accepted, they then proceeded to discuss a long list of thirty-three articles detailing Richard's crimes and defects before agreeing that he be deprived of the throne. Bolingbroke would need more than a signet ring to put him in his place.

The precedent most closely followed by all concerned was that of the deposition of Richard's great-grandfather, Edward II, some seventy years before. Then, though, there was an obvious choice of an heir, his son Edward III. Now Bolingbroke was no such automatic choice. By strict hereditary principles Richard's heir should have been the seven-year-old Earl of March, but his name is barely mentioned. There was some attempt to create or resurrect a strange theory that Edward I was not the eldest son of his father, Henry III. Then, by disinheriting the previous four kings, Bolingbroke could claim descent through his mother from another son, Edmund of Lancaster. This tale was apparently examined and discounted in the weeks before Parliament sat.

There was a strong reluctance to claim the throne by election through Parliament, since what Parliament made it could later unmake. Similarly, right of conquest might give ideas to other mighty magnates that they could do the same. In the end the claim of Bolingbroke to become Henry IV was a cobbled-together version of all three possibilities, which has been argued over by lawyers and parliamentarians ever since.

On 30 September 1399, when the throne was declared vacant, he stepped forward to claim it, 'by the right blood coming from King Henry III, and through that right that God of his grace hath sent me, with the help of my kin and my friends'. Despite the peculiarity of this claim it was immediately accepted by Parliament and the populace, the assembly was dissolved and a new parliament announced for 6 October in the name of King Henry IV.

Exactly one year from the day he departed into exile, on 13 October, the feast day of St Edward the Confessor, Henry was crowned with full ceremonial in Westminster Abbey. Throughout the long ceremony the Sword of Justice was carried by his eldest son, Henry of Monmouth. As one writer has commented, this must have taught the boy the useful early lesson that justice can be a very heavy burden.

Now, however, young Henry was to discover the benefits involved in being a king's son. In short time he became Prince of Wales, Duke of Cornwall, Earl of Chester, Duke of Aquitaine and Duke of Lancaster. It was proposed, and accepted by Parliament, that he be acknowledged as lawful heir of his father, and he knelt to receive a coronet, ring and rod as signs of his authority. Nor were these empty titles. Despite his tender years, it was made immediately apparent that he would be expected to live off the estates transferred to him, to maintain his own household and to take a full part in the administration of both household and estates.

Of the various territories now coming under his sway, Lancaster and Cornwall would be the most productive, Wales and Chester the most challenging. Cheshire had been a centre of support for Richard and there was little sign as yet that the people of that county had transferred their loyalties to a new regime, while in Wales he would have to balance the sensitivities of the Welsh against the egos of powerful English lords holding lands along the border.

Even before he took up his duties, however, one decision had to be made. In late October the commons proposed that Richard be put on trial for his alleged misdeeds. Instead, a special meeting of the lords was held at which each in turn was asked what should be done with the former king. Fifty-eight individual names are recorded as agreeing to the proposal that he should be imprisoned in some secret place where no rescue could be attempted, and that none who had previously served him should have access to him. Although some accounts declare he was not there, it appears the prince's name is enrolled with the rest.

On 27 October this decision was announced to the commons

and approved. Two days later Richard was taken from the Tower and, by various stages, to imprisonment in Pontefract Castle in the heart of Lancastrian territory.

If Henry IV thought he could now rest easy with the crown on his head, he was soon to be disillusioned. His overwhelming acclamation by Parliament and people may have misled him into leniency to those formerly close to his predecessor. As one writer has noted, a more ruthless operator would have had their heads off at once, along with that of the young Earl of March. Instead they were merely demoted, losing the titles Richard had heaped on them in 1397. In return, four of them, including Richard's half-brother the Earl of Huntingdon and his nephew the Earl of Kent, hatched a plot to seize the king and his heir at the Epiphany feast at Windsor in January 1400.

No doubt they thought an early strike would have the best chance of unseating a new king and returning Richard to the throne, but they had sadly misjudged the mood of the country. The plot was betrayed, probably by one of the conspirators, Edward, Earl of Rutland, eldest son of the Duke of York. The king, warned with hours to spare, escaped with his family to the safety of London, raised an army and set out after the plotters. It seems he need hardly have bothered. One group containing the earls of Kent and Salisbury fled westward as far as Cirencester and, failing to raise any support, were dragged from the sanctity of the abbey and beheaded by an angry mob. The Lord Despenser, brother-in-law of Rutland, managed to reach Cardiff, took ship for the Continent but was instead landed at Bristol, and there suffered the same fate. The other chief conspirator, the Earl of Huntingdon, uncle of Kent, who had remained in London, tried to escape eastwards, only to be put to death in the same way at Pleshey Castle in Essex.

Within a month Richard himself was dead, officially having 'pined to death' and refused food. Unofficially it seems that Henry had learned a hard lesson and taken steps accordingly. The body was brought to London and exposed to public view, though only part of the face was visible, the rest of coffin being sealed in lead. After lying in state in St Paul's, it was handed over to be buried obscurely at the Dominican priory of King's Langley in Hertfordshire.

We have no way of knowing if the young Prince of Wales truly believed the official story. What we do know is that one of his first acts when he became king was to have the body of Richard exhumed and reburied with all due state in Westminster Abbey in the tomb designed for him and where his wife already lay.

It was to be in Scotland rather than Wales that Prince Henry would get his first military experience. At the time of the accession of Henry IV, the Scots had such problems at home that very little was expressed in the way of approval or disapproval. With a weak and incompetent king, and a power struggle between his son the Duke of Rothesay and his brother the Duke of Albany, there was little mind to renew ancient hostilities with England. By the summer of 1400, however, Henry had determined on a strong raid into Scotland to try and force the Scottish king to do him homage. A renewed threat from France and the history of alliances between those two countries was one reason for this. Another was the urging of a disaffected Scottish lord, George Dunbar, whose bid to have his daughter married to Rothesay had been trumped by the Earl of Douglas, leading him to transfer allegiance to Henry. A successful campaign would also enhance the new king's prestige at home, and maybe unite the country behind him.

It was not a successful campaign. Money was short and the

Scots refused to fight, shutting themselves up in impregnable strongholds. Henry crossed the border in mid-August, and after two weeks of fruitless sabre rattling the English army was in Newcastle again on the 29th of that month, with only a vague promise of future negotiations to show for their efforts, and having stirred up troubles on the border that would be a drain on men and resources for years to come.

Prince Henry had accompanied his father to Scotland, but it was on their way back to London that they received news which was to concern him and his new responsibilities much more closely. On 16 September Owen Glendower, a little-known Welshman, had proclaimed himself Prince of Wales, and set off a violent revolt against the English that was to spread throughout the whole of that country.

This Glendower was not some wild Welsh chieftain but a comfortably middle-aged landed gentleman with extensive estates and manor houses near Oswestry. What stirred him now to take up arms against England has never been fully explained, but its origins seem to lie in the landholding arrangements along the border between Wales and England.

For centuries the border counties, from Flint in the north to Monmouthshire in the south, had been held by powerful English lords, the so-called Marcher lords. The Mortimers, Fitzalans and Talbots were prominent among them, and, in general, as long as they kept the border quiet, they had remarkable freedom to do as they wished with the lands under their sway. Opportunities for misunderstanding, insult and oppression were legion, and raids back and forth across the borders were frequent occurrences.

One of these lords, Lord Grey of Ruthin, had a land dispute with Glendower. This had been submitted to the new king for settlement, and with Grey being a member of Henry's council, the decision had gone his way. Glendower, feeling 'his pleas slighted and his oaths scorned', had taken some revenge on the cattle and crops of his opponent. Then it appeared that Grey had delayed a summons for Glendower to supply men for the Scottish campaign, and when they had not appeared on time had denounced him as a traitor.

These and similar slights seem to have produced the spark to set alight a rebellion that was to fill the next ten years of Prince Henry's life, and which would give him the soundest of educations in all the arts of war.

Initially at least it seemed a very minor problem. Henry IV diverted his army from Northampton to north Wales, but the immediate crisis was over before he even got there, stamped out by local forces from Shropshire and Herefordshire. Nevertheless he carried out a swift punitive raid through all the northern counties of Wales, while Glendower and his supporters retreated to the mountains. This was followed by confiscation of all the estates of the rebels which were then given to Henry's half-brother, John Beaufort, Earl of Somerset.

This was the situation inherited by the young Prince of Wales when he took up his duties towards the end of 1400. In theory he was overlord of all the Welsh and in supreme command of all actions against the rebels. In practice, the fourteen-year-old had a governor, Hugh le Despenser, appointed by his father to guide him, and Henry Percy, Hotspur, son of the Earl of Northumberland, as justiciar to enforce the royal will. His council was also appointed by the king, and it seems likely that, at least at first, overall policy would have been dictated from Westminster, but it is clear from letters between the two that Prince Henry took a full part in council meetings and decisions. With Hotspur some twenty years his senior and one of the most famous soldiers in England, it also seems likely that the justiciar became something of a mentor to the boy. No doubt he could have done a lot worse than model himself on a man whose reputation for valour and uprightness was jealously guarded, even after his death.

The prince's headquarters were established at Chester, which should have been the heart of his own territory and a source of support and finance for him. Cheshire had been Richard's own county, however, and Wales, too, had strongly favoured him, and this planting of the royal household here may have been intended to discourage the men of Cheshire from joining those in Wales in open revolt against the English king. Glendower was quiet for now, apart from the usual ongoing border-raiding activities, but it was reported that the Welsh in England, even students at Oxford and Cambridge, were all being drawn homeward in his support.

On 1 April 1401 hostilities were resumed. It was Good Friday, and while all the garrison of Conway Castle were at prayers, the castle was taken over by the rebels, led by the Tudor brothers, Rhys and William. This was not only a strategic loss but a psychological blow to the English and immediate steps were taken to recover the castle. Prince Henry himself, along with Hotspur, took part in the four-week siege that led to its surrender on 28 May, but as a sign of the king's displeasure Hotspur was stripped of his lordship of Conway and of nearby Anglesey.

The rebellion was spreading, however, through north and west Wales and down towards the south. Despite having informed his son that Wales was his responsibility, King Henry turned out himself in September 1401. The two raided as far as Aberystwyth and Harlech with the same result as the previous year. Glendower gave before them, removing into the hills, and flowed back after they had gone, to reoccupy the land once again.

This policy of raid and withdraw may have been the only option open at the time, with Henry permanently short of money and Parliament unsympathetic to raising funds for a Welsh campaign. Pitched battles, though, were a rarity in the Middle Ages. Certainly it was not in Glendower's interests to face the English king in the field, where he was outweighed in men and arms and armour. His advantages of speed, mobility and knowledge of terrain were, then as now, best served by a guerrilla campaign.

There is some evidence that Hotspur was in touch with Glendower at this time and seeking to broker an end to the hostilities. The mood of Parliament was against this, however, and nothing came of it. Instead, from an English point of view the situation worsened.

Throughout 1402 troubles for the king seemed to flow in like Atlantic storms, one after another to break over his head. In April Lord Grey of Ruthin, originator of the troubles, was taken by Glendower and held captive for a large ransom. Soon after, Hotspur resigned from Wales saying he was needed more in his own northern lands to hold back the trouble on the Scottish border. He also complained loudly that the king had failed to provide money to pay his soldiers in Wales, and similar problems were reported by Prince Henry.

Then in June a force led by the Marcher lord Edmund Mortimer was ambushed by Glendower in mid Wales, and Mortimer himself taken prisoner. This was by far the most significant captive of the campaign. Edmund was effective head of the House of Mortimer, uncle of the young Earl of March, Richard's designated heir (still held securely by King Henry), and was, through descent from John of Gaunt's elder brother, closer in line to Richard's throne than Henry himself. He was also brother-in-law of Hotspur, and, as Henry seemed to drag his feet over a ransom for Mortimer, this added another complaint to Harry Hotspur's growing tally against the king.

Encouraged by his successes, Glendower turned his attention to the south, marching into Glamorgan in August and finding support all the way. In retaliation, and using all the money he had available, King Henry assembled armies for a three-pronged attack intended to deal with the Welsh rebel once and for all. Prince Henry was to lead an army westwards from Chester, the king himself set out from Shrewsbury and a third force marched from Hereford.

This time it was the weather that defeated them. The Welsh were nowhere to be found, but such storms arose as to lead to a legend that Glendower was a wizard with mastery over the forces of nature. Wind and rain devastated the armies, and at one point the king's tent blew down while he slept within, nearly causing him to be impaled on his own lance.

Again the English trailed back over the border, only to hear that Hotspur and his father, Northumberland, had won a famous victory over the Scots at Homildon Hill, taking numerous prisoners including the Earl of Douglas. What should have been good news turned into another clash with Hotspur when, in October, the king demanded that Northumberland and his son hand over their prisoners, including Douglas, to be ransomed. There were clear precedents for this and Northumberland surrendered his prisoners, but Hotspur flatly refused to do so. He repeated the old complaint that the Percy family was financing Henry's wars in Scotland and Wales, and he challenged the king about ransoming his brother-in-law, Mortimer.

Parliament was sitting at the time and readily approved a ransom for Lord Grey, but nothing was said about any other. Shortly afterwards the Mortimer tenants on the Welsh border were informed by their lord that he was transferring his loyalty to Glendower, and in December of that year Edmund Mortimer married Glendower's daughter.

This was a huge blow for King Henry. Not only was it an open challenge to his authority, but it also left a great gap in the buffer zone between England and Wales and deprived the English of all the resources of the Mortimer estates.

Prince Henry, meanwhile, had a new governor, Thomas Percy, Earl of Worcester and brother of Northumberland. He was also rapidly learning to do without the support of his earlier mentor. In the spring of 1403 he was appointed the king's lieutenant for the whole of Wales, and perhaps to celebrate this led a raid on Glendower's own estates near Oswestry, burning the manor house and ravaging the land all around. Increasingly he was using his own resources to pay his men, and increasingly he was also, no doubt, realising that this was no way to deal decisively with so mobile an opponent. Advancing as far as Aberystwyth and Harlech, he found no one to fight, for, while he was busy in the north, Glendower was making himself master of all the western counties down to Carmarthen, only being kept from Pembrokeshire by the actions of Thomas, Lord Carew. Another conflict was brewing, however, which, for a time at least, would make Glendower the least of the problems of Prince Henry and his father.

In exchange for their Scottish prisoners, Henry had granted to the Percys the estates of the greatest of them, the Earl of Douglas. The drawback to this was that they had first to conquer those estates, and that is what they, Northumberland and his son

Hotspur, had set about doing in 1403. As late as the end of June Northumberland had written to the king asking for more resources for the campaign, and reminding him of what benefit it would be to the Crown if it was to be successful. It was the letter of a mildly aggrieved yet loyal subject.

So it came as a complete surprise when, in early July, Hotspur abruptly took his forces from the Scots borders down to Chester, and raised his banner against the king. He issued a proclamation with a list of grievances, among them the accusation of illegal taxes and corruption, the failure to ransom Edmund Mortimer, and the failure to negotiate an end to the Glendower rebellion. The chief claim, however, was that King Henry was no king at all. He was referred to throughout as Henry of Lancaster, and accused of breaking the oath he took at Doncaster in 1399 that he had come only to claim his inheritance and not the crown. Hotspur, therefore, intended to take back that crown and restore it to its rightful owner – to Richard 'if he lives', or otherwise to the young Earl of March, Richard's rightful heir. Since Hotspur had seen Richard in his coffin it is unlikely he would have believed he was still alive, but a rumour had begun in Scotland that he had escaped from Pontefract and some had even identified a poor wandering man as the former king, since which time he had been kept carefully secret by the Scots, and the rumour heavily promoted.

The supporters claimed for Hotspur's act of treason showed that a considerable conspiracy must have been put together, probably over a number of months past. Northumberland was an obvious one, supporting his son, but Thomas Percy, Earl of Worcester and recently governor of Prince Henry, had also slipped away from Shrewsbury to join his nephew, and Glendower and Mortimer were also named, along with Hotspur's former prisoner the Earl of Douglas. Of these, however, only Worcester and Douglas were actually at Chester. Northumberland was bringing an army down from the north, and Glendower from the farthest corner of Wales. In the meantime there was a prize ready for the taking – Prince Henry of Wales, recently returned to Shrewsbury Castle.

It no doubt seemed like an easy target, a sixteen-year-old boy with a small force and in a most strategic place. Hotspur, however, had miscalculated in two important ways. First, both Northumberland and Glendower moved slower than he might have wished to their rendezvous at Shrewsbury, and second, King Henry was not where he had supposed him to be, far away in the south of England.

Having received Northumberland's letter, Henry had decided to go north in person to his assistance. It was at Nottingham, therefore, that he received news of the revolt on 13 July, and he immediately turned westward, at the same time calling out all the Midlands levies in his support. The threat to his son was clear to him, and some have suggested he may even have been uncertain as to which side the prince would choose. Be that as it may, by a series of forced marches, urged on by the Scottish Lord Dunbar who had much to gain and nothing to lose by supporting the English king, Henry arrived at Shrewsbury ahead of the rebel army.

Any doubts about his son's loyalty seem to have swiftly disappeared, and when, on 20 July, Hotspur arrived to find the king already firmly in control, it was soon apparent that the young prince would be lining up beside his father to face the first battle of his life.

On 21 July Hotspur lined up his forces on a slight ridge some three miles north of the town, adjacent to where the battlefield church stands today, and where a field of peas and three small ponds would hamper the approach of the enemy. Even now the king offered negotiations to avoid a conflict, though he must have been aware that all the time Hotspur's reinforcements might be drawing closer. By some accounts it was Worcester, employed as embassy between the two, who destroyed any chance of a settlement, deliberately misrepresenting the king's offers to his opponents. In any event it was late afternoon before the two armies engaged each other in what had become known as the 'English method' of battle.

Each army was fronted by an array of archers, who began the action with flight after flight of lethal arrows. The Prince of Wales, heading the forces to the left of the king, found himself facing his own famous Cheshire longbowmen, now backing Hotspur in the name of the long-dead Richard.

The prince would, of course, have been in full plate armour with a visored helmet, but at some point he must have raised the visor, either to breathe easier on a hot day, to obtain better vision of the action around him, or simply to show his face to rally his troops. Whatever the reason, the action could have cost his life for he was struck full in the face by an arrow.

An expert has assessed that it must have been deflected, or possibly it was only half-drawn or at the limit of its range, for a fully drawn arrow would surely have killed him. Instead this smashed through the facial bone below his eye, missed both brain and spinal cord, and lodged in the thicker bone at the back of the skull.

Despite this serious wound the prince refused to leave the field, and indeed led his men so well that they broke through the flank of Hotspur's forces and turned to come at them from behind, trapping them between the armies of prince and king. In the wild confusion of the fight that followed it was hard to tell who was friend or foe.

Hotspur's one aim was to slay the king, but he was foiled in this by the use of several decoys dressed in the royal livery. On the fall of one of these the cry went up, 'The king is dead,' only to be refuted by Henry himself from another part of the field. In fact it was Hotspur who was slain at Shrewsbury. Worcester was taken prisoner along with the Earl of Douglas, and the defeat of the rebels was total. It is claimed that Prince Henry wept over the body of his former mentor, which was then in rapid sequence buried, exhumed, beheaded and quartered, with the head set over the gateway to York and the remaining parts displayed around the country as an example to other traitors.

The prince, though, had his own troubles to think of. The shaft of the arrow had been pulled from his face but the head was still embedded in his skull. There was a strong possibility that the wound would turn septic and kill him after all, in the same manner as Richard the Lionheart had perished some two hundred years before. He was, in fact, saved by the skill of one John Bradmore, who later wrote an account of how he did it.

First the wound was reopened and enlarged little by little, using probes made from the dried pith of the elder wrapped in purified linen and infused with rose honey. Then Bradmore designed and had made special metal tongs with a screw down the middle to enable them to be opened to the width of the arrow shaft. These were inserted into the wound some six inches deep, and then the screw turned until the tongs engaged the arrowhead. Gently moving this to and fro, the metal could at last be withdrawn – and all this in the days before anaesthetics. No doubt the prince was drugged and immobilised in some way, but the whole long-drawn-out process must have been excruciating. Even then it was not finished. White wine was squirted into the wound, and over a period of another twenty days further probes of decreasing length, made of barley flour, honey and flax fibres, were inserted, allowing the wound to gradually close up and heal. No doubt this was followed by a long period of recuperation, and it is unlikely that the prince took any part in the further actions of the king that year.

In the north Northumberland was permitted to surrender at York, though stripped of castles, offices and estates. In Wales Glendower, who was little affected by the failure of the Percys' rebellion, consolidated his hold on the southern counties. Though Henry set out in September in an effort to retake Carmarthen, he was humiliatingly forced to turn back through lack of money to pay his troops.

This lack of money was to continue to block progress until Parliament could be persuaded to take the Welsh rebellion more seriously. In January 1404 Prince Henry was put in overall charge of operations in Wales, but with only a small force, largely paid for by selling his own jewels and plate, there was little he could do. Glendower, in the meantime, was going from strength to strength.

A treaty had been sealed with the French, and French ships had helped him take Cardiff, Aberystwyth and Harlech. He had been crowned Prince of Wales in Machynlleth and had called his first Welsh parliament. Early in 1405 the so-called 'Tripartite Indenture' was issued. This was an agreement between Northumberland, Mortimer and Glendower to depose Henry and divide up England and Wales between them. Northumberland would take the north of England down as far as Warwickshire and Norfolk, Mortimer would have the south and Glendower would have Wales.

Northumberland, however, was about to overreach himself, backing another rebellion, this time led by Richard Scrope, Archbishop of York, and Thomas Mowbray, Earl of Norfolk. There was to be no pardon after this, and when the revolt was ended by the efforts of Ralph Neville, Earl of Westmoreland, Northumberland fled with his grandson, first to Scotland, then to Wales, France and back to Scotland again. His power was gone, though, long before his life was finally ended in one last rebellion, at the Battle of Bramham Moor in 1408.

In Wales, in the meantime, 1405 was known as the year of the French, although Prince Henry, now in his late teens, was beginning to make his presence felt and enjoyed some success. In February Glendower's son was captured, in March Glendower was defeated at Grosmont in Monmouthshire, and in May the prince himself led a victory against Glendower's forces at Usk. After this, however, he turned his attention to the north, moving his base back to Chester. With more money from Parliament at last coming through, a new policy was being formulated.

In August of that year, following the terms of their treaty, a French force landed at Milford Haven in the west and marched across the country, almost reaching Worcester before coming to a halt. For several days they confronted the forces of King Henry, freshly arrived from mopping up Scrope's rebellion in the north, and there were a number of skirmishes but no battle. In fact the king was desperately trying to raise more men and money, and the French too seem to have run out of resources, and in the end both sides withdrew without a fight.

This was the high point of Glendower's rebellion and he was never to hold such sway again. Gradually the French forces withdrew, finding less profit than they had expected in the campaign. The last of them was gone early in the next year. At the same time Prince Henry was proving a figurehead that could unite all the scattered loyalties of the English lords, and was also bringing a fresh approach to the problem.

The policy of raid and withdraw, so clearly ineffective, was now replaced by a steady encroachment on the land. Castles were taken, garrisoned and held, forming fixed points for defence and further advance, and more importantly for blockade. Slowly supplies of weapons were reduced, trade cut off and the lifeblood of the rebellion shrunk to a trickle. This, of course, cost money, and regular payments from Parliament helped. The prince was also thanked regularly by Parliament for his efforts.

Gradually Glendower was forced back into his chief strongholds, and now siege came into play. Aberystwyth came under siege in 1407 and was almost brought to surrender before being relieved at the end of that year. The siege was renewed, however, with increased vigour in the following year, even using cannon brought by sea from Bristol. This was almost the first time cannon were used in Britain, and though they were not as effective as the prince might have hoped, they were employed again at the siege of Harlech, which also began in 1408.

In September 1408 Aberystwyth fell and forces were concentrated on Harlech, the headquarters and home of Glendower. Surprisingly, given his earlier tactics, Glendower himself, his family, his chief supporter Edmund Mortimer and his family were all within the castle during the siege. Prolonged bombardment damaged the castle walls, but it was starvation and the exhaustion of supplies that finally led to its surrender in March 1409.

Mortimer had died, probably of starvation, but his wife and daughters were taken prisoner and died later in London.

Glendower himself and a son managed to slip away, but although occasional raids into Shropshire and Brecon tried to continue the rebellion, it was by now effectively over. The last reliable sighting of Glendower was in 1412, but he was reputedly still alive in 1414 and is believed to have died and been buried somewhere near his old estate in the Dee Valley in 1415.

The conflict in Wales had occupied most of Prince Henry's teenage years, and though he was not always personally present, most accounts give him full credit for the change of tactics that led to victory. Certainly the weapons of blockade and siege were down to him, along with the innovative use of artillery. We might also say that his persistence with these weapons over a period of years showed a tenacity of purpose that was to stand him in good stead in the future. No doubt he drew his own lessons from these years – the need for a regular supply of money and other resources, the need for secure bases, the use of siege and the need for long-term planning. What he also acquired was a group of skilled and trusted captains, who in turn gave him their own personal trust and loyalty, and many of whom would again be at his side in all the conflicts to come.

3

KING IN WAITING
1409–1413

Whether Henry IV was a keen or reluctant usurper of the English crown, it is certain that he got very little joy from his achievement; indeed, the first half-dozen years of his reign seem to have left him a broken man. In his youth he had been a vigorous and athletic figure, a bold huntsman, a champion in the lists with a taste, besides, for books and music. He had needed all that vigour to hold down his new kingdom, dashing from Scotland to Wales, from north to south, to stamp out the wildfires of rebellion and challenge. By 1406, though, the tide seemed to have turned in his favour. The French had left, Glendower had passed his peak of achievement and Northumberland was broken. A plot to abduct the young Earl of March and his brother and carry them away to Mortimer and Glendower in Wales had been thwarted the year before, and a happy accident had even given him sway over the Scots.

The Duke of Rothesay, heir to the Scottish throne, had been imprisoned by the Duke of Albany and subsequently died (probably murdered), leaving another son, eleven-year-old James, as the new heir. Recognising the danger to the boy, his father intended to send him abroad to France for his safety and education, but in the course of his already hazardous journey James was captured by English pirates and sent to the king. Henry naturally decided he could give the boy equal safety and education and held on to him. With Scotland still divided by factions, he could thus ensure a reasonable security for the border by threatening either to send back the lad or to keep him in England, according to the need at the time. In fact young James was to spend the next eighteen years of his life in England, sometimes in the Tower, but more usually in fairly relaxed captivity.

In 1407 things got even better, with the murder of Louis of Orleans setting the French factions at each other's throats and removing any threat of an attack on England. Well before this time, however, Henry had fallen victim to a mystery illness that was to afflict him on and off for the rest of his life. What this was, or indeed if it was one illness or several, has been argued over by medical men ever since.

The first attack took place immediately after the trial and execution of Archbishop Scrope in 1405 and has been described as everything from a stroke to a nervous breakdown. For almost a month the king was gravely ill before apparently making a full recovery. From then on, however, he is recorded as suffering from a disfiguring skin disease, variously depicted as a rash, weeping sores, boils and a tumour under his nose. For writers at the time there was no mystery to this. The king had dared to lay hands on an archbishop and God had struck him down. The usual contemporary verdict was that the king had some form of leprosy.

What evidence there is, however, does not support that diagnosis, not least because there was never any attempt to treat the king as a leper. The skin disease often came at times of stress, and eczema or psoriasis have been suggested as causes, or even basic lack of hygiene. Nor would leprosy lead to the repeated bouts of 'grave illness' which left the king unable even to walk for weeks at a time.

The second of these is recorded in April 1406, and then again in June 1408, while in the winter of 1408/09 he was so ill that he sent for his sons to come to his bedside, and composed his will. Epilepsy, malaria and venereal disease have all been suggested diagnoses, while the king's declaration that he felt his skin was on fire has led some to see this as St Anthony's fire, another name for the bacterial skin infection erysipelas. This can attack through any break in the skin, causing a violent red inflammation (particularly of the face), fever, fatigue, weakness and even death.

Whatever the cause, one probable result of this repeated ill health was to draw Prince Henry into closer involvement in government than he might have expected during his father's lifetime. He is first recorded as attending a meeting of the king's council in December 1406, though he may have been present at earlier sessions in a less formal capacity. It is almost certain that he returned to London during the winter months even at the height of activity in Wales. Very little campaigning would be possible at such times, and, if Parliament was sitting, he was entitled to be present.

In fact the parliament of 1406 was the longest of Henry's reign. Called in March, it sat through to December with breaks for Easter and the summer. It is on record that the prince was formally thanked for his work in Wales at the beginning of April, and was present in June and again in December, so we may conclude he was reasonably well experienced in such matters. It was a difficult year for the king, however, and it may be that he welcomed the presence of his eldest son as a moderating voice in that chamber.

Money was the issue. The commons in particular were determined to cut down the king's expenditure and to be assured of value for money. At the very beginning of his reign Henry had put himself in a weak position. Criticising the extravagance of Richard and his money-raising methods, he had assured the commons he would not ask for money for the first year. This may have bought him some popularity, but it left him struggling for money ever after, and permanently in debt to nobles, the Church and even his own son.

Now, desperate for cash to pay for expensive wars, he found the commons determined to bargain hard before granting anything. Possibly weakened by his illness, the king was forced into concession after concession. He would limit his household. He would be advised by his council. He would name the council and, by implication, have it approved by Parliament. Worst of all, he would open his accounts to audit. No king of the time had ever yielded so much. Perhaps it is no wonder we find his son's name among the council he nominated at the end of the year.

Archbishop Arundel became Lord Chancellor at the beginning of 1407 and immediately set about putting the royal finances in order. Much has been made about a division between the prince and archbishop, and the later ousting of the old guard by the new, but certainly at this point they seemed to work well in tandem. Although the prince was busy in Wales this year, still he found time to be present at about two-thirds of the council meetings. Indeed, the failure of the first siege at Aberystwyth has been ascribed to the fact that the prince, thinking the castle sure to surrender very shortly, left the conclusion in the hands of deputies while he returned to Westminster for council business.

One of the first acts of the king in 1407 was to confirm the legitimacy of his Beaufort half-brothers. Since this had already been done at least twice before it seems odd that it needed mentioning again. This time, however, there was a sting in the tail. The Beauforts were declared to be legitimate for all purposes except for any possible succession to the Crown. Such a possibility was remote anyway, as King Henry had four strong sons of his own and the succession had already been confirmed as to his heirs male. There is a suggestion that it was Archbishop Arundel who promoted the exception, thereby causing a degree of coolness in their future relations, but we can only speculate as to why. The rise of this late third family of John of Gaunt had not been popular with some of the older nobility, and the archbishop may simply have been reflecting that feeling.

It is certain, however, that their star was rising, along with that of the Prince of Wales. Family had always been favoured by King Henry – possibly in his position he felt that no one else was so trustworthy – and he had certainly put his children to work at an early age. Henry was sent to Wales at thirteen, and Thomas to rule Ireland at about the same time, while young John was given responsibility in the Scottish borders. Only Humphrey escaped this early burden, being given instead a scholar's education. His daughters, too, were married off early to form alliances in Europe.

Prince Henry seemed to have the same idea. As he became more and more involved with the council, it was family he turned to – not his younger brothers, though their turn would come later, but his 'uncles', the Beauforts. The eldest, John Beaufort, became a regular attender at council meetings. So too did his brother, Henry, now Bishop of Winchester, who seems to have been a political mentor to the young prince in the same way as Hotspur had earlier been his military mentor. When Parliament was called in October

1407, even the Speaker elected then was a cousin of the Beauforts, one Thomas Chaucer, son of the more famous Geoffrey.

This parliament, while still urging austerity on the part of the king, seemed well enough content to vote an increased grant of money for royal use, and in return Henry promised he would not call on them again for the next two years. In the meantime government would be by king and council, and, when the king was seriously ill, by council alone.

By some accounts the king became increasingly an invalid over the next few years and almost completely relinquished power. Others suggest this is overstated and that, apart from a few months of acute illness, his hand was still firmly on the tiller. Whichever is true, it is clear that it was during this period that Prince Henry came to prominence in the council, an apprenticeship in government to go along with his earlier apprenticeship in war.

Over this time, too, some divisions began to appear between the prince and the archbishop, who had worked so well together before. It may have been simply a generational problem. By this time Arundel was fifty-six with a lifetime of service behind him. Henry was in his early twenties and had already demonstrated in his principality that he had his own ideas and was not afraid to put them forward. His steady promotion of the Beauforts may also have irked the archbishop, and, while they agreed that royal finances urgently needed reforming, they may well have disagreed about how this was to be done. The fact that most accounts attribute any progress in this area to the prince may also have been hard for the older statesman to swallow.

One particular area seems to show how far the breakdown in relations had gone. It was a particular concern of the archbishop, as a churchman, to stamp out the heresy of the Lollards. When he discovered Lollard teachings were being studied at Oxford University, he took strong action to prevent this, and it may have been a surprise to him to find the prince in opposition to this action, supporting the freedoms of the university.

On 21 December 1409 Arundel's chancellorship came to an end. By most accounts he resigned, though there is a suggestion that his hand was forced. What is clear is that the prince's party, as it has been labelled, was now firmly in control of the council. After a gap of some four weeks, which may suggest the king had some sympathy for his old friend, a new Chancellor was appointed from among the Beauforts – not Bishop Henry, as might have been expected, but his younger brother Thomas, now joining the council for the first time.

In fact the council that was named in May 1410 was packed with the prince's friends. Bishop Henry was there, along with two other bishops, of Durham and of Bath and Wells. Thomas, Earl of Arundel, son of the earl executed by Richard, had served the prince in Wales, as had Lord Burnell and Henry, Lord Scrope, nephew of the late archbishop. When these last two were later replaced, Henry Chichele, then Bishop of St Davids, joined the council, along with Richard, Earl of Warwick. The former had earlier been involved in diplomacy aimed at securing a bride for the prince, while the latter had fought with him at Shrewsbury and in Wales.

This was the council that would effectively govern the country for the next two years. It is probably a mistake to think that King Henry had completely retired from the scene, but to start with, at least, the relationship between king and prince seemed to help the council to work very smoothly.

The relationship with Parliament seemed equally smooth. This may have been down to the prince's popularity in the country

– he was repeatedly thanked for his efforts in Wales – or possibly because his policies and the demands of the commons happily coincided. It no doubt also helped that Thomas Chaucer was again elected Speaker.

The parliament of 1410 had two main concerns: finance and the defence of the realm. The king, they said, should husband his resources, not give away lands but use their revenues for the support of his household. The prince, too, had money as a priority. He had already learned how essential it was to ensure a regular supply in order to achieve anything in war or peace. He made it clear to the commons that the council would be prepared to resign en masse unless money was made available to them, and several times suggested that more was needed, but in general the aims of reform and efficiency were the same.

As for the defence of the realm, this again was a shared concern. Wales, Scotland, Ireland, all needed attention, as did the remnants of English territories in France, chiefly Calais and parts of Aquitaine, while piracy around the English coasts was a menace to both trade and to the coastal population. The parliament made a rather pointed demand that those with military responsibilities for these areas should take up residence there and do their duty. A contrast is noted here between Prince Henry and his brother Thomas, the former once again being thanked for his service while the latter was more or less told to go away and try harder. This seems unfair, since Thomas had been kept notoriously short of funds and probably had the harder task.

At about this time a breach occurred between the brothers, partly as a result of a dispute between Thomas and the Beauforts. He had recently married the widow of John Beaufort, and claimed through her a share in a substantial inheritance. This was contested by Bishop Henry. As a result, Thomas was not one of his brother's 'party', and almost alone of the younger generation would side with his father and the recently ousted Archbishop Arundel in future matters.

The council members had been required to swear an oath to Parliament that they would give the king good and impartial advice so that his rule should be effective for his good and the good of the kingdom. The prince alone was exempted from this, due to the 'highness and excellence of his honourable person'. Whether this was supposed to make the council answerable to Parliament as well as to the king is not clear, but as long as all proceeded harmoniously the question never arose. In the meantime the council, if not the government of the realm, was undoubtedly under the prince's control, and both benefitted from a unity of purpose rare at the time.

The first clear divisions appeared in 1411 and France was the cause. Of the two factions fighting there for control, neither was strong enough to defeat the other, and both began casting around for allies. England, however, had its own agenda and support for either side would come at a price.

Initially it seemed as though Burgundy, led by John the Fearless, would be the beneficiary. Prince Henry certainly favoured the alliance. John offered his daughter as a bride, together with support for English interests in France, and the Flemish trade connection would have been helped as well.

There are two different versions of what happened next. In one the king decided that he himself would lead an expedition to France, maybe not exactly in support of Burgundy, but not against it either. This was ordered in August, but by the time the fleet and supplies had been assembled in September he had either changed his mind, or become too ill to pursue the campaign. In the other version the king remained uncommitted to any alliance and it was the prince who authorised the more limited expedition that set out at the end of September.

This was led by the Earl of Arundel, accompanied by the Earl of Warwick and Bishop Henry Chichele, and was specifically in support of Burgundy. With striking success they defeated the opposing Armagnac faction at St Cloud on 9 November, not only opening the way to Paris for the Burgundians, but also revealing the weakness of the French forces. By the time they returned triumphantly to England in December, however, they found that all had changed at home.

On 30 November King Henry had abruptly returned to the forefront of government, dismissed his Lord Chancellor, the prince and the majority of the prince's friends from the council, and reinstated Archbishop Arundel. For the next eighteen months Prince Henry would have no role at all in government, even when the king suffered another bout of illness in December 1412, and his friends and supporters were likewise eclipsed.

Many reasons have been put forward for this sudden change, and probably all of them have some validity. At one extreme we are told the prince's behaviour was so bad, his arrogance and assumption of power so blatant, that the king could no longer tolerate it. There is a suggestion that the prince had called on his father to abdicate, though in some accounts the suggestion came from Bishop Henry Beaufort, who also found himself in disgrace at this time. 'Abdicate' was, of course, a dangerous word to use to a king who had been so closely involved with the 'abdication' of his predecessor.

Both the prince and the bishop strenuously denied this claim, and the prince seems to have spent much of the next year apparently seeking a reconciliation with his father. Unless all his conduct during this time was one mighty charade – and there is a writer who accuses him of deliberately 'harassing the last hours of his dying father' – the rift seems to have been all on one side.

It may be that King Henry felt threatened by his son's youth and popularity. He himself was at the time only in his mid-forties, but clearly aged by responsibilities and illness. The contrast may have been hard to bear. The prince's way with Parliament might also have caused him alarm. In the reform of royal finances, too much may have been promised or given away. There is a sharp exchange recorded between the king and the Speaker of the Commons at that time assembled, where the king declared that, though they might speak their minds freely, he would tolerate no 'novelleries' nor any attack on the liberties and franchises of the monarch.

It was undoubtedly the French expedition that brought matters to a head, and the question of who, ultimately, was in charge of royal policy. The fact that the prince felt able to go ahead with this without specific authority from his father would no doubt have piqued his pride. Similarly the fact that ambassadors sent to negotiate with the English were instructed to deal with both king and prince would have shown Henry how far his own position had been called into question by giving the prince and council such a free hand.

For whatever reason, the change was made. Smoothly but suddenly there was a new Chancellor, Archbishop Arundel, and a new head of the council, Prince Henry's younger brother, Thomas, who had never been part of the prince's party, and may perhaps have been his father's favourite.

And with these changes there came an equally sudden change

of policy towards France. Although in January 1412 the Duke of
Burgundy requested continued support, instead the king transferred
his backing to the Armagnac faction. This might have been purely
to assert his right to choose his own policy and go contrary to that
of his son, or it might be that the Armagnacs simply put in a higher
bid. Certainly the treaty that was signed in 1412 offered a good
deal to the English king – recognition of his right to the Duchy of
Aquitaine and a promise to assist in its recovery, a further promise
of full support for any military expedition Henry might make to
assist the Armagnac cause, three months' wages at an agreed level
for the men of such an expedition, and royal alliances by way
of marriage with their 'sons and daughters, their nephews and
nieces, their relatives and kindred'. In exchange the king promised
three thousand archers and a thousand men at arms to be fitted
out and sent with all speed to the aid of the Armagnacs. We are
told that King Henry required each of his sons to sign this treaty,
which must have been a bitter pill for the prince to swallow, more
especially since the head of this expedition was to be his brother
Thomas.

His protests, however, were ignored and he seems to have
taken himself away from court altogether at this time, while the
expedition was being assembled. In June 1412 he sent a letter
from Coventry to friends and supporters around the country,
claiming that certain persons, 'sons of iniquity', were spreading
false stories about him, and trying to make a split between himself
and his father by claiming he wanted to usurp the throne. Instead
he protested his complete loyalty and his love and respect for the
king.

Two weeks later he followed this up by a visit to London with
such a crowd of retainers at his back as to cause comment in

several of the chronicles of the time. In some accounts he was trying to threaten and overawe his father, in others simply to try one last time to dissuade him from the French expedition. In that he failed. Despite being granted an interview with the king – to which Henry was carried in a chair, being too ill to walk – and being assured there was no doubt about his loyalty, a few days later Thomas was dubbed Duke of Clarence and royal lieutenant in Aquitaine, and sent on his way with the king's blessing.

Unfortunately for Henry and for Thomas, even before the expedition had landed in France the warring factions had come to a temporary truce. Now the presence of English soldiers was an embarrassment to all, and, after firing off some furious letters about the breaking of treaties, Thomas was paid to take his men home.

In the meantime stories continued to circulate about the prince. He was accused of misappropriating the wages of the garrison at Calais while holding the office of Captain of Calais, and apparently came to London again in September, armed with rolls of accounts, to clear himself. Some writers merge this with his earlier visit and again the details vary. According to an often repeated, if over-dramatic story, at one of these meetings the prince, having taken Holy Communion and confessed his sins beforehand, fell on his knees before his father, handed him a dagger and told him to take his life rather than that he, the prince, should cause him any worry or suspicion. Needless to say, in the story, the dagger is thrown away and the king and his son end in tearful reconciliation.

It is to other stories no doubt circulating at this time that we must attribute Shakespeare's 'madcap prince'. They are so many and so varied that no doubt some of them are true, but hard evidence, as opposed to hearsay, is almost impossible to find.

Drunkenness, frequenting taverns in Eastcheap with men of low birth, brawling and robbery, serving 'Venus as well as Mars'; all these accusations are thrown at the young prince, and, given his age, would be very easily believable if they did not sit so strangely with his character before and after this period. Perhaps reaction to his father's apparent ingratitude for long and faithful service might be an explanation if the stories proved to be true.

There are some fragments of fact available. The prince's presence in Eastcheap is easily explained since he lived there, when in London, in a property called Coldharbour, given to 'my dearest son' by King Henry in 1410. The place was previously known as Poulteney Inn. There are some records of brawls in the area that were broken up by the authorities, but the names attached are those of the prince's brothers Thomas and John. Similarly there are no records of any royal bastards attributed to the prince, which is probably unusual for the time he lived in, when even Bishop Henry Beaufort was acknowledged as a father.

Perhaps the strongest evidence in favour of such stories comes from the comments in several chronicles about the change in the prince's behaviour when he became king, how he suddenly changed into 'another man, zealous for honesty, modesty and gravity'. How much of this change they witnessed for themselves and how much they were relying on earlier tales of wildness we do not know, and we also have the prince's claim that his name was being deliberately blackened at the time to balance against this.

If such a claim is true, it is hard to see who would be behind these stories. *Cui bono?* is a valid question. Who would benefit by opening a rift between the prince and his father? The obvious candidate would be Thomas, who stepped into his shoes in the council and at the head of the French expedition. Though that brought him little kudos, it made him considerably richer. He had also been named the king's lieutenant in Aquitaine, another stab at his brother, who had been Duke of Aquitaine since 1399. There is never the slightest suggestion, though, that he expected or intended to replace the prince as heir to the throne, and when Henry became king he served him loyally for the rest of his life. At the most it might have been a brief brotherly spat, aimed at getting his own back on a brother constantly praised while he was criticised.

Another target might have been the Beauforts, who had enemies enough of their own, for they too fell from grace along with the prince. One very strange story tells of a man discovered hiding in the prince's room at night, a supposed assassin. On being questioned, he claimed to have been sent by Bishop Henry, which seems patently absurd. By some convoluted thinking it has been suggested the bishop sent him in order to implicate someone else in a plot on the prince's life, the unfortunate man being drowned by the Earl of Arundel soon after. It does seem more likely, however that it was Bishop Henry who was being framed.

Whatever rift there was between the king and his heir seems to have healed during the autumn of 1412, whether because of the prince's visits or because the division over French policy had now been resolved. The health of the king, however, was steadily declining. We are told he suffered greatly in body and in mind, the latter being attributed to a guilty conscience.

In December he had another severe attack of illness, but despite this began to plan a pilgrimage to the Holy Land. It had apparently been foretold to the king that he would die in Jerusalem. The prophecy, if there was one, worked out a little differently than he might have expected, however.

In March 1413 he collapsed while praying before the tomb of

Edward the Confessor in Westminster Abbey. He was carried to the abbot's lodging, to a room known as the Jerusalem chamber, and there he died. Once again all manner of stories and legends have grown up about his death, some accounts dragging it out over several days. In one he confesses to the murder of Richard. In another, repeated by Shakespeare, the impatient prince tries on the crown while his father still lives. In yet another he asks his son how he intends to hold on to the crown, having no right to it, the answer being, 'I will guard it, as you did, with my sword, all my life.'

What seems to be clearly established, however, is that at the time of his death the king was at peace with all his sons, and bequeathed to his eldest not only his crown, but also his blessing.

4

SETTLEMENTS AT HOME
1413–1415

On 9 April 1413, Passion Sunday, Henry V was crowned at Westminster Abbey in the midst of a snowstorm – an 'unprecedented storm with driving snow, which covered the country's mountains, burying men and animals and houses … creating great danger and much loss of life'. Well, England can do that in April, but it set a challenge to those looking for omens for the coming reign. Did it show the icy temperament of the new king? Was England in for a bitter winter of unprecedented severity? Or, as one suggested, did the passing of the coronation snowstorm indicate that spring had come and good times were ahead? With hindsight we could add a few more suggestions. The reign would certainly bring an exciting challenge for many, and future generations would come to see Henry himself as a whiter-than-white example of kingship.

For, however exaggerated the earlier stories of his wild youth, it was immediately clear to all that, from the day of his accession, the king was a new man. Some even likened it to the transformation of Thomas Becket centuries earlier, when he became Archbishop of Canterbury. The story is told that on the very night of his father's death Henry sought out a monk, or some say a holy recluse, at Westminster Abbey and spent the entire night in prayer – rather like the vigil kept by a man before receiving his knighthood.

What is certain is that he emerged the next morning decisively in control of himself and his kingdom. His hand was set firmly on the tiller and never for a moment thereafter was his grip at all slackened. After something like fifty years of loose and variable government, the collective sigh of relief from the nation might have been the breeze to melt all that snowfall.

He was a young man, twenty-six years old, but already rich in experience of military matters and government. There is a general agreement that he was taller than average, graceful and slender but strong. The best known portrait that we have of him was painted many years after his death but is claimed to be a copy of a contemporary likeness. It shows a rather severe face with long nose, square jaw, full lips, hair cropped short above the ears and a piercing gaze. He must have been marked by the wound received at Shrewsbury but that side of the face is not shown, perhaps deliberately. Some have described it as a soldier's face, a cold face, and suggested that the king was unlovable, but surely that can't be true. It is difficult to paint charisma, even harder to describe what makes a man a natural leader, but whatever it was the new king had it in abundance. Those who served him, with very few exceptions, served him for life, and with an intense and personal loyalty that is probably key to the admiration felt by succeeding generations. Even at the time of his coronation he had already achieved something his father had never had – popularity.

The story of his trying on his father's crown while the king lay dying has been interpreted by some as a hint that, if he did not take it at once, it might be snatched away by another claimant. There is, however, not the slightest suggestion of such a threat at the time. Indeed, Henry seems to have had enough confidence in his own right to reign that one of his first acts was to free young Edmund Mortimer, the last heir apparent of Richard II, who had been held captive by Henry IV for most of his life. Not only was he freed but, on the day prior to the coronation, he and his younger brother Roger were made Knights of the Bath, and soon afterwards all his family estates were returned to him.

Such mercy, a sign of the strength of the king's position, was to be extended to others as well. A large group of Scottish prisoners (though not the youthful King James) were sent home. Edward, son of the old Duke of York and a serial plotter and betrayer of plots, was restored to his dukedom, and his brother created Earl of Cambridge. Hotspur's son, another Henry Percy, would eventually be restored to the northern estates of his grandfather, and even Owen Glendower was offered a pardon, though he did not come forward to accept it.

In a similarly decisive way the new king rearranged his government. On the first morning of his reign Archbishop Arundel was thanked for his work and dismissed, the chancellorship going instead to Bishop Henry Beaufort. Others, too, lost their places on the council and the earls of Arundel and Warwick and Lord Henry Scrope were restored to power. The next day a parliament was summoned to meet on 15 May. The king was starting as he meant to go on.

Not everyone was happy with this smooth transition, of course. In July one John Whitelock was tried before the King's Bench accused of plotting against the king. He had been caught posting bills inciting rebellion in the name of Richard II, allegedly still alive in Scotland. Little had been heard of this line of challenge for some time, but a band of supporters of the former king were known to be in hiding in Westminster, and Whitelock was one of them. Found guilty and condemned, he subsequently escaped, only to appear again on the same errand three years later. There was never any real likelihood of danger to the king, but it may be that his ceremonial reburial of Richard's body at Westminster Abbey at the end of the year was more than just a reverent gesture to a well-loved man. In spite of this the name was still invoked as a figurehead for unrest for a number of years, until the pseudo-Richard being supported in Scotland himself died in 1419.

While this first challenge could be easily brushed aside, the second had to be treated more seriously. It came from the Lollards, a religious sect who traced their roots back into the previous century. Most agree that the name Lollard is derived from a Dutch word meaning to mutter or mumble and referred to their method of praying, but one ingenious writer has traced an equally possible derivation from a Latin name for a weed. It is certain that, at the time, the Lollards were regarded as weeds, infesting the good crop of Christian belief and threatening to overwhelm it, and, as such, they had to be plucked out and destroyed.

For western Europe at the time Christianity was the bedrock on which society was built, and not just Christianity but one particular branch of Christianity, the Catholic Church, headed by the Pope, the successor of St Peter. By the late fourteenth century, however, there were some serious flaws in this system, obvious to anyone who was prepared to look for them. One who looked long and hard, first from an academic and then a practical viewpoint, was John Wycliffe, and it is to him that the Lollards traced their origin.

John Wycliffe was an Oxford scholar of some note, who had

spent his academic life studying orthodox theology and the Bible. He became briefly drawn into the political world, representing the Crown on a foreign mission and in a legal dispute, and it was this as well as his studies that led him into his first area of controversy. Not only was the Church immensely wealthy at this time but it was powerful too, and in ways that went well beyond religion. As we have seen, bishops and archbishops were routinely appointed to the highest posts in the land, and, with the Pope as head of the Church and the king as head of the State, conflict of interests was almost inevitable.

Now, in the 1370s, Wycliffe declared that the Pope, and indeed the Church in general, had no business meddling in secular matters. Nor was its wealth at all in keeping with the design laid out in the Bible. Pope and Church should be poor, as Christ was poor. In fact he went further and pointed out that there was no pope mentioned in the Bible at all.

Many agreed with him, not only among the poor but among the landed magnates too, who resented the power and wealth of the clergy. John of Gaunt became his protector, and when in 1377 he was summoned before the Bishop of London to explain himself, both Gaunt and the Earl of Northumberland accompanied him.

No one could deny that some Church reform was needed. For the whole of Wycliffe's life the Pope had resided not in Rome but in Avignon under the influence – some would say control – of the French king, and during this time of exile had behaved more like a king himself than a religious leader. An immense palace had been built, a household of hundreds established, the best food and richest clothing purchased, and art commissioned on a lavish scale. All this was paid for by widespread corruption and by a variety of money-raising schemes, in particular the sale of 'indulgences', regarded as a shortcut to heaven for those sinners who found repentance too burdensome.

Having come into conflict with the Church, however, Wycliffe went further. The Bible, he declared, was the source of all grace, and only those in a state of grace could properly instruct others. If the Church could not deal with its own corruption the State should do so. The sacraments were not essential and nor were priests; pilgrimages and 'saint-worship' were useless; and finally, the worst heresy of all in the eyes of the Church, contrary to doctrine, the bread and wine used at communion were still bread and wine after consecration and only symbols of the body and blood of Christ.

By 1378 he had been condemned by the Pope, though still protected by John of Gaunt and Oxford University. Indeed his many followers at the university had begun to spread his word far and wide. The first sign that this might involve conflict with the State as well as the Church came in 1381, when some of his ideas were taken and adapted to suit the purposes of the Peasants' Revolt.

One John Ball, a former Catholic priest who had adopted Wycliffe's ideas and begun preaching around the countryside, was at the time imprisoned in Kent for heresy. The mob freed him and found his anti-clerical ideas much to their liking. Accompanying them to London, he preached a sermon on Blackheath, including the now famous declaration, 'When Adam delved and Eve span, who was then the gentleman?' Clearly, if the Church would not voluntarily give up its wealth there were many who would be happy to relieve them of it.

Wycliffe had never intended to establish a rival church. He had no control, however, over how his words would be interpreted, and maybe had not anticipated the uses to which they would be put. If the State had a duty to put the Church in order, surely then, if the State failed, others had a right to put the State in order. This was dangerous, revolutionary stuff and Wycliffe soon saw his noble supporters drop away.

Despite being summoned before archbishop and synod in 1382 – a meeting punctuated by an earthquake – no real action was taken against Wycliffe himself. He and his supporters were expelled from Oxford and his books and papers were burnt, but he was allowed to retire to his living at Lutterworth in Leicestershire and continue with his greatest work, the translation of the Bible into English.

There were a number of trials for heresy – none of which ended in martyrdom – and further purges of those with unacceptable ideas from Oxford, but little effective action was taken during the reign of Richard II, though the new doctrines continued to spread, both during Wycliffe's life and after his death in 1384. Indeed, so secure did his supporters seem that there was a group openly referred to as Lollard knights present in Parliament during the latter years of the reign.

A more robust opposition came in with the accession of Henry IV. In 1401 the infamous statute *De Heretico Comburendo* was passed, outlawing both the translation of the Bible into English and the possession of an English Bible. It also authorised for the first time the burning of heretics. Archbishop Arundel, Henry's close ally, was a bitter opponent of all Lollards and it may have been partly for his sake, and to appease the Church in general, that the law was passed.

Before the ink was even dry, one William Sawtrey had been sacrificed in this way. He was a Catholic priest who had converted to Wycliffe doctrines and refused to recant. Accompanying him in prison, another priest, John Purvey, was less firm. Recanting his heresy, he was set free, and indeed so restored to favour as to be given a new living in Kent. This seems strange since he was the man who had, only a few years before, revised Wycliffe's translation of the Bible into vernacular English. Soon after, though, he disappeared from his parish to continue preaching the new doctrines.

In 1407 Archbishop Arundel made a further attempt to control the hotbed of Lollardy that existed in Oxford University. His Constitutions of Oxford banned the writings of Wycliffe and his supporters, forbade any new translation of the Bible and banned any unauthorised preaching or teaching. The university should be purged of all unorthodox views, and strict censorship imposed. The result was a standoff that lasted three years, with the university claiming to defend its ancient liberties and Arundel equally intractable. Only a threatened intervention by king and pope and some diplomacy on the part of Prince Henry eventually smoothed over the situation.

The Lollard knights raised their heads again in the parliament of 1410, attempting to draw the teeth of *De Heretico Comburendo* and once again attacking the wealth of the Church. By this time, too, there was a Lollard sitting among the lords. Sir John Oldcastle, from an old Herefordshire family, had married the heiress of Lord Cobham, and on his death inherited his place in Parliament, along with rich estates in Kent, Norfolk, Wiltshire and the Midlands. Herefordshire was an area where Lollardy had become firmly established and it seems clear Sir John was already known for his beliefs. He was also, however, a close friend of the Prince of Wales, having fought under him against Glendower.

There are some who have called Henry a religious fanatic. They point to his scrupulous performance of religious duties, his interest in the liturgy and music of the Church, and in particular his insistence that all his victories were due to God and not to his own efforts. It seems more likely, though, that he was simply a typical product of his age. England had never been noted for religious sects and heresies; in fact Wycliffe is generally regarded as the first, a 'proto-Protestant'. To most men, therefore, the Church was right because it had always been right. There had been a few standoffs in the past between king and pope, but the idea of denying basic tenets of faith was unthinkable. From one viewpoint, of course, this was because the Church exerted such tight control over both religion and society, but whatever the reason behind it, this is simply how it was. It is true that Henry took his religious duties seriously, but then he took all his duties seriously. He seems to have been, in general, a serious young man.

As far as persecution of the Lollards is concerned, it is notable that at no point was Henry the instigator of events, and he mostly appears to have done his best to avoid the consequences of conflict. In 1410, for example, although rebuking those presenting anti-clerical petitions to Parliament, he made no move against them, which, as head of the council, he might well have done.

So too, his name is linked at this time with one of the most famous Lollard martyrdoms, that of John Bradbury. Bradbury was a tailor from Evesham whose misfortune was to be selected as an example to all potential heretics. Brought before Arundel and a convocation of bishops, he refused to recant his views on a central tenet of faith, the real presence of Christ in the Eucharist, and was condemned to be burnt. That the Prince of Wales should be present at the execution was not that surprising. What was more unusual was that, when Bradbury was already tied to the stake, he should then attempt to reason with the man and persuade him to recant and save his life. Failing in this, the faggots were lit; then, with the victim crying out in anguish, Henry had the fire put out and attempted again to persuade the man to save himself. A free pardon and even a pension for life were offered, but Bradbury refused to be moved. In the end the prince gave up his efforts, the fire was relit and the man perished. Though some have suggested that this demonstrates Henry's fanaticism, perversity and even cruelty, that does seem to take a rather uncharitable view of the affair.

It was Arundel again who sparked off the most decisive move against the Lollards soon after Henry's accession to the throne. Having made little headway against the so-called 'hedge priests' and lower orders of these heretics, it seemed an ideal opportunity when clear evidence appeared against the highest in rank among them, Sir John Oldcastle. Again, some have laid his denunciation at Henry's door, but this seems unlikely. Not only was Oldcastle a friend and former companion at arms, he was also at the time an intimate member of the king's household, and we have evidence that Henry spent some time trying to talk him round before agreeing to his prosecution.

Oldcastle, though, was not apologetic about his faith. He knew what he believed and was recklessly unafraid to say so. His hearing before Arundel and a panel of clerics in September 1413 was short and to the point. The Pope, declared Oldcastle, was the head of Antichrist, the archbishops and bishops his limbs and the friars his tail. Not surprisingly he was condemned as a 'most pernicious and detestable heretic'.

Henry decreed that he should have forty days' grace to reconsider before suffering the penalty fixed by law. Well before this deadline, however, Oldcastle was gone, escaped from the Tower of London, allegedly with the assistance of William Fisher, a parchment maker from Smithfield. Immediately, so the chronicles tell us, he began calling on supporters to join him in an attempt to overthrow the king.

A plot was hatched to seize – or some say kill – the king under cover of a mumming play during the Christmas festivities at Eltham palace. Then an army would gather during the night at St Giles's Fields north of Charing Cross to complete the takeover. What was intended after that remains rather vague – Oldcastle as regent for the king, or possibly a complete overthrow of the status quo to appeal to the more extreme supporters.

In the event neither happened. Somehow the plot was betrayed to the king, who must surely have cast his mind back to that other Christmas plot against his father. This time the end was rather less savage. Moving quietly to Westminster, Henry marshalled his own forces and arrived at St Giles's Fields shortly after midnight. We are told that Oldcastle expected support to flood in from all quarters, particularly from the nearby London. The king, however, had taken the precaution of locking and guarding the city gates, and we have no way of knowing whether or not Oldcastle was correct in his estimates.

Certainly the many thousands he might have hoped for did not arrive, and apparently some of those who did joined the king's forces in error and were promptly arrested. One estimate puts Oldcastle's supporters at no more than a few hundred, and when they found themselves facing determined opposition they fled. Some were killed, many captured and others, including Oldcastle himself, escaped.

For the next four years he evaded capture, probably hiding in his own familiar territory of Herefordshire, and some suggest that at first he was in touch with that other fugitive, Owen Glendower. For Lollardy in England, though, St Giles's Fields marked the end of open defiance. Among those rounded up was John Purvey, who died of natural causes before he could be condemned. Others were not so lucky, and from now on, though it did not disappear entirely, Lollardy moved underground.

We have a number of contemporary accounts of Oldcastle's rebellion, all of them totally hostile to Sir John. He was a 'traitor to God and man', a 'follower of Satan' and a 'man of bloody and unheard-of treachery'. By contrast, the king was God's chosen instrument to destroy the Lollards. To modern ears there seems more than a whiff of propaganda about these accounts, and one writer has gone so far as to suggest that the whole plot was made up simply to enhance Henry's status as an orthodox Christian prince. This seems unlikely given all the circumstantial detail, but it certainly did the king's image no harm at all to be seen as a strong leader favoured by God and a champion of the religion favoured by most of his subjects.

Orthodox Christianity needed all the champions it could get at the time, being challenged by more than just a few Lollards, for this was the time of the Western Schism. Wycliffe had found one corrupt pope unacceptable. By the time of his death, there were two.

In 1377 Pope Gregory XI, inspired by Catherine of Sienna, decided to end the papal exile in Avignon that had lasted more than half a century and return to Rome. He died in March of the following year, and at the conclave of cardinals meeting to choose his successor a mob burst in and forced the election of an Italian, Urban VI. This might not have been a problem except that the election seemed to go completely to his head. Criticised over his behaviour a little later, he is reported to have replied, 'I am the Pope. I can do anything, absolutely anything I like.' Within a year a large group of mostly French cardinals had returned to Avignon and elected a rival French pope, Clement VII.

Immediately both popes began seeking for support among the countries of Europe. In England it was felt an Italian would be more likely to favour English interests than a Frenchman, and the Roman pope was acknowledged. Other countries supporting Urban included Ireland, Denmark, Hungary, the Holy Roman Empire, the Nordic countries and Portugal. Clement could claim backing from France, Burgundy, the Spanish kingdoms, Scotland and later Owen Glendower's Wales. Spilling over from religious considerations, it became natural that countries allied together in war would choose the same pope, and those in dispute would back different ones. It became more or less a bargaining chip.

There were opportunities for settlement in 1389 and 1394, when first Urban and then Clement died. They were, however, replaced by an Italian, Boniface IX in Rome, and a Spaniard, Benedict XIII in Avignon. Gradually, however, support for Benedict began slipping away, with, in particular, France withdrawing recognition in 1398.

When Boniface died in 1404 another chance was missed. The Roman cardinals hesitated to name a successor, and only did so, selecting another Italian, Innocent VII, when assured by delegates from Avignon that Benedict had no intention of resigning.

From all sides now pressure was being brought to bear to end this scandalous situation. Both Benedict and Innocent had their own troubled times, and each blamed the other for continuing the schism. Innocent died suddenly in November 1406, and in the conclave that followed, each of the cardinals swore that, if elected, they would resign as soon as Benedict did the same, or if he died.

The choice fell on the eighty-year-old who became Gregory XII. Immediately he proposed a joint resignation. A meeting was suggested, a time and place eventually agreed, and then each began making excuses. In the end no meeting took place, and, finally losing patience, cardinals from both Rome and Avignon met in Pisa in May 1408 and proposed a meeting of the 'Christian world' to resolve the issue once and for all. In the same month the French king announced that he had abandoned both popes and would fully support such a move, and while Henry IV did not withdraw his support from Gregory, he too approved the idea.

The Council of Pisa, as it became known, opened in March 1409 and was attended by patriarchs, archbishops, bishops, doctors of theology and ambassadors from all Christian kingdoms. First the theologians established that such a council would have supreme authority to settle the issue (a point on which the University of Paris contributed much learned argument) and then, led by the Patriarch of Alexandria, declared that both popes were heretical schismatics, not worthy of their offices. They were declared deposed and the Holy See vacant. In June another conclave was held and a new pope, a Greco-Italian, was elected by fourteen cardinals from Rome and ten from Avignon. He took the name Alexander V.

Both Gregory and Benedict had tried and failed to set up rival councils. Both had eventually sent delegates to speak on their behalf – and neither resigned nor accepted the decisions taken at Pisa. Instead of two popes, the Church now had three.

In May 1410 Alexander dined with Cardinal Cossa, a Neapolitan who had been a leading figure at the council. Shortly afterwards he died unexpectedly and, despite the cardinal's somewhat murky backstory and a rumour that he had poisoned Alexander, Cossa was elected Pope John XXIII. This was the situation when Henry V came to the throne, but by then there was a new player in the game.

Sigismund was King of Hungary, King of the Germans, and would later be crowned Holy Roman Emperor. He had fought the Ottoman Turks on behalf of Christianity (and to protect his own kingdoms) at the fateful Battle of Nicopolis in 1396, and was anxious to reunite the divided Christian kingdoms so as to take further action against these encroachers on Christian lands.

Bowing to pressure from Sigismund and from a number of cardinals, in 1413 John XXIII called another council to achieve what the Council of Pisa had so obviously failed to do. To emphasise its neutrality it was to meet at Constance, a German imperial city, away from both Italy and France, and for the next year Sigismund was heavily involved in gathering support for it. With his influence in the eastern part of Europe, he felt it was important that France and England should also be involved, as 'the three heads of Christendom' who 'should unite together for the general good'.

Henry, too, as a true son of the Church, felt it important to be part of this movement, the more so since, as well as the reunification of the papacy, other themes to be debated by the council were the Lollard heresy and Church reform. Nor was he losing sight of England's other interests. There was long-standing distrust between Sigismund and the Duke of Burgundy, which led the former to favour the Armagnac cause in France, and to generally favour French interests above English ones. Partly this was due to the disastrous outcome of Nicopolis, brought about by the Duke of Burgundy's refusal to listen to tactical advice from Sigismund. In part also it was due to the later attacks on Sigismund's German lands by Burgundians ambitious for expansion. It would be of great benefit to Henry's future plans, however, if the German king could be turned into an ally, and support for him in the council would be one way to achieve this.

The English delegation was therefore chosen with some care. Had it been a year or two earlier, Henry Chichele, then Bishop of St David's, would have been an obvious choice. Though there are stories of his humble origins, that he had been 'a poor plough boy, eating scanty meals off his mother's lap', this seems to have been an exaggeration since his father later became mayor of Higham Ferrers in Northamptonshire. Nevertheless he had been a scholar at Winchester School and New College, Oxford, an ecclesiastical lawyer, and for some time past a royal envoy, regularly engaged on diplomatic missions abroad. In 1411 he had accompanied the Earl of Arundel's expedition to France, and earlier he had been an envoy to both Pope Boniface and Pope Gregory, so he was well versed in the state of the papacy. In February 1414, however, the mighty Archbishop Arundel had suffered a stroke and died, and Henry had immediately proposed Chichele as his successor, the appointment being duly made in April of that year. As archbishop he could not be spared, even for something as important as the council which was assembling in the autumn of 1414.

Instead the English delegation dispatched in October of that year was led by Robert Hallum, Bishop of Salisbury, an experienced cleric known to favour reform in the Church. Along with him went the Bishop of Bath and Wells and the newly appointed Bishop of St David's, and, to show the particular interest of the king, his close friend Richard, Earl of Warwick.

The Council of Constance opened in November 1414, presided over by Sigismund and John XXIII. The early sessions were devoted to establishing its authority, but then, in February 1415 a procedural change was made that greatly enhanced the English influence. Some countries, particularly Italy and France, had sent large delegations, while others were of more modest proportions. In order to avoid being outvoted by the very people who were blocking progress already, it was decided that voting would be by 'nation'. At this point the Spanish countries, still solidly backing the Spanish pope, Benedict XIII, had not sent any representatives, so the four 'nations' identified as having a vote were Germany (including some Scandinavian and Polish representatives), France, Italy and England. From being one of the smallest groups, the English now became one of the most powerful.

Although assembled under the auspices of John XXIII, the decision of the council was that all three popes should abdicate. John reluctantly agreed to this, but then, not trusting the 'nations', fled from Constance and in his absence was tried and found guilty of heresy, selling religious offices, schism, piracy and immorality. Soon after he was persuaded to give himself up and he was imprisoned for some time in Germany.

In July 1415 Pope Gregory sent representatives, giving them his authority to summon and preside over the council (thereby clarifying its authority), and to tender his resignation. This was immediately accepted, the former pope then being reappointed a cardinal and retiring to live out his days in peace.

Pope Benedict alone stood out against the council. He refused to stand down and was excommunicated, and Sigismund spent some time trying and failing to persuade him to step aside for the good of the Church.

While this was proceeding the council was also addressing the problems of heresy. In early sessions the doctrines of John Wycliffe were condemned once again. He was declared a heretic and it was directed that his remains be dug up and burnt – which sentence was only carried out in 1423, the ashes being thrown into the nearby River Swift. Closer to hand, though, they had a follower of Wycliffe, Jan Hus, a Czech priest and philosopher. He had adopted and preached Wycliffite doctrines at Prague University, at that time in the kingdom of Bohemia, whose king was Wenceslaus, elder brother of Sigismund. Strongly linked with pressure for Czech independence, and encouraged by support from Oxford University, Hus insisted his views were not heretical, and had offered to go to Rome and defend them before Pope Gregory. Now, with a safe-conduct given by Sigismund, he had travelled instead to the council at Constance, expecting an opportunity to speak on the reform of the Church. Once there, however, he defied an order not to say Mass, was arrested and tried for heresy. Despite an eloquent defence of his doctrines, he was found guilty, condemned and burnt to death on 6 July 1415. By some accounts Sigismund was absent when this took place, but certainly the Czech people held him responsible for the death of their leader, and the so-called 'Hussite Wars' that followed Sigismund's accession as King of Bohemia in 1419 were a bloody consequence of this.

By mid-1415 the council had achieved a good deal of what it had set out to do. It would continue for a further three years and have a profound effect on the English nation, but now the mind of Henry V was focussed on a different matter, one which would concern him for the rest of his life. Henry was thinking of France.

5

FRANCE
1413–1415

By the time of Henry V, the histories of England and France had been intertwined for centuries. William the Conqueror, setting out in 1066 to claim the throne of England, was a vassal of the French king and did homage for his Duchy of Normandy. Though there was never any question of his overlord claiming the kingdom he won, as happened later with England and Ireland, still William introduced the English to all things French. The feudal system, the French language and French customs, all became dominant in England, and even, possibly, the suggestion that blunt Anglo-Saxon words were rude and unfit for polite society.

The situation became more complicated under William's grandson, Henry II. Already count of both Anjou and Maine before he inherited England, by marrying Eleanor of Aquitaine he added that territory as well to his empire. At the height of his power he held almost the whole of western France, considerably more than the French king himself. He could have ridden from the Scottish border to the Pyrenees without leaving his own lands. The fact that he was still theoretically the French king's vassal was an obvious cause of friction between the two, quite apart from the fact that he had won a large part of his empire by marrying that king's ex-wife.

Of course, it didn't last. Henry's son Richard had no interest in the empire except as a source of money for his crusading in the Holy Land. His brother John, who succeeded him, was inept, and John's son, Henry III, inherited what was left at the age of nine. Normandy itself was lost in 1204, and by 1229 there remained only Guienne and Gascony, part of his grandmother's Aquitaine, for which Henry was required to do homage to Louis of France.

The French kings were due their own problems, however, and they came in the form of Louis's grandson, Philippe IV. Philippe, always short of money, hit on the plan of seizing the wealth of the Order of Knights Templar. These former crusader knights had amassed great treasure, and since they had retired to Europe all manner of stories had grown up about their secretive and possibly occult practices. Whether these were true or not, they gave Philippe an excuse to act. In a single night he descended on the Templars, seized their property and arrested every one of them. Then, by means of torture, they were induced to confess to heresies and gross sins and were put to death. In March 1314 Jacque de Molay, the last Grand Master of the Templars, was burnt to death beside Notre Dame Cathedral in Paris. In the depths of his suffering, so the story goes, he called down a curse on Philippe and on his descendants to the thirteenth generation. In particular, both Philippe and the Pope, who had supported his attack on the Templars, would be dead within a year.

Whether due to the curse or otherwise, it is a fact that Philippe died in a hunting accident eight months later at the age of forty-six. Two years later his son, Louis X, also died in rather mysterious circumstances, apparently after drinking cooled wine following a strenuous game of tennis. (He is, incidentally, the first named tennis player in history, having had indoor courts constructed especially for him.) He was aged twenty-seven, and his son, John I, was not born until five months after his father's death. John I lived and reigned for five short days. Passing over his sister, Jeanne, then aged four, the crown went next to Philippe's second son, Philippe V, who lasted six years until he too died, at the age of thirty leaving only daughters. His brother, Charles IV, also reigned for six years and also left only daughters.

In the space of fourteen years, then, the last direct male descendants of the Capetian line, stretching back to AD 957, were wiped out, leaving behind them an empty throne and a problem of succession France had not faced for nearly four hundred years.

There were three possible candidates. Probably the closest in line was Jeanne, daughter of Louis X, now grown up and married to the King of Navarre. Another possibility was Philippe de Valois, cousin of the last king and nephew of Philippe IV. And then there was Edward III of England. He was a grandson of Philippe IV, his mother being Philippe's daughter Isabelle.

By direct descent the choice would be between Jeanne and Edward, but Navarre and England were equally unacceptable to the French. Philippe de Valois was duly crowned Philippe VI, the first in the line of kings from the house of Valois.

At the time Edward was in no position to argue. He had come to the throne at the age of fifteen only the year before, following the death of his father at Berkeley Castle. Nor was he on good terms with his French mother, who, by popular repute, had caused that death, along with her lover, Mortimer.

In 1329 he performed a homage of sorts to Philippe for his lands in France. By one account he knelt and said the words but did not put his hands between Philippe's hands, as the ritual demanded. In another he came wearing a sword instead of appearing unarmed and bare headed. Soon it became clear that there would be trouble between them. Philippe wanted Aquitaine, while Edward wanted, at the least, to be free of his overlord.

By 1337 Edward was firmly in control of his kingdom and had reasons aplenty for challenging Philippe, who was not only harassing the English lands in France but also creating problems for the wool trade with Flanders. In that year Philippe accused Edward of harbouring his enemies and not behaving as a vassal should. He proposed to confiscate Guienne. Edward's immediate response was to declare that he would have not only Guienne but France itself. The so-called Hundred Years War was underway.

Initial victories went to England. In June 1340 the French fleet was destroyed at the Battle of Sluys off the coast of Flanders. The French lost 190 ships and some 18,000 men. Though this gave the English the upper hand in the Channel and dispelled any threat of a French invasion, it did not entirely clear the seaways. The French called on Portuguese, Spanish and Mediterranean ships for assistance and raiding and harassment of English merchant ships continued, though on a lesser scale.

It was the presence of a Mediterranean fleet off the south-west coast of France in 1346 that led Edward to launch his forces instead against Normandy, this being in retaliation for Philippe's attack on Guienne the year before. With some 4,000 knights and 10,000 English and Welsh archers, his aim was to make a grand *chevauchée* – a great raid for plunder and prestige – rather than an actual invasion. Faced by such forces Normandy fell without a fight, and, loaded down with loot, Edward was making for

Flanders and home when confronted at a place called Crécy, with French forces determined on battle.

Philippe, with superior though undisciplined numbers, launched a traditional mounted attack which Edward countered by deploying his archers. In the event the French force was cut to pieces and the English victory decisive. The following year Edward, ignoring Philippe's chivalrous invitation to a set battle on equal terms, besieged and took the port of Calais.

The Black Death then intervened, carrying off between a third and a half of the population of each country, but afterwards in 1355 the war resumed in similar fashion. By this time there was a new French king, John II, and the English campaign was led by Edward's son, also Edward, known as the Black Prince. The result was the same. At Poitiers in 1356 the French army was overwhelmingly defeated by the English and Welsh archers. Worse, the French king was taken prisoner, and though it took some time to remove him to England it seems that no attempt was made to rescue him.

With such a catch it might have been thought that Edward would press ever harder his apparent claim to the French throne. Instead, in the Treaty of Brétigny in 1360, he settled for much less. In return for renouncing his claim to the throne and to Normandy, Maine and Anjou, he was to have full sovereignty over a large chunk of the south-west of France amounting to almost a third of the country and comprising Guienne, Gascony, Poitou, Limousin and other territories, as well as the most useful channel port of Calais. In addition, a sum of three million gold crowns was fixed as the ransom for King John.

In general the treaty aimed to clear up the feudal anomalies between the two kings and to concentrate the English territories in one area. However, when the treaty came to be ratified by the kings and their sons in the Treaty of Calais later that year, the all-important clauses relating to the English king's perpetual sovereignty over his lands were taken out and put in a separate document which was never formally ratified.

The honour of King John was not in doubt. Not for nothing was he known as John the Good. When the first part of his ransom was paid he was released from custody and other hostages took his place. One of these, his second son Louis, subsequently escaped and returned to France. Mortified at the dishonour of this action, John insisted on returning to England to resume his captivity. We are told he was met with parades and celebrations, but sadly he fell ill soon after and died the following year.

His son Charles V was a different proposition. The first French heir to bear the title 'Dauphin', he had already had a brief taste of the limelight as Regent of France during his father's captivity. Though physically frail he was shrewd, prepared to listen to advice and a good judge of men. When the war resumed in 1369, each side blaming the other, he rapidly reconquered all the land ceded to England with the exception of Calais and Gascony.

Both sides were set for a change, however. Edward and Charles died within three years of each other, and each was succeeded by a twelve-year-old heir: Richard II in England and Charles VI in France. For a time neither was in a position to continue the struggle with any vigour, and when they grew to maturity both were in favour of a succession of truces and attempts to settle the whole issue. The last such truce was sealed by the marriage of Richard to Isabelle, the six-year-old daughter of the French king. By this time, however, Charles had already been struck by the intermittent madness that was to blight the rest of his life.

In August 1392, while on his way to Brittany under a hot sun, the king was approached by a wild man, some say a leper, who seized his bridle and warned him of enemies plotting his doom. Though forced away by the king's men, he apparently followed for some time, still shouting his warnings. Shortly afterwards a page in the king's train dropped a lance that struck against a helmet as it fell, with a ringing noise. Instantly the king drew his sword and attacked his own attendants, killing four before he could be restrained. When taken from his horse he fell into a coma lasting two days, and when he awoke was appalled to hear what he had done. For a while he seemed to recover but then the madness struck again the following year, and then again and again, becoming more frequent, and generally worse in the summer than in winter. At times he would rush violently about until exhausted, attacking anyone who approached. On other occasions, especially later on, he suffered from a delusion that he was made of glass and would break if anyone touched him. He denied his wife and children, his kingship and even his name. Then the fit would pass, maybe after several months, and he would appear sane again, but listless and prepared to do whatever the person advising him suggested.

In the circumstances a council was appointed to govern the country when Charles was incapable. Presided over by his wife, Isabeau of Bavaria, it initially summoned back to power the king's uncles, who had already served as regents for an extended period before he attained the age of twenty-one. Unfortunately for France they had shown before that they had more interest in their own advancement than in the good of the country. Taxes had been raised and the treasury plundered, and now once again there was to be intense competition to control the king and the government of France.

At first Philippe of Burgundy held sway, his aim being to increase the power of his dukedom along the eastern border of France. When he died in 1404 his son, John, known as the Fearless, pursued an even more aggressive policy of personal advancement. By this time, however, he had a serious rival in the form of the king's brother, Louis of Orleans, who had worked his way into Queen Isabeau's affections, and some say into her bed as well.

It was this Louis who, on the usurpation of the English throne by Henry IV, twice challenged the king to a personal duel. Though Henry might ignore this, he could not prevent Louis and his allies from attacking and seizing large portions of Gascony, leaving England with only a narrow strip of land around the towns of Bordeaux and Bayonne. Nor could he prevent the alliance between France and Owen Glendower in 1405 that took the French army across Wales to within sight of the city of Worcester.

A further opportunity arose for Louis to cement his position at the centre of power when Henry reluctantly returned the widow of Richard II. Isabelle, daughter of Charles VI, was now married for the second time at the age of sixteen, her bridegroom being Louis's son Charles. In fact the marriage was short-lived as she was to die in childbirth a few years later in 1409.

John the Fearless struck back by marrying his daughter to the Dauphin, Louis, but he was still behind on influence when, losing patience with political manoeuvring, and also with the efforts of the Duke of Berry to reconcile the two rivals, he had Louis of Orleans blatantly murdered in the streets of Paris in 1407. Not only did he admit to this crime but he even had sermons preached to justify what he had done. His verbal evidence to the royal court took the following form: 'It is permissible to kill a tyrant. The

Duke of Orleans was a tyrant. Therefore the Duke of Burgundy did well to kill him.'

Young Charles of Orleans was thirteen years old when his father was killed and in no position to avenge him. Following the death of Isabelle, though, he married Bonne, daughter of Count Bernard of Armagnac, and Bernard at once took up the Orleanist cause. An anti-Burgundian alliance was put together, known as the Armagnac party and featuring the counts of Armagnac, Alençon and Clermont, and the dukes of Berry, Bourbon and Brittany. A blockade of Paris was set up to dislodge John the Fearless and it was at this point that both sides began appealing to England for help.

As we have seen, that appeal led to the bizarre result of two separate English expeditions being dispatched, one supporting Burgundy and the other Armagnac. Both sides offered marriages for the Prince of Wales. Both offered advantages to England: aid for English wool interests in Flanders, and help in regaining territories in France by the Burgundians; full restoration of those territories in perpetual sovereignty by the Armagnacs. The fact that the Armagnac party largely consisted of just those people who had annexed the English territories in the first place may be one reason for Prince Henry to favour the Burgundians, while the promise to restore them without cost to himself may have swayed his father towards the Armagnacs.

The second expedition was still straggling homeward at the death of Henry IV, but each had shown the new king just how weak and divided was the French kingdom at the time. The tangled history of the two lands up to this point has led one writer to declare, 'Either the same crown must unite the two kingdoms, or a bold stroke must sever the bond.' There was never a doubt in the mind of Henry V as to which it would be.

Nevertheless there was still some way to go before war could be declared, though it seems that Henry began at once to prepare for that outcome. He was equally happy to see what diplomacy could achieve first, and more than happy to negotiate with both sides at once.

The situation in France in the spring of 1413 was changing on an almost daily basis. Despite the setback for the Armagnacs following the Earl of Arundel's intervention, John the Fearless was beginning to lose his grip on the Dauphin Louis, who was now sixteen years old and starting to show a mind of his own. Perhaps because of this, a riot was incited in Paris where there was strong sympathy for the Burgundian cause. Led by Simon Caboche, a butcher in the pay of Burgundy, a mob burst into the Dauphin's palace, murdered his servants and seized control of first the Dauphin and then his parents. The household and government was then purged of Armagnac supporters and these were replaced with Burgundians.

The revolt was short-lived and its main effect was the opposite of what was intended. In defiance of his father-in-law, Louis threw his support behind the Armagnacs and summoned them to help regain control of Paris. For a brief period Charles VI regained his sanity, long enough to denounce the mob leaders and call for peace, and by August the Armagnacs and Dauphin together had largely recovered their position. Once again there was a changing of officials, with this time Burgundians being replaced by Armagnac supporters. As the Armagnacs marched in, and as rumours grew that he would be put on trial for the murder of Louis of Orleans, John the Fearless fled to the safety of Flanders.

At this point, in September 1413, the ambassadors of Henry V met for the first time with the representatives of Charles VI.

As a preliminary diplomatic skirmish it set out the position of both sides, and, as might be expected, achieved nothing more. The English began with a lengthy lecture concerning the claim of Edward III to the French throne and the outstanding breaches of the Treaty of Brétigny. In return the French recited their Salic law as a bar to female inheritance and suggested that Edward himself had broken the treaty. It might be noted here that Henry was on dangerous ground if he was arguing for inheritance through the female line. If that was the case Edmund, Earl of March, would have a claim superior to his own to both the French and the English thrones. The point does not seem to have been taken at the time.

Following this meeting, French ambassadors, including the Constable of France, d'Albret, arrived in London in December to continue discussions. A truce was agreed that was to last for one year from February 1414, and unusually it was to involve not only England and France but all their allies as well. There had been a tussle about what language should be used for these meetings, with the English insisting on Latin – as if they could not understand French as well as the French. A compromise was reached that all conversations and treaties should be recorded in both Latin and French.

At this stage the French clearly believed Henry's claim to the throne of France was merely an opening ploy and that he would be prepared to settle for much less. Consequently, with both sides declaring that they wanted only peace and the avoidance of bloodshed, it was agreed to continue negotiating. The marriage of Henry with Katherine, daughter of Charles VI (and younger sister of Richard's bride Isabelle), was recognised by all as the best way of attaining this goal, and Henry, Lord Scrope, was dispatched to France to continue discussions with a view to arranging such a marriage. In the meantime Henry agreed he would not marry anyone else for a period of three months.

Back in France, John the Fearless was making another bid for power. Arriving outside Paris with an army, he claimed the Dauphin had sent for him to rescue him from the Armagnacs. Despite producing forged letters to back up his claim, no one believed him and the gates of Paris remained closed. After a fortnight he retreated to his stronghold at Arras.

Now, however, he had provoked a reaction. On 2 March 1414 France declared war on Burgundy. The army marched out led by the king (with or without his wits), bearing the 'oriflamme', the sacred war banner of France, and led also by the Dauphin who, perhaps in defiance of his father-in-law, bore a banner celebrating his mistress.

On the way to Arras the towns of Compiegne and Soissons were recovered from the Burgundians, the latter being sacked with such savagery that one chronicler declared that nothing done later by Henry V in his invasion came anywhere near the brutality shown on that occasion.

Arras itself was put under siege and both sides settled down to try the strength of the other. It may well have been that if either had been strong enough to prevail there would have been no further need to negotiate and offer incentives to Henry of England. As it was the siege ended in a stalemate, with the Peace of Arras, a truce putting an end to military activity, being agreed on 4 September.

In fact John the Fearless didn't sign the treaty for nearly a year, and when he did the signing was so hedged about with verbiage as to be almost meaningless. In the meantime he had sent his own ambassadors to negotiate a separate treaty with Henry. He proposed an offensive and defensive alliance against all but the

King of France, the Dauphin and the duke's close family. Each would provide armed men for the other, and he would assist Henry to regain and extend English landholding in France. He also offered his daughter as a bride for the king.

As usual, Henry did not say yes and he did not say no. He did, however, send Henry, Lord Scrope, freshly returned from negotiating a marriage with one Katherine, to go and negotiate a marriage to another. The ambassadors were also authorised to 'seek, obtain and receive the faith and liege homage' of John the Fearless on behalf of himself and his heirs; in other words, they were to secure the full transfer of allegiance of Burgundy from the French king to the English. It is doubtful whether Henry expected to achieve this. It is not mentioned in official documents, and may have been unreliable even if promised. John of Burgundy had a track record of duplicity and weasel words, and this suggestion may even have been a test of his good faith. After the Peace of Arras, however, the urgency seemed to go out of this proposed alliance, and, though the talking continued, there was very little action for some time.

Separate negotiations were continuing with the French. An embassy sent to France in the summer of 1414 was prepared to offer a compromise. Instead of all of France, to prevent war and bloodshed Henry would settle for the old Angevin empire, with the addition of Flanders and Brittany (to which he had no claim at all), all in full sovereignty, and with the lordship of Provence thrown in. There was also the little matter of 1.6 million gold crowns still owing from the ransom of King John, and a further demand for a dowry of two million crowns to accompany Katherine. The French were prepared to offer some of Aquitaine (without mention of sovereignty) and a dowry of 600,000 crowns.

Throughout this time the demands and propaganda put forward by the English would seem, to an unbiased observer, hypocritical in the extreme. On the one hand Henry was clearly preparing for war – this was discussed in a council meeting as early as the spring of 1414 – while on the other hand he posed as a peacemaker, seeking only his just rights and inheritance, and prepared even to give up some of those to avoid bloodshed. His demands for both land and money were clearly preposterous to the French, and it is a sign of their weakness that they continued negotiating and still expected the proposed marriage to go ahead.

It is probable, too, that the famous 'tennis balls' story was another instance of English propaganda. In this tale, beloved of Shakespeare, the Dauphin was declared to have sent a gift of tennis balls to the English king as befitting his youth, and with a suggestion that he amuse himself playing with them rather than making war. Though appearing in some contemporary chronicles, it seems far more likely that this was only a rumour put about to illustrate the 'derision' with which the French were treating honest English claims. In fact the Dauphin, who was considerably younger than Henry, had enough on his plate at this time without going out of his way to pick a fight with the English king.

In November 1414 the suggestion of recovery of ancient rights by force was put to Parliament by the Chancellor, Bishop Henry Beaufort. Though not unwilling to raise taxes for such a cause, they suggested, as the council had before them, that diplomacy might be tried a little further first. Consequently another embassy was sent to Paris in February 1415, led this time by the bishops of Norwich and Durham, together with the king's half-uncle Thomas Beaufort.

It achieved little beyond an extension of the truce to May of that year. The English conceded that they would reduce the dowry demand to one million crowns. The French offered land amounting to some two-thirds of the old province of Aquitaine and a dowry of 800,000 crowns. They were 'unable to agree'.

In April 1415 Henry wrote two letters, variously addressed to 'Charles, by the Grace of God our very dear cousin' and 'Charles, our cousin and adversary of France'. In each he referred to himself as 'King of England and France', portrayed himself as being wickedly deprived of his rights while striving to avoid division and preserve the peace, and put the blame for rejecting that peace squarely on the shoulders of the French king. 'We shall have to answer before God,' he told him, 'for that we retain by force which rightly belongs to another.' 'Think of eternity,' he advised.

A few days after the second letter, and before any reply had been received, Henry proposed once again to his council that he should invade France in the summer, and this time the proposal was answered in the affirmative.

6

PREPARATIONS
1413–1415

It would not be overstating the situation to say that Henry V began preparing for war with France from the very moment of his accession. The scale of his preparations made it clear that he intended no mere *chevauchée* but a determined attempt on the throne itself, and such an attempt was going to involve the whole range of actions known to medieval warfare, from siege to full-scale battle.

Then as now, victory in war frequently went to the side that changed the rules first, and the English had been doing that to some effect over the preceding hundred years. The traditional method of battle, from the time of the Conquest onwards, had depended on the cavalry charge. Heavily armed – and later heavily armoured – men against an unmounted defensive line; it was all but unstoppable, and only a tightly packed formation of pikemen like the Scottish schiltron had any way of resisting such a charge.

Not only was this effective, but it was also seen as an honourable, chivalrous way of waging war. Only the nobility could afford the horses, armour and equipment required, and the knight on horseback was the very symbol of the times. Among western nations, at least, with all its courtesy and protocol warfare sometimes resembled a sport more than a serious business. Even if unfortunate enough to be captured, the noble could rely on being ransomed by his people, and death in battle was a rarity – at least for the upper levels of society.

In the early fifteenth century most countries still relied on such methods, indeed John the Fearless had acquired his nickname by leading a particularly reckless cavalry charge against the Turks at the Battle of Nicopolis in 1396. Impressive it may have been, but it lost the battle for his side, the charge being broken up by a line of stakes driven into the ground protecting packed infantry formations behind. Stakes, potholes and ditches were all methods of disrupting cavalry when the defending army had time to prepare the ground. The English, however, had found another way of dealing with such a charge.

Archery is, of course, almost as old as mankind. Most armies had contained some archers, usually armed with relatively light hunting bows. On the Continent the crossbow was well known, and in particular Genoese crossbowmen operating as mercenaries were often found with the French army in the early part of the Hundred Years War. The English contribution was in the development of what came to be called the longbow, a formidable weapon and in its day as devastating as in later centuries the machine gun would prove to be.

While a crossbow could fire a heavier missile, it was more cumbersome, more technical and more expensive to produce. It was also slow to load, the bowstring having to be wound back mechanically to the shooting position, or at very least the bow braced with a foot in a stirrup while the string was hauled back.

As a result a firing rate of two or maybe three bolts a minute was usual. By contrast the longbow was lighter and cheaper to produce, and in skilled hands could put ten or a dozen arrows in the air in a minute. Simple mathematics tells us that a force of several thousand longbowmen could send a storm of some thirty thousand arrows a minute towards an enemy, 'so thickly and evenly that they fell like snow', and, willing or not, few cavalry charges could face down such a storm.

The drawback to the longbow was that it took years of practice to achieve such skill. From the time of Henry III, however, the law of England had required all adult males to keep a bow and practise. Later this became a more specific order, that all between the ages of sixteen and sixty must practise at the butts after Mass each Sunday and on holy days. Beginning with a shorter, lighter bow, the novice would gradually acquire the strength and skill to master the full-size war bow. This stood roughly six feet high when unstrung, and had a draw weight of around 150 pounds – about three times the weight of modern competition bows. As a result an arrow storm would have a range of something approaching 300 yards, while at closer distances the force would be sufficient to penetrate armour.

Prudent long-term planning meant that there was a steady supply of men able and willing to use the bow, both for defence at home and as a great reservoir to draw on for service overseas. It is not surprising to find, therefore, that archers made up roughly three-quarters of the army Henry V took to France.

The very day after his coronation Henry issued an order forbidding the export of bows, arrows and other arms to the Scots or to other enemies, and almost at once production of bows and arrows was increased.

A bow would be made from a single piece of wood, preferably yew. Although much romance attaches to the 'English yew bow', in fact the best yew was imported from Spain, where the climate and growing conditions favoured the production of long, straight staves from which a bow could be fashioned. With the more flexible sapwood on the outside, a thicker 'belly' in the centre of the bow tapered towards the ends, which were capped or 'nocked' with horn sheaths to hold the bowstring. When drawn the belly was compressed and the sapwood stretched, so that two forces propelled the arrow forward on the release of the string. The bow would be waxed or oiled to keep it flexible, and carried unstrung in a canvas bag to protect it from the weather. The bowstring of gut or hemp would be carried separately in a pouch, or frequently under the archer's hat – hence 'keep it under your hat'.

Each archer would be equipped with between sixty and seventy-two arrows of two main types, used for different purposes. For long-distance use, particularly against horses or lightly armoured men, a longer, lighter broadhead arrow would be used. Preferably made of a lighter wood such as poplar, the iron arrowhead would be flat with swept-back barbs. These made it harder to pull out an arrow that had lodged in flesh, and in fact wherever possible the arrow would be pushed through and out the other side as an easier option. As well as that, the spinning of the arrow in flight meant that the broadhead arrow carved a larger hole and was easily capable of causing a devastating wound to a charging horse.

For closer-range use the bodkin arrow was a little shorter and heavier, made of ash wood, and with a long, sharply pointed iron tip. The penetrating power of bodkins against mail had led to the introduction of more and more plate armour, but, particularly when tipped with beeswax, these arrows could at close range even penetrate steel plate.

Both types of arrow were fletched with goose feathers, whose natural curve made the arrow spin in flight. This and its slight oscillation through the air, gave it a force on delivery something like the action of a hammer drill.

Many thousands of arrows would be needed for Henry's French campaign and the stockpiling began immediately. At the height of demand for goose feathers an order would go out demanding six feathers from every goose, and bowyers, fletchers and bowstring makers all found plenty of employment during the first two years of Henry's reign.

Smiths and forgers of iron and steel were also in demand. In February 1414 more men were taken on at the Tower of London to speed this work, and not only the royal forges there but others up and down the country became increasingly busy turning out the weapons that would be needed.

The sword was the very symbol of knighthood, around three feet in length, double-edged and made of the finest available steel. Most combatants, even archers, would also carry a dagger, with a long, narrow blade suitable for striking through an opponent's visor or between the joints of armour, or for slitting an unprotected throat.

Lances were also in demand. Some twelve feet long if used on horseback, and about half that for use on foot, they were made of ash and tipped with a point of iron or steel. The upper part of the shaft would usually be reinforced by strips of metal to prevent the lethal tip being hacked off in battle. An increasingly popular variation was the poleaxe. Here the head of the pole was topped by a combination of two and sometimes three separate weapons: a long spike for stabbing, an axe head for chopping and a ridged or sometimes pronged hammerhead for breaking armour.

As well as these more or less conventional weapons, Henry had already proved himself a devotee of cannon, now beginning to appear in medieval warfare. These were made by heating and beating together strips of metal around a wooden core, and then binding the resulting tube with iron hoops. The core was then removed, leaving a barrel into which might be loaded a mass of small lead pellets or, more usually, a stone ball weighing anything from 500 to 800 pounds.

These cannon were the most awkward and cumbersome of weapons, both to move around and to fire. Reinforced carts were needed for their transportation and overland they could be expected to move only a few miles a day, although river or sea transport was quicker. To fire they had to be loaded onto a special wooden cradle, and a separate metal chamber containing packed gunpowder put in place, before a lighted fuse was applied through a touch hole. Even then the results were not guaranteed. A fault in the metal could cause the cannon itself to explode, killing the gunner concerned, as happened some half a century later to James II of Scotland. They were difficult to aim, wildly inaccurate and, since the barrel had to be cooled after each firing, capable of only two or at most three shots a day. Nevertheless, as Henry had proved at Aberystwyth and Harlech, they were capable of doing considerable damage to a castle wall during a siege, and for this reason an order went out in September 1414 to construct cannon for the French campaign.

Nor were the more traditional siege weapons ignored. Trebuchets and mangonels, used for hurling heavy stones and other missiles, would also be needed, along with the tall, multi-storied 'belfries' or towers on which attackers could be drawn up close to castle walls to launch their assaults. Quantities of wood were necessary for these, along with skilled carpenters and others to put them together and repair them when needed.

Armourers were also in demand to fit out the many thousands who would march with the king, the quantity and type of armour varying with the status, wealth and role of the combatant. Archers tended to be very lightly armoured. An open-faced iron cap and a brigandine, a canvas jacket reinforced with metal plates, was the usual protection, leaving arms and legs unencumbered for speed and accuracy of shooting and mobility.

At the other end of the scale a knight or noble would be covered from head to foot in plates of metal known as his harness. This was never a 'suit of armour' in the sense of a single garment. Each piece would be attached separately, from the many-plated sabatons on his feet to the helmet or bascinet, with or without a visor, on his head. The body was protected by a breastplate and backplate, usually hinged on the left side. A skirt of steel hoops hung from waist to mid-thigh, while arms and legs were protected by metal articulated at knee, elbow and shoulder. The neck and shoulders were originally covered by a flexible mail 'aventail', but later this was replaced by a solid metal gorget to protect the throat.

Contrary to popular belief, this armour was not overwhelmingly heavy or cumbersome. It was worn over a thickly padded cloth jacket, the arming doublet, which not only made it more comfortable but also helped absorb the blows from an opponent's weapons. With weight distributed more or less evenly all over, it was relatively easy for a fit man to bear. It did, however, need to be well fitting and correctly attached in order to allow free movement. Its main vulnerabilities were under the arms and in the groin area, and later the arming doublet would have mail attached to the skirt and under the arms to reduce this risk. A blow from a warhammer could also disable a joint by bending the metal plates, leaving the wearer unable to lift an arm or bend a leg.

While all these war materials were in preparation Henry was not neglecting the part to be played by diplomacy in making ready for war. In particular his aim was to isolate France from all her traditional supporters. Negotiations with John the Fearless effectively ensured Burgundy's neutrality, while support for the Council at Constance, pet project of the Emperor Sigismund, may, in part at least, have been intended to achieve the same results as regards the Germanic states on France's eastern borders. Castile among the Spanish nations was a long-time French supporter, and her ships were well placed to disrupt traffic in the Channel and harry the English coast. As early as 1413 a truce was agreed to counter this risk, and in January 1414 another was signed with Brittany to halt attacks on English shipping by Bretons, whose piracy was only matched by that of the Devon sailors facing them across the Channel. Both of these treaties were firmly enforced by Henry.

At the same time as clearing the Channel of potential enemies, the king was also planning to fill it with English ships. Always more interested than his predecessors in the security of the sea, it was partly through his influence when Prince of Wales that the number of royal ships had grown from two to six at the time of his accession. In July 1413 William Catton was appointed clerk of the king's ships, with immediate orders to set about building and repairing vessels for the royal fleet. These were not intended as transport but as fighting ships that would patrol the coastal waters between England and the Continent. By 1415 another six had been added, and, based at Southampton Water, this became over the next decade or so at least the embryo of a royal dockyard.

Home defences, too, were put in order at this time. Castles along the Scottish and Welsh borders were repaired and improved, restocked and fully garrisoned. South coast ports, including Southampton, had their fortifications rebuilt, some acquiring new towers with gun ports rather than arrow slits as a sign of the progressive times.

Henry's second parliament, sitting at Leicester in April 1414, had a strong message of law and order, both at home and on the seas. The king, declared Bishop Henry, opening the session in his role as Lord Chancellor, *has set his heart to keep the laws*. As if to emphasise the point, and in response to a number of petitions relating to lawlessness in the Midlands shires, the Court of King's Bench, the most powerful of the common law courts, spent several months sitting at a number of towns around the area, dealing vigorously with the enforcement of the law.

The Scots were always a danger when English eyes were turned to France, but Henry still had his trump card, the young King James of Scotland. As a sign of their importance both he and the Regent Albany's son, Murdoch, had been promptly returned to the Tower of London almost at the moment of Henry's accession, and remained there more or less throughout the build-up to war. Henry's brother John, newly created Duke of Bedford, together with Ralph Neville, Earl of Westmoreland, had been confirmed in their posts as wardens of the Scottish March, but now Henry proposed a prisoner exchange that he felt would make the ongoing truce even more secure.

Not the young king but Murdoch was offered in exchange for Northumberland's grandson, Henry Percy, who had begun as a guest of the Scots but rapidly transformed into a prisoner after his grandfather's last fruitless rebellion. The king calculated that returning Percy to his hereditary lands and titles (provided of course that he remained indebted to Henry) would add to the stability of the region, as would reuniting Murdoch with his father. In fact the exchange went badly wrong when Murdoch, on his way north, was ambushed and abducted by a renegade Lollard knight. (Some accounts suggest he in fact escaped from his escort.) Though he was soon recovered the exchange was delayed, the Scots invaded the north and were only stopped by the actions of Sir Robert Umphraville at Yeavering. This and the threat that Murdoch would not be returned prevented the incident escalating into the war that Henry had been so anxious to avoid.

Throughout 1414 the build-up to the invasion of France continued unabated. Though Henry had consulted his council in the spring and his parliament in November, each time being told to keep negotiating, still the preparations on all fronts went on.

Having experienced years of campaigning in Wales with insufficient money, the king was determined this would not happen again. There were basically three sources of finance available to him: income from the royal estates, money voted by Parliament and loans. While he was prepared to bide his time about the second of these, the first and third were employed immediately under the supervision of his Treasurer, Thomas, Earl of Arundel.

Rents and profits from royal estates and fines from royal courts were rigorously overhauled from the very start of the reign. Pensions and annuities, almost scattered broadcast by Henry IV, were reviewed by his son, who possibly felt there was no need to buy popularity in that way. In general, when they were continued, some service, military or otherwise, would be expected in return. Meticulous accounts were kept, and the fact that the king himself was likely to review the figures and question any discrepancies no doubt kept his officials up to the mark. For a warrior king, Henry seemed also to possess the soul of an accountant. All of this, however, meant that money flowed into rather than out of the royal coffers.

Money voted by Parliament came in two basic forms: subsidies, and duties on merchandise traded in and out of the country. A subsidy would be paid by anyone with moveable goods valued at ten shillings or more. Typically it would be one-fifteenth of the value of these goods for those in the countryside, and one-tenth for those in towns. Subsidies payable by the clergy, again typically one-tenth, were voted for separately by the convocations for the archdiocese of Canterbury and York.

Duties, normally granted for a period of years, were payable on exports of English wools and hides, and, in the form of tonnage and poundage, on every tun or cask of wine and pound of merchandise imported. Foreign merchants paid proportionately more than their English counterparts. The wool duty was granted for a period of four years from September 1413, while tonnage and poundage, initially granted only for one year from that date, were renewed for a further three years from September 1414.

Soon after his accession one Richard Whittington, a wealthy cloth merchant in the city of London, made a loan of £2,000 to the king. This same Dick Whittington, true to the prophecy of the bells in the children's story, had been Lord Mayor of London twice already and would be again in the future. He was a noted benefactor to both Henry and his father, but was not the only one to contribute in this way. From the spring of 1415 the raising of money by loans became a major priority.

In March 1415 the mayor and aldermen of the city of London were the first to be flattered and cajoled into producing from the city a loan that, in today's terms, would be the equivalent of nearly £3 million. Then in May what was almost a begging letter went out under the king's private seal to individuals, towns and religious communities around the country. The king was setting out to claim his rights, and without further money (to be raised by loans) his enterprise was likely to fail or at least be delayed. The amount of the loan was left deliberately vague – to be suggested by the bearer of the letter – and the money was to be produced as quickly as possible. The result of this was a flood of contributions, ranging from individual loans of some thousands from such as Bishop Henry to loans of a few hundred from important towns such as Bristol and Norwich. These latter would be made up of individual payments assessed by the town authorities, which might be as little as ten pence. In return for these loans, some of which would not be repaid for years, jewels, plate, even crowns were handed over from the royal treasury as security.

One estimate puts the total sum raised by Henry for his wars at approaching £70 million in today's currency, and to this sum a large proportion of the country's population would have contributed, whether by loans, subsidies or otherwise. It was a time when unity and common purpose of the nation was beginning to be stressed, and this was certainly one way in which the whole populace could be made to feel involved in the king's endeavours.

A similar theme can be seen in the recruitment of men for the king's army, which began in earnest in March 1415. The idea of a feudal army, where each man was called upon to serve his feudal lord, up to and including the king, had long been abandoned. Though Henry IV had on many occasions called out the local levies to deal with sudden emergencies, this was at best a short-term defensive solution. Poorly trained men serving for only forty days was not what was needed for an army of invasion. Instead an indenture system had been developed whereby professional fighting men would sell their services to whoever might need them.

An indenture was a document containing two identical copies of a contract to provide specified services on specified terms. One type was an indenture for life whereby the retainer undertook to serve in peace and in war. The other was an indenture to serve for a specific time or in a particular campaign. When all the details had been listed and the document signed by both parties and often witnessed, it would be cut in half with a wavy or 'indented' line, each party taking one copy of the agreement. In the case of any dispute the documents could be produced and matched together, thus making any forgery almost impossible.

It was common when raising an army that indentures would be signed with a few of the king's chief men, who would then go away and recruit the necessary numbers in the same way. What is surprising about Henry's army is that so many separate indentures were issued, some covering barely a handful of men. The king's copy of each was kept in a named leather bag, and all further documents relating to it, such as muster rolls and payments of wages, would be kept together in the same bag. Well over six hundred of these bags were ordered, and though they may not all have been used, there are clear records for 250 of them. What this meant was that, instead of there being many layers between the nobles and the men on the ground, a large number of Henry's army had contracts with the king himself – perhaps another way of making them feel a more personal share in the campaign.

The indenture specified the name of the captain and the numbers and ranks of the men he would bring to the muster. The term 'men-at-arms' or sometimes 'lances' is used to cover all those of whatever rank who were not archers or other specialists. It might refer to an earl, a knight or a simple esquire. Unlike the archers, the men-at-arms were supposed to equip themselves with weapons and horses, and the indenture would state exactly what equipment was required.

From the amount of money raised it might be understood that Henry was expecting a long campaign, and this is reflected in the large number of indentures now issued in April 1415 which were for one year's service. They were remarkably vague, however, about where that service would be given. Like all commanders, Henry did not want to warn the enemy in advance about where he might strike.

Wages had been set for the campaign by the king and his council. A duke would receive 13s 4d a day (roughly 67p), an earl half that, four shillings for a baron, two for a knight and sixpence a day for an archer. Wages were paid quarterly in advance, with half of the first quarter paid on signing on and the rest at the muster. This and a 'regard' or bonus payment for each group of thirty men-at-arms might have helped towards the cost of the equipment.

There was no shortage of recruits. Even the archer's pay was well above what an unskilled man might hope to earn in other employment, and there was always the hope of extra profit from such an adventure. Henry was very strict about looting, but the capture of a wealthy prisoner would lead to a ransom being paid, sometimes there and then in the immediate aftermath of battle if it was not set too high. Lesser folk who felt they would not be able to extract such a payment could sell a prisoner to their superiors, thus ensuring they did not miss out. One of Henry's leading commanders, Sir John Cornwaille, was an enthusiastic buyer-up of ransoms, and his fortune and fine new residence, Ampthill Castle, was built upon such profitable trading.

There was a general expectation that there would be such opportunities for enrichment, and the indenture would also clearly state how the spoils would be divided. In general the king would be entitled to all major prisoners such as the King of France and his immediate family, and in addition a third of the personal winnings of company leaders, and a ninth of those of the men in their companies, provided these were worth more than ten marks (nearly £3,000 today). Despite these restrictions the coffers of several noble families, the earls of Arundel and Warwick for example, were well replenished by the profits from Henry's wars.

With the muster set for July 1415 at Southampton, the final problems to be overcome were logistical – how to feed this vast number of men and how to transport them and their necessary supplies to France. As early as March the king's agents were sent to the Low Countries to hire, quietly and discreetly, as many ships and crews as they could, and send these at once to the ports of London, Sandwich and Winchelsea. It is likely that they acquired in this way some six hundred ships, but that was nothing like enough. On 11 April the king ordered that all ships of twenty tons or more at any port from the Thames to Newcastle should be seized for conversion to transports. This applied whether the ships were English or foreign, and, though some compensation was paid, this did not reduce the consternation felt by foreign owners as something over a thousand ships were impounded. It is an interesting point that, while English ships were sent to Southampton, where the build-up of men and materials might be most obvious, the others went to London, Sandwich or Winchelsea.

At the same time wagons and horses were being acquired in great numbers, together with the grooms, farriers, wheelwrights and others necessary to accompany them. Cattle and oxen were bought and driven to the Southampton area, and over several counties around bakers and brewers were instructed to begin to produce whatever would be needed to feed the king's army. It was a feature of Henry's campaigns that such things were bought not requisitioned, although the payment might be a pledge that would be difficult to redeem. In theory, at least, all abuses were to be reported to officers of the king's household so that justice could be done, something else that tended to make the king popular with the working people. Every lord, knight and esquire was told to supply himself with provisions for three months, and this too was expected to be paid for. Whatever shortfall there was in the advance wages provided had to be made up by the individual concerned.

As all this mass of men, animals and materials began to make their way towards Southampton, the only real comparison, and in the same area, would be the build-up of men and materials prior to D-Day in the Second World War some five hundred years later. It is estimated that around twelve thousand men made up Henry's army, and this figure probably does not include all the non-combatants needed to provide for men and beasts. In Henry's retinue alone there were the grooms needed to look after 233 horses, armourers, a sergeant of the pavilions and his assistants to deal with the tentage, some hundreds of kitchen and other servants, minstrels, chaplains and monks to attend to spiritual needs, a personal physician and twenty-three surgeons. Hundreds of ships were needed just to transport the horses since, at the king's expense, each duke was entitled to bring fifty, an earl twenty-four, a baron sixteen, a knight six, an esquire four and an archer one.

The king himself left London with much ceremony on 16 June, and just when he did not want to see them a bevy of French ambassadors arrived the day after. He met with them at Wolvesey

Castle in Winchester, and though it must have been obvious to all that Henry was not likely to be distracted from his purpose, once again they made a slightly enlarged offer which was immediately turned down. At this point, according to one account, the leader of the delegation, the Archbishop of Bourges, made a final riposte. Not only, he declared, was Henry not the true King of France, he was not the true King of England either, which burst of plain speaking left nothing more to say on either side.

The muster of men took place on 1 July, and on 6 July Henry moved his quarters to Portchester Castle, overlooking the harbour from which he would sail. On 24 July the king made his will, and on the 29th he finally gave the order for embarkation. This whole mass of men, animals and equipment were to be loaded and ready to sail on 1 August.

And then, on 31 July, came the most sudden and unexpected interruption that would stop the whole operation in its tracks. On the evening of that day Edmund Mortimer, newly restored to his freedom and honours as Earl of March, came to the king and told him of a plot to depose him and put Edmund on the throne in his place.

The leading conspirator was Richard, Earl of Cambridge, younger brother of the Duke of York who just for once seemed to have no part in or knowledge of the affair. Equally implicated were Henry, Lord Scrope, and a northern magnate, Sir Thomas Grey. Allegations were also made against a number of others, including Sir Robert Umphraville, who had so recently served the king by putting an end to the Scottish invasion.

Instantly arrested by the king, Grey confessed at once closely followed by Cambridge, but had they not done so the whole affair would have seemed little short of a fantasy. Every rebel from the last twenty years was supposed to play a part, from Glendower to the Scottish lords Douglas and Murdoch, to Oldcastle and the Lollards, and not forgetting Henry Percy. The Earl of March was to be carried into Wales and there proclaimed king as the true successor to Richard. Then Wales, Scotland and the north of England would rise to support him. The weakest of all the weak links in this wild scheme was the Earl of March, who, having spent most of his life as a prisoner, had clearly no intention of risking that or worse again. In fact, freed and pardoned by Henry as an innocent victim of the plot, he then served the king loyally for the rest of his life.

On 1 August the three main conspirators were tried before a jury. Cambridge and Grey were found guilty of treason and Grey was executed. Scrope was found guilty of misprision of treason in that, knowing of the plot, he had failed to reveal it to the king. Scrope and Cambridge then claimed the right to trial by their peers, which trial was rapidly arranged since a large number of their fellow lords were present at Southampton. On 5 August this second court, headed by Thomas, Duke of Clarence, had Cambridge's confession read to them while Scrope pleaded not guilty on the basis that he had intended to tell the king when he had full possession of all the details of the plot. Both were once again convicted, and executed the same day outside the north gate of Southampton. No charge was ever brought against Umphraville, and given his response to the only possible action that might have been interpreted as part of the plot, it may be that he had in fact played the role that Scrope had claimed for himself.

Finally, on 11 August, leaving behind his brother John, Duke of Bedford, as his lieutenant in England, Henry boarded his flagship, the *Trinity Royal*, and gave the signal for his fleet to set sail for France.

7

HARFLEUR & THE ROAD TO AGINCOURT
13 AUGUST – 20 OCTOBER 1415

Of course, the French were not completely in the dark as to Henry's intentions. Ambassadors, merchants, even spies crossed the Channel continually and they would have had to be blind not to see the steady accumulation of the invasion force. From the spring of 1415 Henry was announcing to all and sundry that he needed money to finance his expedition as he was now setting out on his 'voyage', and the French would have been in no doubt as to where that voyage would take him.

With Charles VI of France still incapable, the governing council appointed his eighteen-year-old son, the Dauphin Louis, as his lieutenant and at least nominal commander of all resistance to the English. Orders were given for towns and castles to look to their fortifications and for men to be prepared to fight for their country. The most immediate action, however, was the levying of heavy taxes to pay for all this, which were bitterly resented by those lower down the social scale on whom the burden of payment actually fell.

The failure of the last diplomatic delegation must have suggested that invasion was imminent, and on 28 July Charles d'Albret, Constable of France and a career soldier, was appointed commander in chief of the French army. The Constable of France was the chief officer of the Crown, in theory at least outranking all the nobility and subject only to the king. In practice the fact that d'Albret was not himself of the nobility would prove a serious drawback. On the same day Jean Le Maigre, better known as Marshal Boucicaut, was appointed captain-general. He too was a skilled professional soldier, the title 'Marshal of France' being recognition of his achievements rather than a military rank.

As for the forces that would fight under them, though the French had an indenture system similar to that in England, it was not so well developed and, especially for home defence, the feudal levy system, the '*arriere-ban*', was heavily relied on. This could produce large numbers of men, but it was generally slow to activate and the resulting army lacked the skills and discipline of professional soldiers.

Knowing that an invasion was due was a very different matter from knowing where it would arrive, and in this at least Henry did manage a degree of secrecy. With the whole long coastline of France to defend, and, at least to begin with, minimal forces at his command, d'Albret had to guess, and he guessed very nearly correctly. Disregarding the possibility that the English might launch an attack from their own territory, from Calais or from Gascony, he decided Normandy was the most likely place, and even more correctly that the mouth of the Seine would be the key. This mighty river led into the very heart of France, through Rouen, chief city of the dukes of Normandy from whom Henry himself was descended, on to Paris where waited the unhappy King of

France. D'Albret, therefore, set up his headquarters at Honfleur, the major fortified town on the south side of the river. With him were 1,500 men, while the rest of the forces presently assembled were sent with Marshal Boucicaut to guard the first place inland where the Seine might be crossed, some twenty-five miles away.

It was, however, not Honfleur to the south but Harfleur on the northern side of the river which was Henry's immediate target. Consequently, when in the early evening of Tuesday 13 August his fleet came to anchor at a place called Chef de Caux, there was no one there to oppose him. This might have been seen as a second good omen for the success of the expedition, the first being a flock of swans (the swan being Henry's personal heraldic device) that had passed through the fleet as it set sail, raising a cheer from those on board. Nevertheless the king immediately gave orders that no landing was to be attempted until the following day. Then, under cover of darkness, he himself sent out a scouting party.

The honour of first setting foot ashore went to the king's cousin, Sir John Holland, another grandson of John of Gaunt, through his daughter Elizabeth. Though only a young man, Holland was accompanied by others who were older and more experienced, including his step-father, Sir John Cornwaille, Elizabeth's third husband and a well-respected Knight of the Garter. These two men were to figure prominently in the coming campaign. For the time being, however, their first task was to discover what resistance there might be to any landing at that place, and then to seek out the general lie of the land and the best way to approach the town of Harfleur which lay at a few miles distance from their anchorage.

They found that the people of the area had not been idle in looking to their defences. Behind the shingle beach a system of earthworks and ditches had been prepared but they were completely unmanned. It has been suggested that Henry's delay in setting out and the time taken to gather the fleet together and cross the channel may have worked in his favour here. It is possible that a series of false alarms had led to slackness in the defenders, so that when the real danger materialised they were caught napping. An account by an eyewitness suggests that, had even a small number of resolute men opposed the landing, the campaign might have turned out very differently. As it was, not a single blow was struck, and over the next three days Henry was able to disembark the whole of his army and its equipment, and even to dispatch some vessels back to England to pick up a number of men who had had to be left behind due to lack of transport.

It is clear from the forces assembled and the specialist men and materials he had brought with him that Henry was drawing on all his experience in the Welsh wars when planning his campaign. To take and fortify a secure base before moving on; this was what he had learnt of the way to conquer and hold a large area. Harfleur was to be the beginning, a second Calais from which to conquer France itself – but it was not to be achieved as quickly as he had expected.

The town lay in a valley where the waters of two small tributary rivers, the Lezarde and the Leure, came together before emptying into the Seine about a mile away. Strong walls surrounded it, punctuated by more than two dozen towers, giving defenders a line of sight along their entire length. A river ran through the middle of the town, culminating in a large, fortified harbour that gave the town its prosperity. No doubt merchants and others passing through this port had been able to give Henry a general idea of the town and its fortifications, but it was also from here that ships had issued forth to harass and capture English merchant fleets on their way across the channel – another reason why the king might have felt it necessary to begin his campaign at this place.

For more than half its circumference, on the north, west and south, the town walls were protected by a moat filled by waters from the rivers. A deep, wide dry ditch held attackers away from the walls on the north-eastern side. There were three gates, the Leure gate to the south, the Rouen gate to the east and the Montvilliers Gate to the north.

The approach to the south of the town was through salt marshes containing more or less water depending on the state of the tide. On hearing of the approach of the English forces, a similar water hazard was achieved to the north-west by closing the sluices on the river where it entered the town, thereby damming it and flooding all the land above. At the same time great bastions of timber and earth were built before each of the gates, while heavy chains were hung across the harbour entrance, and sharpened stakes driven into the ground all around there, to deter any assaults by water.

Inside the town its commander, Jean, sire d'Estouteville, had barely a hundred men in his garrison, but while Henry was slowly bringing up his forces and establishing his camp on a hill to the south d'Albret was rapidly sending reinforcements. Weapons, supplies and cannon were sent, and more importantly a new commander, Raoul, sire de Gaucort, and another three hundred men. This de Gaucort was an experienced soldier who had fought with Marshal Boucicaut at Nicopolis and in Italy. Just in the nick of time he arrived with his men at the Rouen gate, while Henry, marooned on the far side of the flooded marshes, could do nothing to prevent him. This was to be the last such entry, however. That same day the king sent his brother Thomas, Duke of Clarence, with a large force of men around to the far side of the town, where they camped on another hillside commanding both northern and eastern roads into Harfleur.

With the town now surrounded or 'invested' by the English it was time for Henry to obey the rules of war accepted at the time, taken from chapter 20 of the Book of Deuteronomy in the Bible. Verse 10 declares, 'If at any time thou shalt go against a city to overcome it, first thou shalt proffer peace.' Furthermore, if the people then opened the gates to receive the besiegers, 'all the people that is there shall be saved'. If, on the other hand, they refused this offer and the city was taken by force, 'thou shalt smite by the sharpness of the sword all things of male kind which is therein'. Women, children and all the property of the town could then be taken as booty, to do with as the besiegers pleased. Despite this stark choice laid before them, de Gaucort and d'Estouteville instantly rejected the offer of peaceful surrender and the siege of Harfleur began.

Now Henry brought into action all his war machines, both the traditional siege engines and the new cannon. Through all the daylight hours, all day, every day the bombardment continued. With the blast of the cannon and the shattering of stone on stone, the noise must have terrified the stoutest hearted within the town, and little by little the defences and the buildings within were smashed and broken. Despite this the garrison kept up their own onslaught on their attackers, so that great wooden shields had to be constructed to protect those operating cannon and catapult alike.

Clarence's attempt to fill the dry ditch with bundles of sticks had to be abandoned when it became clear the garrison were just waiting for his men to advance over this before setting it alight and fuelling the fire with all manner of combustible material.

Nevertheless he managed to throw up an embankment topped with stout timber and close enough to the walls to bring his own war machines forward and, behind the protection of this bank, to launch a bombardment on this side too.

Then, at night when the cannon were silent, the besieged under de Gaucort's instructions crept out to try and shore up the defences by any means to hand. Clay was laid in the streets to prevent the shattering of cannon stones as they hit the ground, which would have an effect like shrapnel, causing death and destruction all around.

Nor was this bombardment the only method of attack. Sir John Greyndor, a knight from the Welsh Marches, had brought in his retinue some 120 miners, and these were now set to work to undermine the town walls and so bring down the defences. This mining was a recognised method of assault during a siege, and was opposed by equally energetic countermining by the defenders, intended to undercut and so to collapse the mine prematurely upon the attackers. Sometimes the two parties came face to face. Unlike a narrow coal mine, these shafts would easily allow a man to stand upright, and fighting in the mines was regarded as a chivalric battle carried on not only by the lower orders but by fully armed and armoured knights.

There are basically only two ways for such a siege to end – either the town will surrender or it will be relieved by a force from outside driving away the besiegers. By the first week in September neither of these had happened. Though d'Albret and Boucicaut had regrouped at Rouen, the general order from the king's council calling men to arms was only issued on 28 August, and there was no sign yet of any large-scale muster. Some local nobility were engaged in minor skirmishes with English foraging parties, and d'Albret had managed on one or two occasions to smuggle a messenger and a few supplies into the besieged town. Apart from that, de Gaucort and his men were on their own.

Nor, despite all King Henry's energies, were Harfleur's defences yet ready to crack. Letters written on 3 September suggesting that the king expected the town to fall within eight days proved to be overly optimistic. The men of the garrison still manned the bastions outside the gates, and the gates themselves held firm. Nor was the mining at Harfleur particularly successful. Mines on the king's side were soon abandoned due to the difficulty of the marshy terrain and the river-fed moat. On Clarence's side several mines were begun but none achieved its objective. Instead the king turned to another engineering project designed to speed up the town's surrender. According to the account of one of his clerks he dammed the river higher up the valley, thereby cutting off the supply of fresh water to the town. It may well be that this contributed greatly to his victory, but it was victory won at a high price, both to the besieged and the besiegers.

There is no exact record of when the sickness began. On 3 September Henry was writing to Bordeaux that all were 'in good health and disposition', but certainly within a week of that date strong men both within the town and without were succumbing at an alarming rate. The accounts vary in their explanations – too greedy eating of oysters from the estuary, or unripe fruit – but there is no doubt that it was dysentery that was spreading so rapidly.

The insanitary conditions in a camp of large numbers of men and animals, based on swampy ground in hot summer weather, would be a perfect breeding place for such a disease. The closing off of the river's freshwater supply may simply have been the final straw. Nor was it any respecter of persons. Rich as well as poor were struck down by the 'bloody flux' as it was called, while the symptoms of violent and bloody diarrhoea, together with high fever, made it easily spread through such a multitude. Within the town the situation was just as bad or even worse.

On 10 September the thirty-five-year-old Bishop of Norwich fell ill and, despite all care, died five days later. A close friend and advisor of the king, he was a senior member of the royal household, and Henry himself was present at his deathbed.

Perhaps taking advantage of this distraction, on the same day de Gaucort launched a surprise raid out of the Leure Gate, temporarily displacing those investing the area who included Sir John Holland and his stepfather Sir John Cornwaille. Before they could be driven back the French had set fire to the English forward position and siege weapons, causing little real damage but forming a provocation that could not be ignored.

The very next day Holland and Cornwaille spearheaded a final determined assault on the bastion before the gate. Already weakened by regular bombardment, it was now fired by the English and overwhelmed by the sheer weight of numbers following Holland's standard. A great melee of hand-to-hand fighting now took place before the French were at last forced to abandon the position and retreat within the town gate. Although this was rapidly reinforced with whatever timber and stone were to hand, English guns could now be brought significantly closer and it was apparent to all that the endgame was fast approaching.

On 17 September, the following day, Henry once again attempted to persuade the town to surrender. De Gaucort and a number of leading burgesses were given a safe conduct to come to meet the king, who once again recited his ancient right to 'his' duchy of

Normandy. De Gaucort replied that he did not recognise Henry's authority, that he had been sent by the French king to hold Harfleur and he was confident that a relieving army would be appearing any day. This last must have been sheer bravado on his part for he would have been aware that the messengers he had managed to send to the Dauphin had brought no such news – some, indeed, had received no answer at all to his desperate requests for assistance.

It may be that this rebuff piqued the king into deciding on an all-out assault on the town – or maybe seeing the condition of its inhabitants he had realised just how close to cracking it really was. Whatever the reason, almost as soon as his visitors had departed it was being loudly proclaimed through the camp that every man should be ready for a final assault the next day. Throughout the night a mighty bombardment was carried on and at dawn Henry's assault began. Even before this, however, and probably unknown to de Gaucort, concentrating his attention on the Leure Gate, a group of burgesses had carried an offer of surrender to the Duke of Clarence on the other side of the town.

It took some hours before this could be communicated around the flooded area to the king, and, since it was then obvious de Gaucort could not carry on alone, negotiations began in earnest for a surrender. A truce was agreed to run until 1 p.m. on the following Sunday, 22 September. Safe conduct would be given to a delegation making one last plea for help to the Dauphin, failing which there would be an unconditional surrender. In the meantime the French would provide twenty-four hostages including d'Estouteville. All this was solemnly signed and sealed and sworn on the Eucharist under the supervision of the Bishop of Bangor, who reassured the vanquished, 'We are good Christians and Harfleur is not Soissons,' referring to the sack of that town by the Armagnacs the previous year.

The waiting was in vain. The Dauphin's army was not yet ready, so the messenger reported, and thus at 1 p.m. on Sunday 22 September, Henry, enthroned and richly dressed, formally received the surrender of Harfleur from de Gaucort, dressed in a shirt and with a noose around his neck. 'Most victorious Prince,' he said, 'I yield unto you with the town, my self and my company.'

Town, self and company – and what was the victorious prince to do with each? A few weeks before the answer would have been simple. Garrison the town, hold de Gaucort and company prisoner for ransom and move on to further conquest – Fécamp and Dieppe, perhaps, along the coast, and maybe Rouen or even Paris. Now things were not so straightforward.

It has been estimated that Henry had already lost some two thousand men from dysentery, among them many leaders of retinues including the Earl of Suffolk. Many more were sick. De Gaucort himself and many in his company were suffering the same illness. The loss of time was almost as serious as the loss of men. It would be October before any move could be made. The campaigning year was ending. As Henry very well knew from his Welsh endeavours, nothing could be achieved during the winter months.

On 23 September the king entered Harfleur for the first time. Barefoot like a penitent he walked through the ruins to what was left of the church of St Michael and offered thanks to God for his victory. Then, with characteristic decisiveness, he made his dispositions.

Church and clergy were to be untouched. All those citizens who would swear allegiance to him would be permitted to remain, though none could own houses or business property in the town. Those rich who would not swear would be held for ransom. The poor and sick, women and children, would be expelled with some money for the journey and all the possessions they could carry. An armed escort would take them some fourteen miles beyond the English lines, whereupon they would become the responsibility of the French. Harfleur would be repopulated by English merchants and tradespeople and become a second Calais. Thomas Beaufort, Earl of Dorset, was appointed warden and captain of Harfleur and the reprovisioning of the town began at once.

Though this might seem harsh to us, it was seen as unusually lenient at the time. Even more lenient was the treatment of de Gaucort and his fellows. By the rules of war their lives were forfeit to the king, hence the nooses round the necks of those surrendering. At the least they would be held for ransom and might expect months or years of confinement. Henry, however, had neither time nor men to spare to deal with a company of some 260 sick prisoners. Instead they were released on their own parole to present themselves to the king or to his lieutenant at Calais on 11 November. It says a lot for the chivalric ideas of the time that there was a firm expectation on both sides that they would do so.

Before de Gaucort could take himself to his sickbed, however, Henry had one more humiliating task for him. He was to take to the Dauphin Louis, now residing at Vernon, about halfway between Rouen and Paris, a personal challenge to settle the whole issue of Henry's claim to France once and for all, through trial by battle. This was not, as some have suggested, a frivolous challenge to a joust. Trial by battle was a serious judicial procedure usually involving combat to the death. Common in Europe, it had been introduced to English law after the Norman Conquest and was frequently used to give 'the judgement of God par excellence' in cases where there was no decisive evidence. It was, in fact, the procedure chosen and then rescinded by Richard II to decide just such a situation between Henry's father and Mowbray in 1398.

Henry's proposal was that, to avoid 'the death of men, the destruction of the countryside, the lamentation of women and children, and so many evils generally', he would personally fight the Dauphin and the winner would be legitimate heir to Charles VI. Since Henry was a seasoned soldier of twenty-nine and the Dauphin an untried boy of eighteen, there seemed little likelihood that he would take up the challenge. However, in the eight days allowed for Louis's response the king had time to plan for his next move.

A decision was taken that the sick, of whom there were many, should be immediately evacuated back to England. A muster of men was held with the leader of each retinue providing a list of those no longer fit to serve. Many of these records survive, listing nearly two thousand men, so the estimate at the time that five thousand were sent home may not be much of an exaggeration. Add to this the two thousand already dead, and the shrunken nature of the great army that had left England some six weeks earlier stands revealed. As a rough average something between a quarter and a third had been lost from each company. Of the eight earls who had sailed with them, one was already dead and three others – Arundel, Mowbray and March – were seriously ill. This reduction in the numbers of fighting men was going to severely limit the king's options for the immediate future.

Of the choices available to him the original plan for further sieges and conquest was already out of the question. It was too late in the season to have any chance of success. At the other extreme, to withdraw to England for the winter and regroup was equally unpalatable. To launch such an invasion and then abandon it, with money spent, lives lost and only one town to show for it, would involve an unthinkable loss of face for the king. There had been precious little profit so far. 'Our town of Harfleur' had been spared looting, and though some would be rewarded with property in and around the town, a few ransoms were otherwise all the pickings of a very thin campaign.

A grand *chevauchée* to Bordeaux in the south, with plenty of plunder along the way, was another possibility, but Bordeaux was some 350 miles away with great swathes of enemy territory, including the Orleanist heartlands, in between. There was another, nearer, English territory at hand, with historical precedents of glory for those who marched that way. Henry would have been very well aware of the exploits of his great-grandfather Edward III at Crécy, and the appointment with his prisoners at Calais suggests he had already made up his mind as to where he was going.

At a council meeting on 5 October the majority were for going home. Clarence pointed out the unknown numbers they might have to face on the road to Calais and argued strongly against the decision. This unusual timidity on the part of Henry's normally belligerent brother might be explained by the fact that his name next appeared on the lists of the sick to be evacuated home. On the other hand, since he then turned up in Calais rather than England it may be that his illness was political rather than medical.

Despite this opposition, Henry's desire to see 'his' lands of Normandy and Ponthieu carried the day and orders were immediately given to prepare for departure. Harfleur must be left secure and Dorset was allocated three hundred men at arms and nine hundred archers for this purpose, together with a number of cannon and gunners. In addition an English fleet was directed to patrol the coastline and estuary.

This garrison left the king with a force of only some nine hundred men and five thousand archers. He declared he was trusting in God and the justice of his cause to see them through, but clearly he was making some assumptions which, in the event, would prove to be overly optimistic.

So far opposition had been minimal. As far as he knew d'Albret and Boucicaut were in Rouen with a few thousand men, while the Dauphin was still attempting to assemble his disunited forces even further away in Vernon. Calais was a good eight days' march away. Before the French could stir themselves he would be well on the way, with possible reinforcements coming to meet him from that English territory. He was still talking to John of Burgundy and expected no opposition there. To complete the march at all would enhance his prestige. If in doing so he provoked a battle with the reduced French forces he was confident his better trained, better disciplined men would win the day.

On 8 October they left Harfleur travelling in the traditional three divisions or battles. Sir John Cornwaille and Sir Gilbert Umphraville, two seasoned campaigners, led the vanguard. The king himself rode with the main body along with some of his younger lords, his brother Humphrey of Gloucester and Sir John Holland, while again the rearguard was commanded by the experienced Edward, Duke of York, and Richard de Vere, Earl of Oxford (much younger cousin of the favourite of Richard II). All were carrying only eight days' rations, probably all were mounted and all unnecessary gear was left behind at Harfleur.

Almost certainly, though accounts seem to vary on this point, they would have been travelling in at least part of their armour.

They were likely to be subject to sudden attack along the way, and to fit correctly all the separate pieces of harness took at least one, and usually two, assistants and something like twenty minutes or more in time. There would be problems in travelling in this way. It would certainly be less comfortable, and armour was always likely to rust in the rain, leading to seized joints and lack of mobility. On the other hand this had to be balanced against increased security. At least the backplate and breastplate would have been worn, and maybe protection for arms and legs as well, though the very heavy great helm would probably only be donned when necessary.

They would have to cover nearly twenty miles a day, and, with the usual (though restricted) baggage carts, servants, clergy and so on following behind, there would be no time for delays or diversions. Discipline was tight. There would be no looting, no women, no destruction. Henry was the King of France, intending to impress his subjects not turn them against him. Food might be commandeered but everything else must be paid for. Indeed, he treated the French citizenry considerably better than did the French army itself, something that was commented on in even the more hostile chronicles.

To begin with Henry's assumptions seemed to be working well. Travelling close to the coast they met with nothing more than a few skirmishes in the first few days. However it seems that the king's plans were known about even before he set off. By 6 October it was known in Boulogne that the English were coming and defences on towns and bridges all along the way were strengthened. Again it may be that the appointment with the prisoners gave the game away. De Gaucort would be sure to pass this on to the French commanders in Rouen, and, while the French army was now at last gathering massively in that place, it is certain that d'Albret and Marshal Boucicaut were at Abbeville on the Somme on 11 October with an advance guard.

The Somme was the greatest of the many rivers that Henry had to cross on the way to Calais and he had counted on using the old Roman ford near the mouth of the river at Blanche Taque, which his great-grandfather had used before him. Just in time, however, a prisoner taken by Cornwailles's vanguard revealed that the French were there ahead of him. The ford had been spiked with sharpened stakes and on the far shore d'Albret and Boucicaut waited with a force six thousand strong. Nor would there be reinforcements from Calais, those who had set out having been killed or captured by local forces.

There was little to discuss for the council meeting now convened by Henry. They were two days' march from Calais. Though they had received some bread and wine on the way their rations were more than half gone. Now, with no other option, they would have to turn away upriver to look for another hopefully unguarded crossing, maybe as far as the head of the river itself, some sixty miles away, moving further from their goal with every step.

At Pont Remy they not only found both bridge and causeway smashed but a belligerent French force on the opposite bank. Since this was led by the father and brothers of de Gaucort it is perhaps as well there was no way across, but from now on they were well aware that their progress was shadowed all the way by their enemies, and the chances of finding anywhere to cross unchallenged were slim indeed.

There was some little respite at a place called Boves, beyond the city of Amiens, which they had carefully avoided. Here, though local forces had marched to join the French army, and the captain of the castle proved friendly, supplying them not only with much-needed bread and wine but also billets in the village.

If this raised their spirits the next day they were rapidly lowered again. A more serious skirmish at Corbie and the capture of some rather talkative prisoners seems to have led Henry to a change of tactics. It was from these men, apparently, that the king first learnt of the size of the army now being assembled across the river at the town of Peronne. After a slow response to the initial call to arms the shameful loss of Harfleur had galvanised the French nobility. With the exception of John the Fearless, who still prevaricated, all had now come forward to fight for king and country. The oriflamme, that sacred banner of France, had been brought from its resting place at St Denis, and the wiser counsels of d'Albret and Boucicaut had been overruled by hot-blooded nobles who demanded nothing less than vengeance. They would neutralise the English archers by riding them down, and then use their overwhelming manpower to put an end to this upstart Henry and his shrunken army.

The king's response was twofold. First every archer was instructed to provide himself with a six-foot stake sharpened at each end, which could be driven into the ground in front of him to deter a charging horse. Secondly the whole army moved away from the river.

In a time before detailed maps Henry must have had some knowledge of the local geography. At Corbie the River Somme begins a big loop, and by cutting straight across this the intention was both to lose those shadowing his movements from the far bank and to get ahead of them. Only in this way could he hope to find an unguarded way across. Now, however, with not even the river as a guide, the morale of his men seems to have sunk to its lowest.

On 17 October we have the only record of a soldier breaking the king's rules against looting. Entering a church he stole a pyx, a small receptacle containing the consecrated host. The response was immediate. He was hanged in front of the whole army as an example to all. It may be this story that later led French writers to conclude that Henry ruled his army through fear and the threat of harsh punishments for any who disobeyed him, though this seems to have been very much an exception rather than a rule.

The following day they reached Nesle, once again close to the Somme, and for the first time when food was demanded from the hamlets thereabouts there was open defiance from the populace. We are told they hung red cloths from their walls (possibly a reference to the red oriflamme banner) and Henry threatened he would burn them to the ground. It might have been this threat that finally produced the information he needed, that within a few miles, there were not one but two fords by which the king and his army might cross the river (and leave the villagers in peace!)

Some have suggested that Henry had known about this all along but if so he seems to have kept the knowledge to himself. Either way, the army had been praying for a miracle and here, apparently, they had found one. Although the causeways had been broken up neither ford was guarded. At last they had outrun their pursuers.

At first light on Saturday 19 October the army began to cross the Somme – first a group of archers, then Cornwaille and Umphraville and their banners and then the men-at-arms of the vanguard. Only when a secure position had been established on the far side could the rest begin to move. In the meantime they had torn down doors, window shutters, sticks, stones and straw to mend, as best they could, the causeways approaching these crossings. The repairs must have been rough and ready in the extreme but eventually it was possible to proceed. To avoid unnecessary delays the king decreed one ford would be used by the army and the other by the baggage train, and to ensure discipline he stationed himself by the entrance to the river where the soldiery would cross.

With three men riding abreast it took all the rest of the day to get the whole force safely to the other side. There was one alarm when a party of French cavalry appeared, and though these were quickly driven off by Cornwaille and his men, it meant the whereabouts of the English would rapidly be reported to d'Albret.

Soon after nightfall the army was safely encamped around the hamlet of Athies a few miles downstream from the crossing point. They were still there the following morning when three heralds rode into camp, sent by the Duke of Orleans, the Duke of Bourbon and Constable d'Albret. Their message was simple and couched in most chivalrous terms. Aware that Henry had been seeking a battle ever since he left Harfleur, they would now be happy to meet him and fulfil that desire at a time and place of his choosing.

8

AGINCOURT
20–25 OCTOBER 1415

Had it been left to d'Albret and Boucicaut it is likely there would have been no battle at Agincourt or anywhere else. The constable and marshal would have been quite happy to shepherd Henry to Calais and send him home. Alternatively, since they were guarding the crossings of the Somme, the plan may simply have been to exhaust and starve his small force until they were brought to surrender. Either way the risk would be minimal, Harfleur could be besieged and retaken and there would be very little damage done.

The fall of Harfleur, however, had produced a sudden and violent surge of patriotism in those who had stood by and let it happen. At a meeting of the royal council, called by Charles VI when he arrived at Rouen on 12 October, a decision was taken that the loss of the town must be avenged by bringing the English to battle. This not only overrode the advice of d'Albret and Boucicaut but also that of the old Duke of Berry, who was now in his seventies and who argued strongly against such a policy. He had seen his own father, King John, captured at Poitiers and knew how these things could turn out, but the only concession he won was that the king and the Dauphin should remain at Rouen well away from the action. 'Better to lose a battle than the king and a battle,' he is said to have remarked grudgingly.

In truth neither Charles nor his son would be much loss on a battlefield. The king's fragile mental state rendered him useless (in the same way as his grandson would be useless at St Albans some fifty years later). The Dauphin by all accounts was fat and lazy and more interested in clothes and jewels than martial matters. Both would, instead, be represented by members of their households.

Without them, however, there was no one decisive voice who could unite the different factions that made up the French army. Indeed, although John the Fearless of Burgundy and Charles of Orleans had each been ordered to send forces for the defence of their liege the king, there was some suggestion that they should not come in person since, as sworn enemies, they would be as likely to attack each other as the English.

Not only was a decision taken at Rouen to fight but a detailed battle plan was prepared, and it seems to be here that the first mention is made of tactics to deal with the English archers. While the plan envisaged a traditional formation of vanguard, main battle and rearguard, one behind the other, and even named the commanders for each, it was proposed that there would also be an elite cavalry force to ride down the unmounted and lightly armoured archers. If this was intended as a 'secret weapon' the surprise element was lost when it was spilled to the English king a week before the battle.

Simple and elegant though it was, the plan was rewritten twice before the actual battle and the most glaring omission was the Duke of Burgundy. Among the named commanders and their duties Charles of Orleans was included but John the Fearless was not. Though he had by this time finally signed the Peace of Arras, there was still a strong suspicion that he might suddenly appear on the side of the English, or, worse still, choose this moment to make a renewed attack on Paris. The area into which Henry was marching was also strongly Burgundian in sympathy, and this was another reason for leaving king and Dauphin safely in Rouen.

Nor would all the commanders listed on the plan eventually make it to the battle. The Duke of Brittany was listed as a commander of the main battle. Mindful of his treaty with Henry, he had eventually set out with a force after several promptings, but proceeded very slowly and never reached the area at all. Philippe, Count of Charolais, listed as one of those in command of the rearguard, was the son and heir of John the Fearless. Despite the Burgundian leader forbidding any of his people to join the French army, most of them, including his two brothers, did eventually answer the king's summons. Philippe, too, was eager to serve, but was apparently locked up by his father to prevent him doing so.

If Henry had anticipated provoking a battle when he left Harfleur, he had clearly not expected the change in circumstance that had come about before the French challenge was actually received. His small but disciplined force had already marched several days more than they had planned for. Their rations were exhausted and the land through which they travelled was quite incapable of feeding some six thousand men, together with their horses and supporters. The accounts tell us that by now they were reduced to eating what nuts and berries they could find on their way. Many of them would be still recovering from the dysentery that attacked them at Harfleur, and to top it all they had just spent a day forcing their way through sodden marshy land bordering the

Somme and wading across that river, swollen by the autumn rains, belly deep on their horses.

Nor had Henry anticipated fighting more than the advanced guard of roughly equivalent numbers to his own. He knew by now, though, that a much larger force was gathering, and the names of the dukes of Orleans and Bourbon announced by the heralds suggested that a substantial part of it was already assembled.

Nevertheless he seems to have received the challenge very calmly. If the French wished to fight him, he told the heralds courteously, it was not necessary to pick a day and a time. He was on his way to England and they might find him on the road or in the open fields any day without difficulty.

The king seems to have anticipated that an attack would be made at once. His men were now told to cover the armour they had been wearing since they left Harfleur with whatever coat of arms they were entitled to. This was a surcoat worn over plate armour and bearing the heraldic device of the man wearing it. On a battlefield it was an essential identifier of friend from foe – and also indicated those most worth ransoming and who should, therefore, be captured rather than killed. It was thus both a target and a defence, and the wearing of it signified a readiness to engage at once in battle.

In fact, though, no attack came, and it is a little puzzling as to why the challenge was delivered at just that time if there was to be no immediate follow-up. Henry's army was probably at its weakest and most vulnerable then, and with the Somme at their backs there would be no possibility of retreat.

A second battle plan seems to have been drawn up by the French at this time, and by a fortunate chance it has been preserved to this day. Similar to the first, it envisages a much smaller force, even deploying valets and servants to make up the numbers. This time there were to be just two battles, side by side, one commanded by d'Albret and Boucicaut and the other by the Duke of Alençon and the Count of Vendome. At each side a large wing of foot soldiers would have in front of them the crossbowmen and other archers. Once again an elite cavalry force of a thousand men would be responsible for dealing with the English archers, and a smaller mounted group would attack the rear of the English and their baggage train.

It may well be that the constable had intended to strike at Henry at his weakest, deploying the troops then available to him. It is likely that the bulk of the French forces did not leave Rouen until the 14 or 15 October, and although it was once thought that these shadowed the English army in their long diversion to cross the Somme, it is now clear that they passed instead through Amiens, probably around 17 October. Nor did they join the advanced guard at Peronne, marching instead to the more centrally positioned Bapaume, so as to be well placed to cut off Henry's route to Calais by whatever road he took.

No doubt d'Albret knew they were coming but he may not have known exactly when or where. Then, as he became aware of the forces pouring in from all parts of the realm, it would have made sense to postpone the encounter for a few days, while his army became daily stronger and Henry's daily weaker.

Throughout 20 October, a Sunday, the English army rested around Athies, possibly expecting an attack at any moment. When it did not come they moved on again the next day, carefully skirting round Peronne where they may have believed the French to be. A short way beyond this, however, they came upon a sight that left them in little doubt as to what awaited them. Just as the French forces had crossed the tracks left by the English near Amiens, so the English now crossed the tracks left by the French, and saw, by the churning of the ground, that many, many thousands had passed that way not long before. A chaplain in Henry's retinue wrote later that they 'raised ... eyes and thoughts to heaven, crying out with voices that expressed our inmost thoughts, that God would ... turn away from us the violence of the French'.

Still, though, no attack came, and for the next three days it seems the armies marched more or less side by side, though far enough apart to be hidden from each other by the lie of the land. Then, on 24 October as the English were preparing to cross the River Ternoise near Blangy, news was brought that the French army was only three miles away on the other side of the river. Crossing as quickly as possible, they climbed the hill on the far side and there, about a mile away, saw, in the words of the chaplain, 'hateful swarms of Frenchmen', 'an incomparable multitude in their columns, lines and divisions ... filling a broad field like an innumerable swarm of locusts'.

The king immediately marshalled his forces as if they were to give battle at once and the chaplains were put to work hearing the confessions of those who thought they faced imminent death. It is at this point that the famous line of Sir Walter Hungerford is recorded, wishing for ten thousand of the archers then in England who would have been glad to join them. The king's riposte was immediate. 'I would not have one more than I have, even if I could ... Dost thou not believe,' he demanded, 'that the Almighty can through this humble little band overcome the pride of these Frenchmen, who boast of their numbers and their strength?'

Once again, though, there was to be no immediate action. After a little the French moved on, skirting a wood and placing themselves squarely across the road to Calais to the left of the English lines, which were now turned to face them. This, then, was the chosen ground, selected not by King Henry but by the French, and, in accordance with all the laws of chivalry, giving no advantage to either side. Had it been earlier in the day it is possible the battle would have been fought at once. Instead the two armies faced each other solidly in full battle array until the dusk of the October evening closed in around them.

It was a cold, wet, hungry night for the English. Eventually stood down when it was fully dark, they sought what shelter they could find in the gardens and orchards of the hamlet of Maisoncelles close by. Although some French accounts say they played music, it is generally accepted that the king enforced a strict and eerie silence on his men, to such an effect that the French feared they were trying to slip away in the night and posted fires and watchmen around to prevent them doing so.

By contrast the French, less than a mile away and spread across the field and neighbouring hamlets of Agincourt and Tramecourt, seem to have been noisily confident throughout the night. It would, of course, be difficult to keep so large a host silent, especially when they had pavilions, food, wine and all manner of luxuries that the English lacked. It should also be remembered that many of the accounts that spoke of drinking and boasting through the night and gambling for prisoners not yet won were written later, when French pride and overconfidence was seen as a major contribution to the outcome of the battle.

Shakespeare made much play of an incognito visit by Henry to his troops during the night. There is no record of such an occurrence, but on the other hand it is clearly recorded that during the siege of Harfleur the king was everywhere, night and day, encouraging his men and seeing every detail for himself. On the march, too, when spirits flagged it was Henry who inspired them to keep going. So it would be entirely in character for him to make such a visit, though hardly incognito – after a fortnight's march with such a small force he must have been known to all – and maybe it was simply too common an occurrence for it to be recorded.

Through most of the night it rained steadily, and it is more than likely that at some point Henry sent out a scouting party to discover more precisely the lie of the land and the forces he would be facing the next day. On the basis of this he drew up his battle plan.

Despite the fact that the French had selected this site, if anything it favoured the English. It was a large, open field, the common field of the three hamlets that bordered it, newly ploughed and sown with corn. Of course in the six centuries since then the physical surroundings have changed enormously, but the accounts make clear that it was well over a mile in length, something over half a mile wide, and flanked with woodlands whose size and density we can only guess at. It was these woodlands that afforded the greatest advantage to the English. Without them the small force could have been attacked on all sides and quickly massacred or forced to surrender. In particular the cavalry aimed at wiping out the archers would have had full opportunity to do so. The protection on their flanks meant that, although Henry's line would be stretched, it could fill the available space across one end of the field and meet its enemies head-on.

Whatever his activities in the night the king was about before dawn, attending to his usual religious devotions, first lauds, the pre-dawn service of psalms and prayers, and then the hearing of three Masses. At this time too, we are told, all French prisoners were set free on parole, to surrender themselves again if victory went to the English or otherwise to remain free.

By now the English army would already be forming up according to the plan the king had devised. We have a number of eyewitnesses for the battle, including one of the king's chaplains mentioned earlier, who wrote a full account quite soon afterwards. Like most eyewitnesses they fail to agree on the details but read together they give a generally good impression of the action.

Unlike the traditional formation, Henry's three battles would fight side by side. Even so they would be spread thinly across the field, each having no more than three hundred men. The king himself would lead the centre battle. The former vanguard, now on his left, would be commanded by Edward, Duke of York, and the former rearguard on his right by Lord Camoys, both solid and reliable veterans of many campaigns. Our witnesses differ as to the placing of the English archers. The chaplain declares that at least some formed 'wedges' between the three battles, implying a triangular formation projecting in front of the line. The other witness, a herald on the English side, declares that the archers formed wings at each side of one solid line of men-at-arms, curving forward so as to allow flanking fire into the body of an attack. It is not out of the question that both are correct. With some five thousand archers at his disposal it would be possible to deploy the bulk on the flanks while still having some hundreds to place between the battles, and there would be some logic in doing so. If indeed they were in wedges and behind the stakes they had been carrying for some days now, they would be able to fire at close quarters into the sides of an attacking force. Again some support is given to this idea by the chaplain's statement that the French attacked in three places where there were banners, implying that there was some division at least between these places.

It is a military cliché that battles are won and lost on intelligence, and certainly the information gained from the prisoners at Corbie would be of great help to Henry. The idea of the sharpened stakes, however, was not his own. John the Fearless was not the only Frenchman at the Battle of Nicopolis. Marshal Boucicaut had also seen the reckless cavalry charge come to grief on the field of stakes protecting the infantry, and moreover had written about it later. Though some have suggested it was Edward, Duke of York, who put forward the idea of stakes to the king, either way it is likely that one or both of them had read the Marshal's account, and it seems ironic that this should have contributed so much to his own downfall at Agincourt.

There are no reliable figures for the size of the army the French put into the field on that day. Estimates vary from thirty thousand to a wildly over-the-top 150,000. They outnumbered the English, however, by at the very least three to one, and possibly six to one. There are even stories of men being turned away. One account details six thousand men from Paris being rejected as being 'of little value', though, given the loyalty of Parisians to the Burgundian cause, it seems more likely that it was their reliability more than their usefulness that was called into question.

Once again the French battle plan had to be altered, and it was here that the lack of a single decisive leader was most felt. By now there were so many leaders present, of differing ranks, regions and loyalties, that it would have taken a very firm hand to override their individual quarrels and jealousies. The two appointed professional commanders, d'Albret and Boucicaut, had not the rank to overrule princes of the royal blood such as the dukes of Orleans and Bourbon, while competing Armagnacs and Burgundians (who had been fighting each other not so long before) equally pressed their claims for prominence.

Confidence in victory caused even more problems. The French were to fight in two battles, a vanguard and a main battle, one before the other, but such was the eagerness to kill or capture the English king and to take prisoners for ransom that everyone wanted to be in the vanguard – and in the end almost everyone of note was. Among many others the constable and marshal, the dukes of Orleans and Bourbon, the counts of Eu and Richemont, one of the two admirals of France and the grand master of the king's household all took their places in the front rank. The main battle was led by the dukes of Alençon and Bar, and a considerable number of counts including Philippe, Count of Nevers, younger brother of John the Fearless.

Both these battles fought on foot, as probably did the wings at each side of the vanguard. One of these, led by the Count of Vendome, largely consisted of officers of the royal household, including Guillaume Martel, sire de Bacqueville, the bearer of the precious oriflamme. The makeup of these two wings and their functions is generally less certain than the rest of the force, but what seems to be clear is that they were either placed in front of – or, pulling rank, placed themselves in front of – the crossbowmen, archers and cannon that on the previous plan had been positioned before them. By doing so, of course, they basically removed all these 'missile men' from the battle entirely. It is recorded that the crossbowmen got off one shot (though their target must have been obscured behind their own forces) and that one unlucky person was killed 'by a gun'.

Somewhere, though again accounts are vague about where,

were positioned the elite force of cavalry envisaged by the original plan. The chaplain describes 'squadrons of horsemen in many hundreds on either side of their front line', though others placed them further back. Indeed, whether this was one group or two, or, by the time the action started, any kind of group at all, has been the subject of much speculation.

By first light both the English and French had taken up their positions facing each other maybe a little under three-quarters of a mile apart. Now the king appeared, fully armoured and provocatively wearing a surcoat emblazoned with the arms of England and France. We are told he rode a small, grey horse and passed up and down the line of his men, reassuring and encouraging them. He told them his cause was just, so their consciences would be clear when they engaged in battle. He reminded them of previous English victories against the odds, of their fathers, mothers, wives and children in England looking to them to uphold the honour and glory of crown and country. He told them he would never be taken prisoner to charge England with his ransom, and he claimed the French had boasted that they would cut off two fingers from the right hand of every English archer so they could never draw a bow again. This last seems to have been pure invention but had the right effect of inducing outrage in the men concerned. It has also been credited as the origin of the two-fingered salute, so much a feature of English defiance to this day.

There was one more formality necessary to satisfy the complicated etiquette of medieval battles. Heralds from each side had to meet together to make at least a show of final negotiation to avoid bloodshed. All manner of claims have been made for this meeting. In particular it has been suggested that Henry offered to give up all claims to France and to hand back Harfleur if he and his men would be allowed free passage to Calais. In view of all his preparations and the rousing of his men this seems extremely unlikely, and, since the meeting took place well away from both forces, in fact no one knows what was said on either side.

Now the king dismounted and all the horses were sent to the rear, where the baggage train had already moved up closer to reduce its vulnerability to attack. Taking his place in the centre, surrounded by his banners of St George, Edward the Confessor, the Trinity and his own personal arms quartering the lions of England with the fleur-de-lis of France, King Henry now donned his great helm, over which had been placed a golden crown studded with precious jewels and fleurs-de-lis.

Although one account claims there were two decoys dressed in similar fashion to the king, it seems fairly clear that Henry stood out among his bedraggled band like a peacock among geese. Indeed his wearing of the fleur-de-lis was seen as so provocative that one group of eighteen Burgundian esquires vowed together that they would between them strike the crown from his head or die in the attempt. They achieved at least the latter part of their wish, all of them perishing in the battle, but not before one had got in a blow that cut off part of the crown.

That was later, though. Now, in the cold, damp early morning, with both sides armed and ready – nothing happened. For two, three, some accounts say four hours the English stood braced and ready for an attack that did not come. On the French side things were a little more relaxed. They had, after all, food, numbers of men and time on their side, all of which the English lacked. Conventional military wisdom of the time said the side which attacked first invariably lost, so the French remained where they were, letting hunger and fear work their effect on their opponents.

They had no need to go to the English. Let the English come to them.

It may be that Henry realised the long wait was eating away at his men's morale, or equally he may simply have decided on a change of tactics. His scouts had no doubt reported the sodden nature of the surface of the battlefield. To charge some thousand yards across that would be disastrous, but he had a weapon that could be used at long range to make the enemy come to him. It was a risk but, as so often with this king, a calculated risk.

At last the order was given: 'In the name of Almighty God and St George. Banners advance.' (Though one account gives the rather more down-to-earth 'Fellas, let's go.') At this each man knelt and kissed the ground, taking a morsel of soil into his mouth. This invariable ritual was performed partly in remembrance of the holy sacrament received in the Eucharist at the Mass, and partly as a reminder of the warning delivered each Ash Wednesday, 'Remember man that thou art dust and to dust thou shalt return.' Then, in full battle formation, they advanced up the field some seven hundred yards to a new position.

This was the time of greatest danger. It is unclear whether or not the archers had deployed their sharpened stakes in their original position, but it seems probable. If so they would have had to pull them out and carry them forward to the new line. A cavalry charge now would surely have had the effect the French intended but none came. The enemy were taken completely by surprise and before they had thought about it the ground had been covered, the archers had hammered in their stakes again and the opportunity was lost.

Now, when all was ready, Sir Thomas Erpingham, in command of the archers, threw his baton in the air and shouted a word most commonly given as 'Nestrocque' as a signal to loose their arrows. What he actually said is open to dispute (and some accounts place this earlier, at the time of the advance). Since he was a Norfolk man, some have translated this as 'Now strike', delivered in a fine East Anglian accent. Others claim it was 'Knee stretch', a signal to the archers to bend their knees to shoot, which seems unlikely since archers do not shoot with bended knees. In one manuscript, attributed to the Burgundian chronicler Monstrelet, writing in the 1440s, the word is given as 'Nescieque', which seems strikingly similar to the Latin 'nescio quid', meaning 'I don't know what' (he said), and maybe that is as close as we will get to the truth. Whatever it was, he was clearly understood by his archers and a moment later some five thousand arrows darkened the sky on their way into the midst of the French host. Battle had commenced.

It seems clear that the French elite cavalry were not at their posts when needed. The suggestion is that after the long wait many had dismounted and their horses were being exercised to keep warm somewhere at the rear of the host. The French chronicles were quick to accuse them of cowardice.

When the call came, only about half the original number could be assembled for the charge. Nor could they carry out their rapid flanking movement into the side of the body of archers. The English now occupied the narrowest part of the field with woods on each side, while the heavy overnight rain had turned the freshly cultivated land into thick mud. Even a willing horse could not gallop at speed over such a surface, and now they were charging head-on into a hail of arrows.

The charge must have proceeded with nightmare slowness while large numbers of horses and riders fell wounded and dying under the arrow storm. Nor could they get at the archers through the hedge of sharpened stakes. One of the leaders cried that the stakes would fall down in the soft mud, but when he charged on he proved to his cost that they did not. Very few followed him. Soon the field was full of fleeing, terrified horses, some wounded, many riderless, all trying to escape the murderous flights of arrows, and many charging straight back into the oncoming mass of the French army.

In accordance with the battle plan the start of the cavalry charge was the signal for the vanguard to advance, but they found the going even more difficult. Carrying roughly their own body weight in armour, slipping, tripping, sinking into the soft mud by some accounts almost up to their knees, avoiding living and dead horses and their own fallen comrades, the advance must have been a crawl. Anyone who has crossed a sodden ploughed field in wellingtons will have some idea of the impossibility of maintaining any kind of pace. Nor could they see well where they were going. With visors closed and heads down against the continuing flights of arrows, vision was extremely limited.

Hundreds never made it to the English lines, going down like corn before a scythe, but there were thousands more behind pushing them on. The chaplain, sitting on his horse with the baggage train at the rear, describes the moment when they crashed into the English front row, with 'such a fierce impact that they were compelled to fall back for almost the distance of a lance'. This was the crucial time. If the fragile English line had broken then they would have been quickly overwhelmed. Instead they held, recovered and fought back against the mass of their enemies, while the archers continued pouring arrows into the flanks of the attackers, their bodkin arrows being even more effective at close range.

Now the French discovered the disadvantage of their numbers. Channelled into three columns by the archers and by their desire to get at the English leaders under their banners, they were crammed together and pushed ever forward by those coming behind. In the brutal melee that now developed there was barely room to raise a weapon at all, and many of those who fell were simply knocked over in the slippery ground and, unable to rise again, suffocated in the crush. 'Living fell on the dead, and others falling on the living were killed in turn.'

Still, the chaplain tells us, the battle was 'continually renewing' and the fighting was intense. On foot alongside his men-at-arms, the king fought as valiantly as any. Having deliberately made himself a target he was often in the thickest of the fighting, losing a fleur-de-lis from his crown and receiving a great dent in his helmet in the process. His brother Humphrey was getting his first taste of battle alongside the king. At one point he was wounded in the groin and we are told Henry stood astride his body, fighting off his attackers, until he could be dragged to safety behind the lines.

As the archers ran out of arrows they emerged to join in the slaughter. Some with daggers and the leaded mallets earlier used to drive in their stakes quickly dispatched the fallen, while others took up axes, swords and lances from the many lying abandoned and fell upon those still engaging in the fight.

Fifteenth-century depictions of the battle tend to show a rather gentlemanly encounter of individual combat, clean death and prisoners calmly surrendering and being led away. There was, in fact, an etiquette about this, as there was for all aspects of medieval battle. The person surrendering should identify himself to his captor, say, 'I yield myself to you', and give him some token such as a glove. It was then the captor's responsibility to remove the prisoner from the field of battle and guard him from all harm. At Agincourt, however, as the chaplain duly noted, 'No one had time to receive them as captives.' Almost all were killed 'without distinction of person'. Indeed, the Duke of Alençon, attempting to surrender himself to Henry in the correct manner, was at that moment struck down and killed by another soldier, possibly one of Henry's bodyguard.

For two to three hours by most accounts the battle raged. This may be an exaggeration, but no doubt it took some considerable time for the English forces to fight their way through the vanguard and the main bulk of the French army. In the three places where the attack was most concentrated, the chaplain tells us, 'piles of dead and those crushed in between grew so much that our men climbed on these heaps ... and slew those below with swords, axes and other weapons'. It is suggested the piles of bodies were stacked higher than a man, though this seems scarcely credible.

At last, though, there was a lull. The remnants of the two French battles were scattered and fled, and the English began the grisly but potentially profitable task of sorting through the heaps 'to separate the living from the dead'. It was at this point that numbers of prisoners could be taken, and even lowly men-at-arms and archers could anticipate some return for all their endeavours.

While this was happening, however, a cry went up that the French rearguard cavalry was reforming in great numbers and preparing to charge again. This may possibly have been the late arrival of Antoine, Duke of Brabant, younger brother of John the Fearless. Slow in reaching the area and hearing that the battle had begun without him, he is said to have spurred ahead of the bulk of his men, borrowed some armour from his chamberlain, wrapped a pennon bearing his arms around his neck and charged to his death.

Whether in fact it was he or, as other accounts suggest, the original cavalry leaders attempting to reopen hostilities, this together with some sort of raid on the baggage train at the same time led to one of the more infamous incidents of the day. The king gave the order to kill all the prisoners.

This was against all the rules of chivalry and caused outcry at the time – not because unarmed prisoners were killed, but because the nobility were massacred along with the lower classes. The military imperative, however, is understandable. Henry's men were exhausted. In front of them an unknown number of the enemy, mounted and unmounted, were regrouping. Behind them large numbers of prisoners were also gathered, while weapons were lying freely all around. The risk that, even at this late stage, they might be trapped between two hostile forces was not one the king was prepared to take. Accounts differ about how and by whom and even how many of the prisoners were killed. The traditional view is that, apart from a few of the highest rank, killed they were, 'lest the captives should be our ruin in the coming battle'.

In fact the 'battle' came to nothing. The more prudent of the archers had no doubt taken the opportunity to resupply themselves with arrows from the many thousands discharged earlier, and this last cavalry charge of maybe six hundred men met the same hail of steel as their predecessors and rapidly fled. Nor did the raid on the baggage train turn out to be more than local pillagers helping themselves to the king's money, jewels, sword of state and even a crown. These two groups, however, rapidly became French scapegoats, blamed by their countrymen for causing the deaths of the prisoners killed in response to their actions.

One final act was needed. Heralds from each side had watched the battle in the role of impartial observers. Henry now summoned the senior French herald, Montjoie, and formally asked of him whether the King of England or the King of France had achieved victory in this full-scale trial by battle. He was told that victory was undoubtedly his. He then demanded the name of the castle visible through the trees, for all battles should bear the name of their location. Being given the name he declared, 'This battle will now and for ever be known as the battle of Agincourt.'

9

INTERLUDE
26 OCTOBER 1415 – AUGUST 1417

There is no way of knowing exactly how many were killed at Agincourt. The heralds, whose job it was to number and name the dead, were concerned only with those of rank. Nobody bothered to count the common soldiers. What is clear though is that the French army, which massively outnumbered the English when living, similarly massively outnumbered them among the dead.

Estimates of French losses have varied from four to eleven thousand. Our English chaplain suggests 1,600 nobles and knights and four to five thousand esquires lost their lives. The meticulous Burgundian chronicler Enguerrand de Monstrelet, writing in the 1440s, records some three hundred names before giving up and admitting 'one cannot know how to record them all, because there were too many of them'.

Nor is it just in sheer numbers that the list is impressive. It reads like a roll call of French nobility. Three royal dukes (Alençon, Bar and Brabant) went to their deaths along with at least eight counts and an archbishop (presumably a throwback to the old days of militant priests), the constable, d'Albret, an admiral, the grand master and the steward of the king's household, and the grand master of the crossbowmen. Guillaume de Martel, bearer of the sacred oriflamme, also perished and that banner was lost never to reappear, no doubt trampled and torn to pieces in the mud of Agincourt.

The local area was almost completely despoiled of its lesser nobility, while from across France fathers, sons and brothers died together. John the Fearless lost both brothers. The master of crossbowmen died with three out of his five sons.

Many more were never identified. They were too disfigured, or came from far away and none of their fellows were left to claim them. The right of the victors to strip everything of value from the slain complicated things. Once arms and armour were removed the dead had a terrible likeness, and this stripping began immediately after the battle. Indeed, so thoroughly was this plundering carried out that Henry made an order that no one was to take more weapons and armour than he could personally bear. All the rest was piled into a nearby barn and set alight. There was no knowing how many of the enemy were still in the neighbourhood and there were enough weapons around literally to supply an army.

When the rain began again the English retired to Maisoncelles for the night, carrying with them not only their plunder and prisoners, but also provisions left behind by the French to give them a first decent meal for days. Then it was the turn of the locals to pick over the battlefield so that by the next day it is recorded that the slain were left 'as naked as the day they were born'. Nevertheless, so great were the heaps of bodies that even two days later some were still being found alive – though none of these survived for much longer.

By contrast the English casualty list, though similarly incomplete, was tiny. Estimates range from one hundred to five hundred, with most agreeing that the lower end was more likely. Only a handful were thought worth naming and the chief of these was Edward, Duke of York. The story that he was old and fat and died of overexertion was invented over a century later. In fact he was in his early forties and had been all his life an enthusiastic huntsman, contributing five detailed chapters of his own to an English translation of a treatise on that ancient sport. If, as some suggest, he suffocated, it would have been for the same reason as many others on that day, for his wing of the battle was a centre of the fiercest fighting and suffered proportionately higher losses than any other. His body was apparently retrieved from a great pile of corpses at that place.

His career as soldier and diplomat went back to the time of Richard II, though sprinkled with a startling number of conspiracies against the Crown. In each case it seems to have been Edward who betrayed the conspirators and who was forgiven surprisingly soon afterwards. One writer has referred to him as a 'serial marplot', though perhaps nowadays those wedded to conspiracy theories might question whether he was performing something of the role of a secret double agent. His absence from the Cambridge plot of 1415 is only one of the odd features of that conspiracy.

The next most prominent casualty was the twenty-one-year-old Michael de la Pole, who had been Earl of Suffolk for just over a month since his father died of dysentery at Harfleur. His title was inherited by his younger brother, William, who had been seriously injured in that same siege and invalided back to England.

Besides these few others were named, one notable exception being Daffyd ap Llewelyn, more commonly known as Davy Gam, a Welshman with lands in Brecon who is believed to have been the model for Shakespeare's Fluellen. Even before this he had led a colourful life, remaining loyal to Henry IV both before and after his accession and being taken prisoner by Owain Glendower for his pains, and later ransomed. He had been knighted on the battlefield but then was killed along with his two sons-in-law.

Of the English dead who were identified roughly two-thirds were archers, many on the flank of the Duke of York's wing. No doubt they were buried nearby but the bodies of the duke and earl would be carried back to England for burial. The usual procedure in such cases, since there was no way of preserving the corpse, was to boil the dismembered body down until the flesh left the bones, and then to carry these home in a casket for interment according to the wishes of the dead man. In the case of the Duke of York his bones were buried in the newly begun church of St Mary and All Saints at Fotheringay, and the church then built around them.

The French dead were not so easily disposed of. Some were claimed by family or retainers and carried away for burial. The local churchyards were quickly full, and even some of the minor lords found themselves sharing a tomb. For the vast majority, however, the only answer was a mass grave on land specially consecrated for the purpose by the local bishop. Many thousands were buried together there without name or rank or mourners. A large calvary erected in the nineteenth century may or may not mark their final resting place.

Nor were the dead the only, or even the main French losses. The most frequently quoted figures put the numbers of French prisoners at between 1,500 and 1,600. These would all have been nobility of various ranks since no one else would be worth holding for ransom, and again included some of the highest in the land. Charles, Duke of Orleans, headed the list, along with Jean, Duke of Bourbon, the counts of Eu and Vendome, Arthur, Count of Richemont (brother of the Duke of Brittany) and Marshal Boucicaut. Most of these had been rescued from the heaps of bodies and most were injured, so the stories of Henry having the leading prisoners wait on him at table that night are likely to be fanciful. As a believer in chivalric ideas, the counterclaims that he had their wounds tended and then dined with them seems more probable.

The following day the English army set out again for Calais. By necessity the first part of their journey, prisoners and all, took them across the battlefield little more than twelve hours after they had left it. The awful debris of battle was as yet uncleared, and probably the English chaplain best sums up the thoughts of most. 'I truly believe there is not a man with a heart of flesh or even of stone who, had he seen and thought on the horrible deaths and savage wounds of so many Christian men, would not have fallen to weeping time and again for grief.'

They travelled slower now. We are told most were on foot, the horses no doubt being used for prisoners and the wounded. With so many of each it would have been impossible to hurry. The more severely injured, possibly Humphrey of Gloucester among them, would have been carried in a litter – a more comfortable way to travel than in a cart with no suspension.

It took three days to cover the forty-five or so miles to Calais, and though the king was joyfully received by his friend and captain Richard, Earl of Warwick, and by the populace, the army he led was not so welcome. The heroes of Agincourt were not allowed to enter the town, and, camping outside, found they had to bargain hard for every morsel the citizens were prepared to provide, treatment which has befallen many returning heroes since then.

This was a time, too, for prisoner exchange. Many a man with a prisoner worth ransoming sold him now for cash to a greater lord who would be better able to feed and shelter him in the time it took for the ransom to be raised. Some would be set free at once on their own parole to better enable them to collect their own ransoms. Others would be held in and around Calais, and only the more valuable would be transported to England and held at the expense of their captors. Some would be there for many years and others would never return, Marshal Boucicaut, for instance, died in Yorkshire in 1421.

Nor would the victorious army return together in triumph. The indentures required only that their passage should be paid for and this was begun at once. Little by little, then, the army made its way home to England, where news of their victory had been broken by Bishop Henry Beaufort from the steps of St Paul's Cathedral on the very day the king had entered Calais.

The king himself, however, remained at Calais, waiting for the day appointed for all the prisoners he had taken before Agincourt to surrender themselves according to their oaths. It is perhaps surprising to the modern mind that, on 11 November, the appointed day, every single one of them did so, Raoul de Gaucort even rising from his sickbed to get himself there.

On 16 November the king and his prisoners sailed for home, and after a notably rough crossing landed at Dover in a snowstorm. Then, stopping at Canterbury to give thanks for his victory at the tomb of Thomas Becket in the cathedral, he proceeded to his royal manor of Eltham, and finally on 23 November to his triumphant entry into London itself.

They had had almost a month to prepare for this and it seems no expense had been spared. The king was first met at Blackheath by the lord mayor, twenty-four aldermen and some thousands of others, all in their finery and bearing the badges of their guilds. Then his route through the city was decorated with the grandest effigies, tableaux and other flights of fancy that the medieval imagination could conceive. Lions, antelopes (the king's personal badge), singing virgins, Old Testament prophets, apostles, wooden castles and representations of heaven complete with golden-faced angels singing appropriate psalms; all these and more greeted the king. In all things, though, it was emphasised that victory was due to God's blessings rather than man's endeavours, and we are told that the king rode throughout with sombre face, first to St Paul's and then to Westminster Abbey to make an offering at the tomb of Edward the Confessor. No doubt all this pomp and triumphalism had more of an effect on his noble prisoners, forced to follow behind the king in this procession. It was the day before the twenty-first birthday of young Charles of Orleans.

The French experience of defeat is perhaps best illustrated by a long poem, *Le Livre des Quatres Dames*, written shortly after the battle, and referring to it as 'the awful day'. In it four weeping ladies reveal that they all lost their lovers on that day. One was slain in battle, one taken prisoner. The fate of the third is unknown – he is clearly among the unnamed dead – but the fourth, the cause of the bitterest sorrow, is the one who put on his armour only to run away from the battlefield.

Recriminations of this kind were heard all over France in the weeks following the battle, and it might be thought that, having sunk their differences to fight and die together, the disparate factions might be further united to present a solid opposition to the English invader. In fact the opposite was true as each blamed the other for the defeat.

In place of d'Albret, Bernard, Count of Armagnac was appointed constable, and since he was the implacable enemy of John of Burgundy this meant there was no possibility of a reconciliation there. The duke began to advance threateningly towards Paris and then, abruptly, on 18 December the Dauphin Louis died, possibly of dysentery. This changed the balance of power completely. The new Dauphin, John, was seventeen years old, married to the niece of John the Fearless, and had been brought up at his father-in-law's court in Hainault, fully sympathetic to the Burgundian cause, since the age of eight.

Nevertheless the appointment of Armagnac as constable was confirmed, and, with one eye on the Burgundians, he began to take steps to recover what had been lost to the English. In January 1416 French ships, together with those of their Genoese allies, began to blockade the mouth of the Seine while an army moved up to the landward side of Harfleur. This was not a siege as such, but it did cut off Thomas, Earl of Dorset, and his garrison from supplies from England, forcing him to forage in the surrounding countryside where he was likely to come under attack.

Exactly that happened in March when, near Valmont, some twenty miles north-east of Harfleur, he and his foraging party comprising most of his garrison met with a large French force led by Armagnac himself. Fierce fighting took place with casualties on both sides until, as darkness fell, the English managed to secure themselves in what has been described as an orchard or a walled garden. Then, with honour satisfied, they slipped away in the night to make their way to the coast and return along the seashore towards Harfleur. Before they got there, however, the French, having guessed their aim, came upon them again close to the site of the original English landing at Chef de Caux. Further fighting ensued with the victory of Dorset's men being assisted by reinforcements from nearby Harfleur. Perhaps it is not surprising that, the following month, a letter urgently requesting supplies and assistance was sent by Dorset to the council in England.

Henry, meanwhile, had not been idle. Even before his return from France planning had begun for his next expedition, originally scheduled for the summer of 1416. With considerable shrewdness Parliament had been summoned by John, Duke of Bedford, to sit from 4 to 11 November. In those heady days following Agincourt they were happy not only to bring forward payment of the second part of the subsidy already approved for February 1416, but also to add to it a new one. Some of this money was to be spent to great effect on the building of ships.

His experiences in Wales had shown Henry the value of ships. There had been, at the time, nothing in the way of a royal fleet, still less a royal navy. Nothing had prevented the French from landing an army in Pembrokeshire to assist Glendower. Later, nothing had stopped their raiding on English south coast towns, and preying on English ships going to and from Gascony. With ships of his own, on the other hand, he had helped to enforce the sieges of Aberystwyth and Harlech. Little wonder, then, that one of his first concerns on taking charge of the royal council as Prince of Wales had been the strengthening of England's sea defences and the building up of a fleet of his own ships.

Some of these would be built from scratch and others rebuilt from existing or captured vessels, and not only the numbers but the size and structure of the ships was changing. The old cogs, single-masted ships, the largest of which would have been around two hundred tons, were being replaced by the much larger carracks of five hundred-plus tons, with high, rounded sterns, three or four masts and a high forecastle and aftcastle. Henry commissioned four of these 'great ships', the *Trinity Royal*, the *Jesus*, the *Holy Ghost* (rebuilt from a captured Spanish ship) and the *Grace Dieu*. The latter, at 218 feet long and 1,400 tons, was the biggest ship yet built at Southampton and somewhat of a failure. It only put to sea once, whereupon the crew mutinied. It made it as far as the Isle of Wight and back, and thereafter remained laid up in the River Hamble until some years later it was struck by lightning and entirely consumed by fire. The others, though, along with many smaller vessels, all saw active service.

These new fighting ships carried men-at-arms and archers, actively seeking out enemy vessels to capture or sink. In between they patrolled the Channel (skimming the seas, as it was called) making it safe for merchant vessels as well as for the passage of armies. Indentures would be signed for service at sea, usually for several months at a time, with the instruction that they should come into port only when it was necessary to take on fresh water or supplies.

Although the Earl of Dorset was nominally admiral, in 1416 he was busy commanding the garrison at Harfleur so it was John of Bedford who was dispatched in August at the head of a sizeable fleet to break the blockade of the Seine and to resupply the town and garrison. The French fleet that put out to meet them off the mouth of the river had eight Genoese carracks against the English four, and in addition had eight galleys and many smaller craft, probably outnumbering the English. On the other hand it is likely Bedford had more fighting men at his disposal since some thousands of these had been assembling at Southampton ready for the king's next expedition which had had to be postponed.

French tactics, too, seemed purely defensive. One writer has commented that they seemed to have learned nothing from the

Battle of Sluys three-quarters of a century before. Once again their major ships were chained together, making a solid battlefront almost as if they were on land. Overtopping the English ships by some way, this gave an advantage to their Genoese crossbowmen, of whom they had some six hundred, shooting down from the heights of these 'sea castles' onto the English below. This was, however, at the expense of any manoeuvrability among the sandbanks at the river mouth.

The battle began at nine in the morning and was fiercely fought for five or six hours, 'man to man, lance to lance, arrow to arrow'. Unsurprisingly in the cramped conditions casualties were high on each side but in the end the English prevailed, boarding some of the enemy vessels while others broke loose and fled back towards Honfleur. In all, three of the carracks were captured, one sank and one ran aground on a sandbank while trying to escape.

This battle, fought on 15 August, not only broke the blockade and enabled Harfleur to be reprovisioned, but also gave a first success for Henry's new policy of clearing the Channel of enemy ships and making it effective both as a line of defence and as a passageway to further conquests in France.

The same day saw a milestone in another of his policies, with the signing of the Treaty of Canterbury with the Emperor-elect Sigismund. The visit of this august person to England had been the cause of the postponement of Henry's summer expedition, but that was counted a small price to pay if he could be persuaded to ally himself with the English claims to the French crown. In fact, though the treaty was seen as a great achievement and a solid blow against France, neither side got exactly what they had hoped for from it.

By the spring of 1416 the Council of Constance, Sigismund's pet project, had achieved only a limited amount of what it had set out to do. The heretical works of the Lollards had been condemned and at least one of their leaders burnt, but this was, in a sense, the least important of the aims of the council. There was as yet no unity of the Church behind one pope, and the reform of the suspect practices of recent times had hardly been touched on.

With two of the three popes disposed of Sigismund had spent some time trying without success to persuade Benedict to resign. His only achievement was in getting the Spanish kingdoms to abandon their support of him, which they had done in December 1415, promising to join with the council instead.

Sigismund had then turned his attention to peacemaking between France and England, reasoning that only by reaching some unity among the 'nations' could progress be made on what, to him, was the most important of the council's aims, the reform of Church practices. 'How perilously,' he wrote, 'is the power of Christianity divided by these wars and lessened by these divisions.'

He began with France, being naturally sympathetic towards them, arriving on 1 March 1416, but soon discovered the difficulties of dealing with a country divided among itself. Moving on to Calais he was warmly welcomed by the Earl of Warwick and soon embarked for England.

Henry had determined to put on the greatest possible show for this potential ally and to woo him with honours and courtesies. Thus it was that he was met at Dover on 1 May by Humphrey, Duke of Gloucester, passed on to Canterbury where he was received by Archbishop Chichele, and thence progressing in order of seniority up the chain of royal brothers (John of Bedford at Rochester, Thomas of Clarence at Dartford) until he met Henry himself with a great entourage of knights and nobles at Blackheath.

During his stay he was lodged at the palace of Westminster in Henry's own apartments, the king moving out to the archbishop's residence at Lambeth for the duration. Then for the next four months a great programme of feasts and entertainments was laid on for his benefit. On 24 May he was accorded the greatest honour, being admitted to the Order of the Garter at Windsor. It has been suggested he did not fully appreciate the significance of this, but certainly he wore the Garter insignia, together with the Lancastrian SS collar given by Henry, on many formal occasions later. When he returned to the Council of Constance this display of English honours caused some consternation among the other contingents.

Henry's aim in all this was to secure the Emperor as an ally, thereby at least ensuring that the eastern border of France would be held in friendly hands, and at best obtaining active support and assistance in his claim for the French throne. Sigismund, on the other hand, was looking for an ally at the council, to press home his plan for reform of the Church before the election of a new pope.

Though from time to time Henry tore himself away to visit the forces now assembling at Southampton and to view the progress of work on his great ships, still it became obvious that the renewal of the war in France would have to be postponed, more especially since he was anxious to impress on Sigismund that he was seeking peace. At the end of May William, count of Holland, Zeeland and Hainault, and father-in-law of the new Dauphin, came to England to join the talks. Gradually, though, Sigismund came to accept Henry's claims as legitimate and to view the French as the obstacles to peace.

The Treaty of Canterbury, signed on 15 August, not only

recognised Henry's claim to France, but also acknowledged his right to use all means necessary to recover what was rightfully his. As an offensive and defensive treaty it also gave Henry the right to call on Sigismund for active support when next he pursued this claim, though in fact the Emperor never did commit any troops to this task.

Nor did Sigismund get the full measure of support at the council that he might have hoped for. By the time he returned to Constance in January 1417 there had been some changes. The Spanish had sent a delegation which now made up a fifth voting 'nation', and they, together with the French and Italians, were pressing for a speedy resolution in dismissing Benedict and electing a new pope. Sigismund insisted that reform of the Church must come first, since it was the abuse of power by the Pope and his governing council, the curia, which had to a large extent created all the problems in the first place. His influence as a supposedly neutral, benign leader was in decline, though, not helped by his clear adoption of the English cause. In fact there was a considerable fuss at the time about whether or not England was entitled to be treated as a nation at all.

A French accusation that England was too small and unimportant and not deserving of one out of five votes to settle the affairs of Christendom was answered in a way that was to have great significance for the development of English identity. The themes of history, Christianity and language were all employed to answer the accusation, and these were all areas where a growing feeling of Englishness was already taking root and would spread and bear fruit in the future. English history, it was claimed (wrongly of course), went back to that great Roman, Brutus, after whom the land of Britain was named. Likewise Christianity had been originally brought to the land by no less than Joseph of Arimathea, the very man who had received Christ's body from the cross, and the flowering thorn tree at Glastonbury marked the exact spot where he had planted his staff.

In fact the status of English saints had been advancing greatly already in Henry's reign. He had fought under the banner of St Edward the Confessor at Agincourt, as well as that of St George (whom England shared with other countries). Similarly, although it is well known that the battle was fought on the feast day of St Crispin and St Crispinian, two French saints, equal prominence was given in England to St John of Beverley, an Anglo-Saxon of the eighth century who had been Bishop of Hexham and later of York, and one of whose feasts also fell on that day. Others such as St Dunstan, St Chad and St Winifred were also increasingly honoured, while the better-known Thomas a Becket was celebrated with great ostentation by the English delegates at Constance on his feast day of 29 December.

Perhaps the greatest impact of the challenge at Constance, however, was felt in the use of the English language. Henry had been actively promoting this for some time by commissioning translations of celebrated works into English. Geoffrey Chaucer, too, had shown in the previous century that English was a suitable medium for literature. However it was still possible for the French to sneer that the vast majority of official documents in England were written in French or Latin.

From 1417 that began to change and the change was led by the king himself. Henry had always written some of his letters in English, his characteristic blunt, down-to-earth style contrasting favourably with some of the more flowery language employed by others. Now he seems to have made a conscious decision that all should be in English. And when he wrote in English he was increasingly answered in English. Gradually the king's chancery started to develop a standard form of the language, while over a period of time Parliament, the city of London, monasteries and guilds all began to express themselves in their mother tongue.

At Constance, in the meantime, matters seemed to have reached an impasse. The English, led by Robert Hallum, Bishop of Salisbury, solidly backed Sigismund in calling for Church reform, a matter which was, in fact, close to his own heart. The Spanish, French and Italians were equally determined the election of a new pope should come first. In particular they wanted no reduction in the role of the cardinals, of which they had many, in carrying out that election.

By the summer of 1417, however, Henry had his mind again on France. A deadlock at Constance did not suit him. He wanted the council's business concluded so that Sigismund might be free to back him in his new French campaign. In mid-July he sent new instructions to his delegates with an abrupt change of policy and a firm direction that they must carry out only his orders and not express their own views. At almost exactly the same time, by coincidence or otherwise, Bishop Henry Beaufort announced his intention to make a pilgrimage to the Holy Land, resigned as chancellor and set out across Europe.

At Constance a brief and unexplained absence of Sigismund caused a small shift in the situation later that month. The other nations took the opportunity of finally deposing Benedict and declaring the papal throne vacant. A matter of weeks later the sudden death of Hallum was a further blow to the reform cause.

It was at his funeral that the proposal was first put forward by the English that the time might have come for the council to move at last towards the election of a new pope. This was, apparently, the first Sigismund had heard of this, though his allies were quick to assure him that this was no desertion but an attempt to negotiate a compromise between the deadlocked parties. The negotiations were clearly going well when it was discovered that Bishop Henry was passing close by, and he was invited to come and lend his silken tongue to the discussions.

Matters now proceeded fairly rapidly. First there was an acceptance in principle that a papal election would take place imminently, with promises of reforms to follow. Then, on 30 October, it was settled that the election would be by the twenty-three cardinals together with six deputies from each of the 'nations'. On 8 November the final details were arranged, and this was followed immediately by the election of an Italian cardinal who would become Pope Martin V. The fact that the English delegates voted unanimously for him and seemed unlikely to change their minds, was seen as highly influential in persuading the other voters to follow suit, and it is generally acknowledged that Martin in large part owed his election to the English influence.

The new pope was enthroned on 21 November, but despite the fact that a new reform commission (the third) was set up immediately afterwards, very little in the way of actual reform was achieved before the council was finally brought to a close on 22 April 1418. It is ironic to think that if Sigismund had had his way perhaps the revolution and bloodbath that made up the Protestant Reformation a century later might have been avoided.

Henry's diplomatic efforts in 1416 were not solely confined to the Emperor Sigismund. Reminding the Castilians of their treaty may have persuaded them to stay away from the Battle of the Seine, and Duke John of Burgundy also needed attention.

Immediately following the Treaty of Canterbury both Sigismund and Henry travelled to Calais to set up a meeting with the duke with a view to persuading him to join the alliance. Having set the precedent of assassinating his political opponents, John the Fearless was so fearful for his own safety that he insisted Humphrey of Gloucester be exchanged as a hostage for the duration of the talks. As usual, pinning the duke down to a form of words was like trying to tie knots in water. He acknowledged that Henry's victories showed that God favoured his cause, so he would, therefore, support his claim to be King of France. However he would only swear fealty and do homage to him as such when Henry had conquered a substantial amount of the land he claimed. He would support him in secret ways rather than openly, and further, if later he was found to be supporting the (other) King of France or his son, this should not be seen as acting against the interests of Henry.

What he meant by this is not at all clear. At the least it seemed he would not actively oppose Henry, which was something. Beyond that he might be agreeing to fight against the other factions in France, or hoping that Henry would fight his enemies for him. Or he might simply be playing on both sides as usual. One commentator has referred to Henry, Sigismund and John of Burgundy as 'the three champion double-crossers of the age'. In fact almost as soon as the meeting broke up, John was in touch with his brother-in-law William of Holland and the Dauphin John, proposing an alliance against both Armagnac and England.

Henry, however, had achieved as much as he was likely to and returned to England determined that the next year would see a resumption of his campaign in France. The theme introduced in the parliament held in March 1416 had been, 'A good beginning is half the deed.' Now a new parliament was summoned for 19 October with the theme, 'The best way to peace is through war.' Further money was voted for the coming year, one and a half subsidies to be paid in February 1417 and a further half in the following November.

At this time, too, Henry rewarded two of his most faithful followers. His half-uncle the Earl of Dorset, still holding Harfleur for the king, became Duke of Exeter, while Sir John Holland, who had served so valiantly in France, was finally restored to the title Earl of Huntingdon, which had been lost by his father (along with his head) in the rebellion of 1400.

Early in the New Year indentures for service in France were once again being issued, this time in general for one year's service. From February ships were being arrested and converted to transports as before.

The sudden death of the Dauphin John in April made little difference to Henry's plans. (Poison has been suggested, though other accounts say it was an abscess to the head.) It did, however, bring about a further power shift in France. The new Dauphin, Charles, was the last surviving son and eleventh child of Charles VI. He was fourteen years old and for the last three years had been betrothed to the daughter of the Duke of Anjou, placing him firmly in the Armagnac camp. Although they would not marry for some time he was already living in the household of the duke, treated in all respects as a son-in-law, and when at about the same time the duke died, the new Dauphin was left in the care of the formidable thirty-three-year-old duchess Yolande of Aragon, who was to play the role of supporter and protector through all the dangerous years ahead.

Immediately John the Fearless began exerting his influence in

northern France, raising support for an advance against the king
and the Armagnacs in Paris. With the country in a state of chaos,
Count Bernard had little attention to spare for Henry across the
Channel. At the end of June an English fleet, this time under the
new Earl of Huntingdon, defeated another French and Genoese
flotilla off Honfleur, clearing the seas for another invasion. As a
bonus they captured four Genoese carracks, a French admiral and
a considerable treasure which had been intended to pay the wages
of the sailors.

Finally Henry set sail in his new ship, the *Jesus*, leading his
forces once more across the channel to claim his kingdom. They
landed on 1 August near Touques, to the west of Honfleur on the
coast of Normandy. The nearby castle surrendered immediately,
but as Henry sent his formal defiance to the King of France he
would have been well aware that the next stage of his campaign
would not be achieved so easily.

10

THE SECOND CAMPAIGN: NORMANDY
1417–1420

Long before, in Wales, Henry V had learned how to take or retake a hostile land. At the time the successful tactics had been his, and they were his again now. There would be no pitched battles this time, no strike for Paris, no swift raid and retreat. Instead siege, blockage and consolidation would be the way forward. The Duke of Burgundy had declared he would only pay homage to Henry when he had taken a substantial chunk of France. Very well, then. He would take it.

It is hard to assess exactly how far those two believed and trusted each other. For a time it suited them to work in tandem, though how much liaison there might have been between them we don't know. It is certain that Henry would have had a considerably harder job – would maybe not have attempted it at all, for he was always a realist – if France had not already been split open by civil war. Given the ambitions of each it seemed inevitable that they would sooner or later end up confronting each other, but for now, with John of Burgundy operating on the eastern side of the Seine, Henry turned away from Honfleur and Rouen and made instead for Caen.

Caen was the second town in Normandy, some ten miles inland but on the River Orne, which gave certain advantages to an attacker. Not only could supplies, and particularly guns, be brought up to it by water, but a branch of the river divided the town in two. On the north side the castle on its steep hill dominated the Old Town, while across the river on the Ile Saint-Jean was spread the New Town. The only link between them was a single bridge guarded by the fort of St Pierre.

The town had been sacked by Edward III in 1346 and its fortifications were new and impressive. Both parts were completely surrounded by walls, and on hearing of Henry's landing it had been well stocked with food and re-garrisoned. There were, however, two weak spots. On each side stood an abbey (his and hers abbeys founded by William the Conqueror and his queen Matilda) which, although also fortified, rose higher than the town walls. Artillery mounted there could fire straight into the town itself. There was a plan to burn down the suburbs outside the walls and mine the abbeys themselves, but the Duke of Clarence arriving too quickly with an advance guard put a stop to that. One chronicle tells a story that a monk from one abbey, aghast at the prospect of it being destroyed, showed Clarence a secret way in to enable him to save it. It adds the rather improbable detail that he found the duke sleeping in full armour in a little garden, presumably on his own, with his head on a stone.

Be that as it may, both abbeys were seized by Clarence and became the headquarters of the king and his brother at opposite sides of the town. By 8 August the town was ringed with English camps – the king, Warwick and Mowbray the Earl Marshal on the west; Huntingdon, Salisbury, Sir John Cornwaille and the Duke of Gloucester to the south; Talbot, Umphraville and Neville to the north; and Clarence, Willoughby and Pembroke on the east. The siege of Caen began.

Once more Henry deployed his guns, including some lighter pieces on the abbeys, and the walls and town took a pounding though the French fought back with artillery of their own. On 4 September simultaneous attacks were launched by the king in the west and Clarence in the east. The king was held up by some fierce fighting, but Clarence, making a bridge of boats across the river, managed to carry a breach and get inside the New Town. Then, joining with men of the Earl of Warwick, they seized the fort of St Pierre and fell upon the rear of those defending the western side. Even now the defence went on as the English had to fight street by street into the Old Town, while the defenders gradually fell back to the castle in the rear, to which some of the townspeople had also managed to retreat. The town was now given up to pillage, though Henry's strict orders that no violence was to be done to priests, women or children seems to have been obeyed.

The castle held out until 20 September when, with no prospect of relief from the Armagnac forces of the king or Dauphin, terms were negotiated to allow the governor and garrison to leave with their arms and horses. On taking possession of the castle, Henry found there were quantities of money, jewels and other valuables left behind which had been placed there for safety by people from the town and countryside around. It is reported that Clarence was rewarded with a good part of this for his role in the taking of the town.

The people of Caen found themselves in very much the same position as those of Harfleur before. Since Henry regarded himself as their rightful king, those who opposed him were treated as rebels rather than patriots. However, once the fighting was over he was prepared to pardon any who agreed to acknowledge his sovereignty, in general allowing them to keep their property. A new garrison and governor would be put in place and English settlers invited to take the place of those who had died or refused to submit, but Henry would then offer them the same 'good governance' as he had offered his English subjects on his accession. Oppressive taxes would be cancelled, trade encouraged and an administration put in place that was often more efficient than the one they had had before. In contrast to other areas of France, where chaos was reigning, those parts of Normandy conquered by Henry were relatively well off, particularly if their submission was quick and easy.

At about the same time as Caen was surrendering the nearby towns of Bayeux and Lisieux also submitted, and with a firm foothold along the Normandy coast Henry now marched south into the heart of the duchy. Within a matter of weeks the towns of Argentan, Sées, Verneuil and Alençon were all in his hands. The latter put up some show of resistance but surrendered in a matter of days when it was clear no help would be expected from Paris.

Paris had trouble enough of its own, with John of Burgundy steadily advancing on it and spreading his influence through all of north-east France. At about this time, too, he got another boost to his ambitions. Earlier in the year the French queen, Isabeau of Bavaria, had been reported to her temporarily sane husband for having an affair with a young courtier. The denouncer was Bernard, Count of Armagnac, whose dislike of the queen was only surpassed by her hatred of him. The unfortunate young man was tortured and then murdered by being sewn in a sack and thrown into the River Seine. Some say this was by order of the king and some say by the Dauphin, but since Bernard of Armagnac likely spoke for them both this may amount to the same thing. The queen was then exiled from the court and held in rather austere surroundings until, in November of that year, she so far overcame her earlier aversion to John the Fearless as to appeal to him for help.

The gallant duke sent eight hundred horsemen to rescue her and from this time on she was a firm supporter of the Burgundian cause. She declared herself the true Regent of France, a role she had earlier legitimately fulfilled, and it is possibly at this time, too, that she called for her son to join her, a request that was firmly turned down on his behalf by his mother-in-law Yolande of Aragon. 'We have not,' declared Yolande, 'nurtured and cherished this one for you to make him die like his brothers, or to go mad like his father, or to become English like you. I keep him for my own. Come and take him away if you dare.'

Fiercely protective of her young son-in-law, Yolande was equally fighting for the rights of her own son, for whom she had become regent on the death of her husband in May 1417. Though her dislike of the English was clear, she had now to join with the Duke of Brittany in treating with Henry, whose advance had led him to the very borders of Normandy.

While Henry was still at Alençon he was visited by the Duke of Brittany to remind him that they had an existing truce, and to extend that truce for Brittany, Maine and Anjou until the following September. The king was happy to do this. With his southern and western borders secure he would be free to turn his attention elsewhere.

It was late in the year by now and most armies had been stood down for the winter. Henry, however, had one more target in mind. On his journey south he had left unconquered the town of

Falaise, rightly feeling that this might take some time to achieve. Now, though, with the countryside around already subdued, he set out to besiege the town. The Earl of Salisbury had been sent ahead with an advance guard to hinder any preparations that might be underway to withstand an onslaught, and on 1 December the town was surrounded and the siege begun.

Once again facing a walled town and a castle perched on a rocky crag, Henry was thorough in his dispositions. Log huts roofed with turf protected his men from the worst of the cold, while a market established in the camp kept them fed. As the guns blasted away at the walls and town, fierce resistance was met with from its governor, Olivier de Maunay, who launched frequent sorties at the besiegers with losses on both sides.

After a month the town was forced to surrender, but the governor and garrison withdrew to the castle to hold out for a further month. Usual mining operations were not possible against the great rock on which the castle stood, but the English set to with pickaxes and, despite the efforts of the defenders to rain down fire and boiling pitch on them from above, so undermined the walls that de Maunay was eventually forced to surrender. As punishment for this Henry kept him in prison until he had raised a ransom sufficient to pay for the damage to both castle and fortifications.

By now it was February and, putting in place an English commander and garrison, Henry withdrew to his headquarters at Caen to see out the season of Lent. In the meantime, however, he sent out three separate forces to consolidate his hold on all the other areas of Normandy west of the Seine. Gloucester and the Earl of March went westward to the Cotentin peninsula, which quickly submitted with the exception of the port of Cherbourg.

Despite an intense battering from the artillery used by Gloucester, Cherbourg held out under siege for five months. Meanwhile the Earl of Warwick took Domfront and all the lands up to the borders of Brittany, while in the boldest move, Clarence was sent eastward towards the Seine, on the far side of which the forces of John the Fearless were clearly established.

It is to be noted that by Easter 1418 Henry had kept an army in the field for roughly nine months, including the whole of one winter. This was almost unprecedented at a time when campaigning was usually confined to definite seasons. Those who had signed indentures for one year's service were already approaching the end of their time and new indentures would be issued, while in England the Duke of Bedford was actively recruiting fresh men on the king's behalf. Reinforcements were needed not only for the king's future plans but also to replace those now left as garrisons in the places already taken. In May 1418 the huge sum of £26,000 was dispatched to France to cover the pay and provisioning of what was becoming a standing army.

In May, too, the biggest shift of power for some time took place between the rival French factions. On the 29th of that month the many Burgundian sympathisers in Paris rose up in revolt against the Armagnacs and a party of the besieging Burgundian army was let in. There followed a period of ransack and massacre which John the Fearless made no attempt to control, during which almost everyone with Armagnac sympathies, including Bernard of Armagnac himself, was put to death. The mob was later thanked by the duke for their good service.

The poor mad king was delivered up to John the Fearless who, with both king and queen in his control, was now the effective ruler of France. The Dauphin, however, had escaped, escorted by an

Armagnac captain, Tanneguy du Chatel, who was himself to play a significant role in the future. In fact, with the single exception of the fourteen-year-old new Duke of Anjou, the Dauphin was by now sorely lacking in noble supporters. All those who could have advised him or led armies on his behalf had either died at Agincourt or soon after, or were prisoners in England, leaving mercenary captains like du Chatel to take up both roles.

With an eye to the enhanced power of his supposed ally in Paris, Henry now moved his newly reinforced army eastwards towards the Seine. It was quite possible that, with his rival effectively disposed of, John of Burgundy might now break his truce and turn on the English, and Henry intended to be in as strong a position as possible before that happened.

In late June the strategic town and castle of Pont-de-l'Arche on the Seine was besieged and it fell some three weeks later. Now, having control over the river to the south and thereby cutting off aid from Paris, the king turned his attention northwards to the great prize of Rouen, ancient capital of Normandy.

The people of Rouen were not caught unprepared. The previous winter they, like so many others, had expelled the Armagnacs and gone over to the Burgundian side, and they had since been reinforced with some four thousand Burgundian soldiers. Determined to learn the lessons from other sieges, they ruthlessly executed the plan that had been half-heartedly attempted at Caen, razing to the ground the suburbs that had grown up outside the town walls and creating a wide, desolate space all around. The walls themselves were around five miles long, completely surrounding the old town, and were studded with towers and barbicans. Rubble from outside was brought in to repair any damage to these fortifications, and fine new artillery was deployed, along with many crossbowmen under the command of Alain Blanchard, who was to become something of a folk hero in France.

From the English point of view there were six gates into the town, all of which would need watching, and from any one of which sorties could be launched to attack the besiegers. Where the River Seine flowed past, Henry had chains slung across it to prevent any access by water, and once again a bridge of boats was used by the English to connect the various camps of the besiegers, as had been successfully done earlier at Pont-de-l'Arche.

The estimates of numbers inside the walls on that July day when the English king arrived with his army vary enormously. Different accounts of the siege give totals from seventy thousand down to twenty thousand. Though Rouen was a major centre and quite possibly did have, in peaceful times, a population of seventy thousand, no doubt many of these had left as the threat of attack drew closer, particularly when the extensive suburbs had been destroyed. On the other hand it is likely that refugees from other parts of Normandy might have added to the numbers. An order was given that every family in the town must provide itself with enough food for ten months or leave the town. Where they were to get it from, when it was not yet harvest time and the English were in control of most of the countryside, was not specified. As events were to prove, there was nothing like that amount of food stockpiled, though by all accounts some poor people, possibly the refugees, were expelled before the siege began.

Similarly exaggerated figures have been quoted for the size of the English army, in some accounts reaching as high as forty-five thousand. Since Henry brought fewer than twelve thousand with him the previous year and this force, though recently reinforced, would have been depleted by garrison duties and by the numbers still occupied with Gloucester at Cherbourg, a more realistic figure would be about seven thousand.

The siege effectively began on 29 July, though the encirclement was not totally complete until the outlying fort of St Katherine was taken by the Earl of Salisbury with heavy losses on 2 September. It quickly became clear, however, that it was not going to go the way of earlier sieges. The wide, desolate area created outside the walls, together with the French artillery and crossbowmen, kept the English guns too far away to be effective. Indeed there is evidence that they were never used. Rouen was not going to be battered into submission, it would have to be starved to death.

The constant sorties from the town in the early weeks of the siege led Henry to order the digging of a great ditch all, or at least most of the way, around the outside, to be topped with a palisade. Then it was simply a matter of waiting.

The hope, indeed the expectation of those inside was that the Duke of Burgundy would soon appear with a mighty army to lift the siege. When in late October food began to run short and there was no sign of him, the first of two 'appeals' was smuggled out. Addressed to the king and also to the Duke of Burgundy, 'who has the government of the king and his kingdom', it begged for urgent assistance. More than that, it carried a fairly blunt threat that if such assistance was not forthcoming they would be prepared to transfer their allegiance to Henry, and that in that eventuality they would become the bitterest of enemies both to the French king and to John of Burgundy.

Stirred into action, the duke began assembling an army. On 17 November the oriflamme (presumably a new oriflamme) was taken from St Denis and the army set out northwards as far as Pontoise. And there they stopped. Clearly if they had marched on to Rouen there must have been a battle, but whether John the Fearless did not want to fight his 'ally' or, with the recent memory of Agincourt, was afraid to do so, we don't know. There was a half-hearted attempt at negotiations mediated by the Bishop of Beauvais which came to nothing, and then, having exhausted the food available at Pontoise, the army marched on to Beauvais and Rouen was abandoned to its fate.

By now there was real starvation inside the sealed-up town. We have an account of the siege in the form of a long poem written soon afterwards by one John Page. Nothing is known of him except his own claim that 'at that siege with the king I lay' and that there was an archer of that name in the retinue of Sir Philip Leche when they embarked in 1417. Apart from giving us full details of the disposition of the English lords and men about the walls, he also paints a stark picture of the plight of those inside as the siege dragged on from November into December. 'Their bread was full nigh gone, and flesh, save horse, had they none. They ate dogs, they ate cats. They ate mice, horse and rats.' When all this failed, 'then to die they did begin, all that rich city within. They died faster every day than men might them in earth lay.'

In early December, in a desperate move to hold out a little longer, the gates of the town were briefly opened and, according to John Page, 'many a hundred' poor people were expelled. Women with children and old men, they could go as far as the ditch but no further, for Henry would not allow them through, and though out of pity the English soldiers gave them some bread 'though they had done some of our men to death', they were soon ordered to stop. Once again the more ruthless side of Henry showed through. 'I did not put them there,' was his response when he was asked to show mercy, and he put the blame for the many deaths from cold and starvation squarely on the shoulders of the garrison commander, Guy Le Bouteiller, who would not surrender the town to his rightful lord.

The one exception he made to this was on Christmas Day, when 'because of that High Feast' he sent food and drink to those in the ditch, who then declared that this 'excellent king ... hath more compassion than hath our own nation' and 'God, as Thou are full of might, grant him grace to win his right'. Sadly the truce lasted only that one day.

Late in December a further appeal was sent from the town to John of Burgundy on the same lines as before, but this time adding that if no help was received they would surrender in a matter of days. There is evidence that his reply came in the form of a secret order that they should do the best deal they could with Henry for they could expect no help from anyone else.

As John Page wryly notes, where all else fails 'hunger breaketh the stone wall', and in early January negotiations were opened. Apparently a group of citizens inside called from the walls until they attracted the attention of Sir Gilbert Umphraville. Discovering that his ancestors had come from Normandy they decided they could trust him to carry their request for terms to the king. There was to be no compromise, however. Death or surrender were the only options, and it was finally agreed on 13 January that, if no relief came in six days, the gates would be opened to the English. Of course there was no relief, and so on 19 January the Duke of Exeter took possession of the town and castle on behalf of the king. Henry himself came in solemn procession the day after, riding through crowds that the chronicles tell us were more like the dead than the living, up to the great cathedral of Notre Dame to give thanks for all he had achieved.

Once again under the rules of war the English would have been entitled to plunder the town but there was no sack in Rouen. In fact the terms imposed were seen as surprisingly merciful. Only one man was to be hanged, the commander of crossbows, Alain Blanchard, who had rashly made a habit of hanging English prisoners from the town walls. A priest who had solemnly cursed Henry with bell, book and candle was imprisoned, but the rest of the garrison could leave, without their arms or armour, taking with them any citizens who refused to swear allegiance to the English king. Those who did so swear could in general keep their property, though an overall fine of three hundred thousand crowns was demanded. Best of all, the order was given that the people of Rouen should be fed.

In fact, true to their earlier threat, the vast majority of the citizens did take the oath of allegiance, and Henry's hand was further strengthened over the next few months by the mopping up of the last areas of resistance in Normandy. Soon, with the exception of a few tiny spots – Mont St Michel, for instance, which held out for a full twenty-five years until finally relieved by the French – all of the duchy was his. Now it was time to talk.

Of the three players in the game Henry was by far the strongest. He had already defied and outfaced John of Burgundy, while the Dauphin's party was still licking its wounds from the year before. It was with Burgundy, then, that Henry prepared to negotiate.

After a preliminary sending of envoys, a meeting of the principals was arranged at Meulan in May 1419. Not only John the Fearless was to attend but also King Charles VI and Queen Isabeau, along with their daughter the seventeen-year-old Katherine, whose marriage with Henry had been under discussion for the past half-dozen years. Katherine was the tenth child of Charles and Isabeau and the youngest daughter, being some twelve years younger than her sister Isabella, who in 1396 had been the child bride of Richard II.

A field was elaborately set out for the meeting at Meulan, with pavilions for the French at one end and for the English at the other. In the middle was a large negotiating pavilion for the principals and their chief advisors. In the event Charles was, as usual, too ill to attend and the outcome of the meeting was mixed. By all accounts Henry was very taken with Katherine but not to the extent of modifying his demands. These now included all the lands promised in the Treaty of Brétigny plus his recent conquests in full sovereignty, plus the hand of Katherine and a dowry of eight hundred thousand crowns. The French offer seemed to have advanced not at all since their last discussions on the subject in the summer of 1415. The only concession achieved by the meeting was that Henry might possibly be prepared to renounce his claim to the throne of France if he got all the rest.

A further meeting was arranged to take place in July but by then John of Burgundy was having second thoughts. It is quite likely that he felt agreeing to Henry's demands would be giving far too much away. He was, after all, supposed to be speaking on behalf of the French king, and there was always a possibility that his own supporters might abandon him and go over to the Dauphin if he was seen to be caving in to English demands.

For whatever reason, when an envoy from the Dauphin proposed that they should join forces against the common enemy he was not unwilling. By some accounts it was Tanneguy du Chatel, now effective leader of the Dauphin's forces, who made this proposal. The result was a meeting at Pouilly-le-Fort near Melun on 11 July, where the former sworn enemies John the Fearless and the Dauphin Charles agreed to work together for the expulsion of the English.

1. Monmouth Castle, birthplace of Henry V.

2. The castle, along with many others, was inherited by Henry's grandfather, John of Gaunt, from his father-in-law, Henry de Grosmont.

3. The coronation of Henry IV's second wife, Joan of Navarre, as Queen of England. Arthur, Count of Richemont, her son from her first marriage, fought against Henry V at Agincourt.

4. The Battle of Shrewsbury, 21 July 1403 was the first of Henry V's battles. As Prince of Wales, aged sixteen, he fought on after suffering a severe facial wound, contributing substantially to his father's victory.

Above left: 5. Site of the Battle of Shrewsbury facing the ridge where Hotspur placed his forces. To the right is the battlefield church built as a memorial to those who fell in the battle.

Above right: 6. Kenilworth castle, favourite residence of Henry V. He came here to recuperate after the Battle of Shrewsbury.

Right: 7. Fighting in Wales against the forces of Owen Glendower not only gave Henry V valuable military experience but also a group of trusted commanders who would later serve him faithfully in France.

8. Westminster Abbey. Here, on 9 April 1413 in the midst of a snowstorm, Henry V was crowned King of England.

9. Less than ten years later his body was laid to rest here, close to the tomb of St Edward the Confessor. His chantry chapel, constructed by Cardinal Henry Beaufort was later dwarfed by Tudor extensions.

Above left: 10. Richard de Beauchamp, Earl of Warwick, was a close friend of Henry V. Here, in 1414, he kneels before the king to receive from Bishop Henry Beaufort his letters of appointment as Captain of Calais.

Above right: 11. Henry showed his close interest in the Council of Constance by appointing Warwick among the ambassadors he sent to the council. It was set up to end the Western Schism and reform the Catholic Church.

Right: 12. English and Welsh archers using the longbow revolutionised fighting techniques during the Hundred Years War. Few could stand against an arrow storm from massed archers.

Above left: 13. Henry V, writing to the French king before the Agincourt campaign, called himself 'King of England and France.'

Above left: 14. The weak and mentally feeble King of France receives Henry's letters from an envoy.

Left: 15. Sigismund, King of Hungary, King of the Germans and later Holy Roman Emperor, visited England in 1416. In return for Henry's backing at Constance he supported his claim to the French throne.

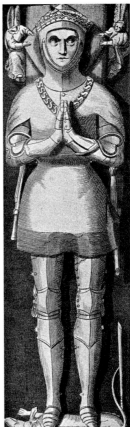

Above left: 16. Battles at sea, like those on land, were fought by archers and men-at-arms. French and Genoese ships had to be cleared from the Channel to allow for the passage of Henry's armies.

Above right: 17. Thomas, Duke of Clarence, Henry's eldest brother, fought at Harfleur and in later campaigns, but was invalided home before Agincourt.

Right: 18. John, Duke of Bedford, Henry's middle brother, was his trusted lieutenant in England during the French campaigns, and later Lieutenant of France for the infant Henry VI.

Above left: 19. Henry V was the first to commission royal fighting ships to patrol the Channel. Their design improved greatly during his reign.

Above right: 20. Humphrey, Duke of Gloucester, Henry's youngest brother, was brought up a scholar rather than a solider. He saw his first action at Agincourt, was badly wounded and saved by the king.

Left: 21. A brass of John Peryent and his wife made in 1415 shows the typical armour of the time. In battle the face would be covered by a visored helm.

22. An archer carried his arrows in a canvas bag to protect them from the weather.

23. An arrow was fletched with feathers from a goose's wing, the curve of the feathers spinning the arrow in flight.

24. From the left: a mail-piercing arrow, a bodkin arrow and a broadhead arrow. It was most likely a bodkin arrow that wounded Prince Henry at Shrewsbury.

Above left: 25. Plate armour was put on from the feet upwards. Here a squire adjusts the greave (leg armour) so that it fits exactly, allowing free movement.

Above right: 26. A modern re-enacter demonstrates similar plate armour and a typical weapon for close-quarters fighting.

27. Calais, an English possession in northern France. Though Henry was welcomed here in October 1415, his heroes of Agincourt were forced to camp outside.

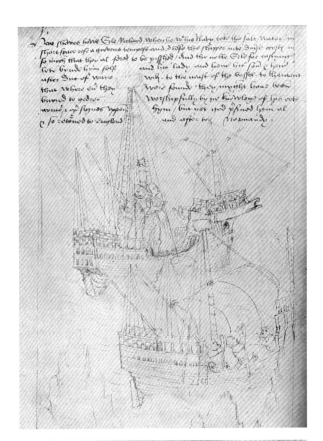

28. The most important prisoners from Agincourt were brought to England, crossing the Channel with the king in a November storm.

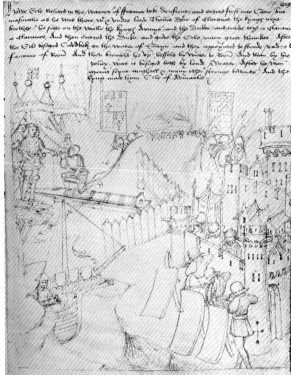

29. Siege of Caen 1417. Henry mounted cannon to fire over the town walls, but the siege ended in savage street-to-street fighting.

30. Henry was a pioneer of fifteenth-century cannon. Though cumbersome and unreliable they could smash defensive walls, firing stone balls weighing several hundred pounds.

31. Siege of Rouen, July 1418 to January 1419. With cannon proving ineffective, the ancient capital of Normandy was starved into submission.

32. A joust from around 1415, watched by the ailing King of France. With closed visor, a charging knight had a very restricted field of vision.

Above: 33. The head of a lance. This most effective weapon could be used for stabbing or hacking at an opponent or for smashing armour.

Left: 34. On 2 June 1420 Henry V married Katherine of France in a simple ceremony at Troyes.

35. The White Tower at the Tower of London. Among prisoners held here were Richard II and King James I of Scotland. After Agincourt Charles, Duke of Orleans, and Jean, Duke of Bourbon, were imprisoned here for a time.

36. A prisoner's view from the Beauchamp Tower at the Tower of London, probably named after Thomas de Beauchamp, Earl of Warwick, imprisoned here by Richard II.

37. The son that Henry never saw. The infant King Henry VI is presented to Parliament. He was not officially crowned for another seven years.

38. Effigy of Richard de Beauchamp, Earl of Warwick, on his tomb in the Beauchamp Chapel at the Collegiate Church of St Mary, Warwick. An illustrated Pageant of his life is a useful source of information about the times in which he lived.

Each was to raise an army and a further meeting was arranged for 10 September at Montereau to finalise the details of their campaign.

Henry's reaction to this was typically decisive. On 29 July his previously arranged truce with John the Fearless came to an end. That same night he sent a force to capture the town of Pontoise, which until very recently had been the duke's headquarters in the area. Refugees streamed towards Paris, soon to be followed by the English army itself. On 3 August Clarence with an advance guard appeared outside St Denis only six miles from Paris, and the royal court, king, queen and princess all, fled to the safety of Troyes near the Burgundian border. A week later the English army was outside Paris itself. While the Parisians looked to John the Fearless to save them he was still collecting his army and preparing for his meeting with the Dauphin.

It says a lot for the lack of trust between these two that the security arrangements for this meeting were stringent. It was to take place on a bridge over the Seine which was barricaded at each end. Only the duke, the Dauphin and a few of their most senior advisers and household were to be allowed onto the bridge. What could go wrong?

At 5 p.m. each party entered the fenced-off area and proceeded to the centre of the bridge. In a show of courtesy to the son and heir of his king John the Fearless knelt before him, and then, as he rose to his feet, he was struck down and killed by Tanneguy du Chatel. In the hubbub that followed at least one other Burgundian was killed and others were wounded, before the shocked and horrified Dauphin was hustled away by his supporters.

The accounts of this killing are as confused as the incident itself. There is a suggestion that as the duke rose he put his hand on his sword, perhaps because it was in the way, and that in that extremely tense atmosphere this was interpreted as an imminent danger to the Dauphin. Others have accused Tanneguy du Chatel of plotting the whole thing so as to prolong a war which was personally profitable to him and to his fellow mercenary captains. Be that as it may, at the time is was seen as a deliberate murder, and the whole alliance and meeting just an elaborate plot by the Dauphin to kill the hated Burgundian leader. There is some evidence that in fact the Dauphin took some time to get over the shock of the murder, but to his contemporaries he was the villain of the piece, and all the repercussions that followed were blamed on him.

It was certainly a game changer. A century later the prior of the Charterhouse at Dijon, showing off the damaged skull of John of Burgundy, is reputed to have declared, 'This is the hole through which the English made their way into France.' When next Henry's ambassadors met with the French king's council in Paris on 27 September, his demands had altered considerably. With the Dauphin effectively out of the equation due to his reputed involvement in the murder, Henry now proposed to take both the crown and the kingdom. He would marry Katherine without a dowry, since she would bring all of France with her, and he and his heirs would be acknowledged as the rightful heirs to France. He promised, however, that his two kingdoms would be kept deliberately separate, each with its own laws, customs and administrations. When it was protested that he had previously been prepared to settle for a good deal less, the reply was simply that circumstances had changed.

To turn this proposal into fact Henry had to convince four separate groups: the French court, and in particular Queen Isabeau; the Burgundians under their new duke, Philippe; the Parisians; and the English. Of these the last two were the easiest. To the Parisians, with Henry camped on their doorstep and exerting a stranglehold on their trade and their very lives, it was obvious that he would get what he wanted one way or another. If it could be done peacefully, so much the better.

The English themselves were beginning to feel the effects of the prolonged war effort. The year 1419 was the first in which there was no large contingent of new troops recruited for service in France, and in the parliament that assembled in mid-October concern was expressed about the amount of coin that was being sent out of the realm to pay for the ongoing hostilities. It was proposed that wool be sent instead, which could then be sold to raise the necessary money. Serving soldiers, too, were beginning to express a hope that there might soon be peace so that they could all go home.

It is often said that the twenty-three-year-old Philippe of Burgundy immediately threw his support behind Henry, but in fact the process was not quite so instant. Following a meeting of his representatives with those of the English king in early October, it was made clear to him that if he did not enter an alliance with Henry, negotiations might be opened instead with the Dauphin. To help persuade him, though, it was emphasised that there was no question of deposing Charles VI, which would be treason on the part of Philippe. In fact, it was said, France would be stronger and more united under Henry, who in addition promised to join with the new duke to avenge the murder of his father.

Philippe called a meeting of all his advisers at Arras but the options were clear. Under no circumstances could he support the Dauphin Charles, and Henry's proposal was the only real alternative. In early November his decision was delivered to the Earl of Warwick, the English envoy at Arras, and on 24 December a general truce was announced between France and England.

Immediately the blockade of Paris was lifted and work began to turn this general agreement on principle into a workable treaty. A known and trusted envoy, Louis Robesart, was sent from Henry to the French court, now in Troyes, to persuade Queen Isabeau to accept the English king as both son-in-law and heir. Once again accounts differ as to her reaction. In some she had already disinherited her son Charles, even declaring that he was not the true son of Charles VI. According to this version she bore him a bitter hatred, blaming him for the death of the young courtier drowned in the Seine, and for the seizure of her treasures when she had been exiled by Bernard of Armagnac. In other accounts she was more reluctant to take the dramatic step proposed. In general the chronicles are not kind to Isabeau, accusing her of extravagance, flightiness and promiscuity, though how much of this may be propaganda for the various competing factions trying to obtain control of her husband and son is not at all clear.

Whichever version is true, Robesart did his job well. On 23 March 1420 Duke Philippe of Burgundy arrived at Troyes. On 9 April an agreed text for a treaty was sent to Henry, now at Pontoise. Amendments were made and agreed on 5 May, and soon after Henry set out for Troyes, bypassing Paris on the way, to arrive on the 20th of that month.

The following day, amid much ceremony, the treaty was signed and sealed in the cathedral of St Peter at Troyes. Once again Charles VI was too ill to attend, and in his absence it was signed by Queen Isabeau, who thus added to her crimes in the eyes of many Frenchmen by giving away the country to the English. In a neat touch, Henry sealed the treaty with the seal used by Edward III on the Treaty of Brétigny.

It was the conclusion of five years' hard effort and was the high point of his reign.

11

THE LAST CAMPAIGN
1420–1422

The Treaty of Troyes was very much an echo of the proposals put forward by the English the previous autumn. It provided specifically for the marriage of Henry and Katherine (who were formally betrothed immediately after the signing) and for the disinheritance 'for his enormous crimes' of Charles 'who calls himself Dauphin'. The English king was to rule as regent for Charles VI in his lifetime, and after his death Henry and his heirs would inherit the throne in right succession. In the meantime he would drop the title 'King of France' and be known as 'Regent and Heir of France'. It was also made clear that there would be no change to the laws and institutions of France. Henry would be advised by a council of the French and would govern with the three estates of France, the *parlement* of Paris having supreme legal authority.

Not only was this treaty signed by the principals on behalf of France, Burgundy and England, but all French nobility, town officials and senior clergy were required to swear an oath to accept it, this order being issued in the name of Charles VI. It sounded like a full and final peace settlement but of course it was no such thing.

France in fact was as divided as before. Those 'in the obedience of Charles VI' would be governed by the treaty but all the lands south of the Loire remained loyal to the Dauphin. Even closer to Paris, particularly in fortresses along the Seine and the Marne, pockets of resistance held out on his behalf. Nor was it entirely plain sailing within 'the obedience'. Though the rank and file of the clergy were in general happy to accept the new arrangements – particularly as Henry was offering them special protection and privileges – a number of bishops refused at first to take the required oath, and the Bishop of Paris in particular was vocal against the treaty. Among the Burgundians, too, there was a measure of dissent. Some towns and nobles needed a personal visit from their new duke to persuade them to swear the oath, while the Prince of Orange flatly refused to do so and took his men away home.

Others were prepared to argue the niceties of the case. The right to the crown could not pass through a woman, and even if it could, how could it be transmitted through Katherine who still had two elder sisters and a brother living? The matter was even debated in the papal court and, despite the debt he owed to the English who had secured his election, Martin V never did accept the treaty.

The Dauphin's response was more blunt. In 1421 he issued a Manifesto Against the Treaty of Troyes containing a long list of reasons to oppose it. The crown belonged rightly to King Charles and to the Dauphin and should not be given away to strangers and ancient enemies. The honour and crown of France should be guarded by faithful and loyal subjects who should bear any pain to guard the honour of the fleur-de-lis and the crown. Giving away the crown was treason and would lead to eternal damnation. The 'damnable' treaty, full of 'malignity and fraud and deception', must be resisted by every good citizen, 'especially by the Pope, the prelates and the princes, by peers, notables and citizens and all who hate tyranny and uphold virtue and freedom'. Whatever others may have hoped for, the Dauphin was not going to take his disinheritance as final.

In the meantime on Trinity Sunday, 2 June 1420, Henry V of England married Katherine of France at Troyes. No doubt this came as something of a relief to his subjects on both sides of the Channel. He was in his mid-thirties, constantly engaged in perilous pursuits, and it was high time he produced an heir. At the time his heir apparent was his brother Thomas, Duke of Clarence, who had been married for some time but still had no legitimate child. (His illegitimate son John was with him in France.) Neither of his younger brothers had yet married, though under the terms of the treaty one was due to marry the sister of Philippe of Burgundy.

Henry's wedding seems to have been a fairly simple affair – it has been described as a soldier's wedding – attended by the English nobility in all their richest finery but by few of the French. The Duke of Burgundy in full mourning black must have struck a sombre note. As was usual at the time, the household appointed for the new eighteen-year-old queen was made up largely of the subjects of her new husband, with just a few French ladies-in-waiting. It was to be some time, however, before she had finally to leave her parents and native land to travel to England.

Only two days after the wedding Henry and his fellow army commanders left Troyes to continue with their unfinished business. Their immediate targets were the three Dauphinist strongholds, Sens, Montereau and Melun, spread along the River Seine to the south of Paris. Sens, the first to be attacked, offered very little resistance, and in fact its downfall was more like a social occasion for the royal party with both kings and both queens in attendance.

The whole group then moved on to Montereau, a place of particular significance for Philippe of Burgundy as the site of his father's murder. Although more resistance was found here the town fell on 23 June and the castle on 1 July. The body of John the Fearless was then exhumed from its hasty grave, sealed in a lead-lined coffin and taken away to Dijon by the new duke for a proper burial.

Though Philippe had gone the bulk of his men remained with Henry, who now moved on northwards to Melun, one of the closest of the Dauphin's fortresses to Paris. This town, commanded by Sire de Barbazon, one of the leading Dauphinist officers, was not going to give in without a struggle. The siege began around 9 July and has been described as one of the hardest of Henry's career. Some of the fiercest fighting took place underground in the mines and countermines dug to bring down the walls of the town. As we have seen, fighting in mines was seen as the height of honourable combat, the added danger making the fighters 'brothers in arms' under the code of chivalry. One particular encounter was to save the life of Sire de Barbazon. Coming up against a particularly strong and able opponent he asked his name, only to be informed he was fighting the King of England himself. Immediately he withdrew, and later, when the town surrendered on 18 November and his life was forfeit, he could rightly claim that the king was his brother in arms and thus that he should be spared. This was duly granted but he was then to spend the next ten years as a prisoner.

Melun held out for some eighteen weeks on the expectation that the Dauphin, who by now had assembled a large army, would be marching to their relief. In fact although always about to set out he never came, thereby remaining safely out of reach of the combined armies of England and Burgundy, which were sitting outside the town and hoping for a decisive battle.

The terms of surrender were not as generous as usual. Whether this was because Henry was for the first time outside 'his' duchy of Normandy, or because he wanted to impress the French, or simply that he was annoyed the siege had lasted so long, we don't know. For whatever reason those who were to be ransomed were held prisoner until they actually produced the money, and there was an unusual number of hangings.

Among the latter was a group of Scottish prisoners. The previous year the Dauphin had appealed to Scotland to renew the old alliance and a force of Scottish soldiers had been sent under the command of John Stewart, Earl of Buchan. Some of these formed part of the garrison at Melun, and despite Henry producing their king, the by now twenty-five-year-old James, to order them to surrender, they had refused to do so. On slim or non-existent grounds Henry now decided to treat them as rebels and a number were executed.

With the way to Paris now cleared, Henry finally made his entrance into that city on 1 December 1420. Beside him rode the King of France, joyfully greeted by his subjects, while, behind, the strength of the new regime was amply demonstrated by Philippe of Burgundy, the dukes of Clarence, Bedford and Exeter, the earls of Warwick, Huntingdon and Salisbury, and many other notables. 'No princes were ever welcomed more joyfully,' wrote an eyewitness. The following day a similar welcome greeted queens Isabeau and Katherine and their entourage.

On 6 December the estates general of France, clergy, lords and commons (or at least those of them within 'the obedience') assembled to debate the treaty. Charles VI appeared in person to address them and urge them to ratify it, which they duly did. Then, just before Christmas, the Duke of Burgundy and other members of his family made a formal accusation against the Dauphin and some of his chief officers. Before a *'lit de justice'* – a solemn meeting of the *parlement* of Paris – they were accused of the murder of John the Fearless. Needless to say they did not appear to contest the charges and in their absence were found guilty of treason against the honour of the King of France.

Christmas was celebrated in Paris, with the English king and queen holding court at the palace of the Louvre and the French in the lesser surroundings of the Hotel St Pol. There was some muttering about this on the part of those still suspicious of the treaty arrangements. The English were treating the French king shabbily and not giving him the honour that was his due. Nor did everyone take to Henry as the English had. He was thought to be cold and aloof and his plain speaking did not impress. One complained that he had only two answers to any matter that was put to him: 'It cannot be done' or 'It must be done'.

Immediately after Christmas Henry made arrangements to set out for home. He had been away nearly three and a half years and an anxious English parliament held earlier in December had urged his early return. Leaving the Duke of Exeter as Captain of Paris with charge over the French king, he initially spent nearly a month at Rouen putting the administration of the duchy of Normandy on a firm footing. Then, accompanied by his queen, by his brother Bedford, Bishop Henry Beaufort, the Scottish King James and the earls of Warwick and March, he set out northward for Calais. Clarence was left in France as his lieutenant, and to assist him he had some of Henry's most seasoned commanders, the earls of Salisbury and of Huntingdon and other most experienced men.

On 2 February Henry and his party landed at Dover to the delight of his English subjects. Once again their king had returned triumphant, and once again his mere presence in the realm immediately silenced all those who had been complaining about the length of the war and the drain on the country's resources.

Three weeks later Katherine was crowned Queen of England by Archbishop Chichele in Westminster Abbey. The king had no part in the service and there is no record of him attending. Nor was he present at the grand banquet that followed, where it was King James of Scotland who sat beside the queen. A charitable view might be that Henry didn't want his presence to overshadow his wife on her big day.

Even before that day the king had once more taken into his own hands the reins of government, meeting with his chancellor among others on 18 February. The Bishop of Durham, Thomas Langley, had replaced Bishop Henry Beaufort in the post in 1417. A safe pair of hands, he had already served as chancellor under Henry IV and devoted the best part of twenty years to royal service. In fact the arrangements Henry had made for his kingdom before he left in 1417 had worked so well there had been very little to ruffle the calm in his absence.

In October of that year the so-called 'Foul Raid' of Scots upon the north of England had taken place, led by Archibald Douglas and aiming to take the castle of Roxburgh and attack Berwick. They retreated rapidly, however, when John of Bedford approached with an army rapidly assembled from local levies, though they caused devastation in the places they passed through on their way home.

In November 1417 Sir John Oldcastle had finally been captured near Welshpool in the Welsh marches. Severely wounded, he was carried to London in a litter and appeared before Parliament on 14 December. His defiant speeches did little to help him and he was condemned out of his own mouth as a traitor and heretic, being sentenced to punishment for both. According to a contemporary account he was then dragged to St Giles's Fields on a hurdle, hanged with an iron chain around his neck and simultaneously burnt in a raging fire.

Now a parliament was summoned to assemble in May and in the meantime Henry set off on a tour of his kingdom. Part pilgrimage, part money raiser, it was also felt appropriate that the king should show himself to his subjects after so long an absence. Beginning in Bristol he travelled northward through Hereford and Shrewsbury, then across the Midlands to Kenilworth, Coventry and Leicester where his wife joined him. They celebrated Easter there on 23 March and then continued on through Nottingham and Pontefract to York.

It was while Henry was visiting a holy shrine at Beverley that news was brought to him of a catastrophe in France. For the first time the English had lost a battle against a force of French and Scots – and worse still, in that same battle his brother Thomas, Duke of Clarence, had lost his life.

As king's lieutenant in France Clarence had no doubt been following instructions to press southward against the frontier with the Dauphin. One account suggests he was conducting an old-fashioned *chevauchée* and collecting considerable plunder along the way. Another says he was pursuing the forces of the Dauphin, trying to bring them to a decisive battle. He certainly succeeded in that.

On the day before Easter while camped near the town of Vieil-Baugé he was informed that the combined Franco-Scottish force was not far away. At the time a major part of his force, including all the archers, were scattered about the countryside foraging for food and plunder. If the next day had not been Easter Sunday, the holiest day of the year, when fighting was out of the question, Clarence might have listened to the advice of the Earl of Salisbury and Sir Gilbert Umphraville to assemble his forces and draw up a proper battle formation before engaging the enemy. Instead he allegedly told Umphraville, 'If you are afraid go home and keep the church yard. For you have been with the king too long to make me lose my reputation and my name; you have always gained a reputation and I have none, so you would lose me fame by inaction.' Then, instructing Salisbury to collect up the men and follow, he set off at once in pursuit of a glory to match that of his brother.

His force of at most 1,500 mounted men was initially held up at a river crossing by a small group of French and Scots. Then, when they had forced a passage they found themselves facing some five thousand in full battle array. In tactics it was the reverse of Agincourt. Apparently Clarence and his few horsemen with no support attempted a cavalry charge on dismounted men-at-arms and archers. Once again the modern tactics prevailed. Not only was Clarence killed, but alongside him Sir Gilbert Umphraville, who despite his forebodings had refused to let him go to his death alone, and Lord Roos, another seasoned campaigner. The arrival of the Earl of Salisbury with archers and men-at-arms retrieved some part of the English losses, but the Earl of Huntingdon and John Beaufort, Earl of Somerset, were among those taken prisoner. Worst of all, perhaps, was the damage to the reputation of the

English army which was now seen to be less than invincible, at least when not led by the English king.

All the chronicles make much of the fact that Henry was not panicked by this news, indeed he kept it to himself for twenty-four hours while no doubt considering what was best to be done about it. Nor did he immediately rush back to France or even to London. Continuing with his tour, he and the now-pregnant Katherine visited Lincoln, King's Lynn and Norwich, with an excursion to make offerings at the important shrine at Walsingham, before returning to the capital in time for the meeting of Parliament.

It is likely that the king had always meant to return to France quite soon. He had, after all, substantial unfinished business there. What he needed now was men and money, and probably he had been prospecting for both in the course of his tour of England. Certainly he made no request for any extra subsidy from Parliament, instead obtaining what he needed by loans. This gave Bishop Henry Beaufort an opportunity to re-establish his loyalty and dispel the coolness that had arisen between him and the king since the spring of 1418.

The cause of this, probably unwittingly, was the Pope, Martin V. No doubt in gratitude for the bishop's role in obtaining his election, in December 1417 he appointed him not only cardinal and personal legate in England, but also confirmed his position as Bishop of Winchester. This put Henry Chichele, the Archbishop of Canterbury, in a very awkward position as he pointed out to the king early in 1418. As cardinal, Beaufort would outrank him, whereas as Bishop of Winchester he was subject to the archbishop's authority. The position was untenable. The king agreed and told Bishop Henry in no uncertain terms that he must not accept the appointment.

There was never a suggestion that the bishop might defy his king, but it was the first discordant note between the two in ten years of working together, and Bishop Henry had been doing all he could to mend the situation. Now, despite still having large loans unpaid from earlier campaigns, he made by far the largest single contribution to the current needs, more than eight times greater than the next largest, which came from the city of London.

On 9 June Henry set sail from Dover, having made a new will as he had on each previous campaign. With him were the Duke of Gloucester, King James of Scotland, the earls of Warwick and March and some four thousand men. Once again John of Bedford was left in charge in England. It is at this point that one of the contemporary chronicles ends, and the last few sentences are full of foreboding for the future. 'Our Lord the King, after stripping every man throughout the realm who has money, now returns to France. Woe is me! Great men and the treasure of the realm will be foredone about this business ... I pray that my liege lord may not become partaker, along with Caesar and Alexander ... of the sword of the wrath of the Lord.'

Arriving in France, even after so short an absence Henry found the atmosphere had changed. The victory at Baugé had put new life into the Dauphinists and encouraged others to give them support. In May a treaty was signed with the Duke of Brittany and as a result Henry could no longer rely on peace on his western border. Nor was the Burgundian alliance as strong as formerly. There had been trouble in Artois and Picardy, where the Treaty of Troyes had not gone down well, and although the new duke was probably easier to deal with than his father, relations between Henry and Philippe were also strained at the time.

The cause of this, Jacqueline of Hainault, was a niece of Philippe and sole heiress of William of Holland, who had died in 1417. Married off to her cousin the Duke of Brabant, a secure Burgundian supporter, she had soon decided her husband was not to her taste and left him to seek protection in the court of Henry V. Now she was actively petitioning for an annulment of the marriage, first to Martin V, and when that failed, applying to the disgraced 'pope' Benedict, still living in Spain. Despite requests, Henry had refused to return her to her husband, though his stance on this was not helping the unity of his cause.

Meeting with the duke, it was decided that Philippe would concentrate on restoring peace to Picardy while Henry would take his forces to tackle those of the Dauphinists who were now besieging Chartres. Once again it was hoped that the enemy might be brought to a pitched battle to allow the 'judgement of God' – which Henry was sure would be in his favour – to settle the whole matter.

Marching towards Chartres, the king paused at Paris to consult with his captain there, the Duke of Exeter, and to meet with Charles VI on whose behalf he was supposedly acting. It was reported that the town of Dreux to the west of Paris, which was held for the Dauphinists, had been causing problems for the capital, so that became the first target of the new campaign.

Dreux was besieged on 18 July and intensely bombarded, surrendering on 20 August. Then, having cleared the countryside around, Henry marched on towards Chartres. Once again the Dauphin was not prepared to face a second Agincourt and the besiegers melted away across the Loire where, try as he might, he could not get at them. The crossing was solidly held against him at Beaugency, and when he passed on to Orleans he found the town well fortified and prepared, and soon decided he had not the men and equipment he would need to carry out a successful siege. By this time the Dauphin had retreated even further to Tours and it was clear Henry had little chance of catching him and even less of bringing him to battle.

At this point, campaigning deep into France, it may well be that Henry was also experiencing problems of supply. In Normandy he had made great use of the rivers to bring men, provisions and equipment close to where he needed them, but now all this had to be brought a considerable distance overland. Possibly looking ahead to the vast areas of France he still had to bring under his control he might have had the first qualms about what he was attempting to do – or maybe, being Henry, he simply took the thought away with him as a logistical problem to be solved when the time came.

Returning to Paris, he soon set about a more immediate target. The town of Meaux, roughly thirty miles to the east of the capital, straddled a horseshoe bend in the River Marne. It was another of the pockets of Dauphinist support in the region, and replacing the enemy garrison with a friendly one would greatly increase the security of the whole area. Forcing a surrender, however, would be no easy task.

The town lay on the outside of the horseshoe to the north, and while this was well fortified and defended there was also an inner Marché, effectively on an island since a canal had been dug across the neck of land to join the two sides of the bend. The garrison was headed by the so-called Bastard of Vaurus, more robber-baron than army commander but unscrupulous and effective in either role. Neither he nor the Scots and Irish in his garrison could expect any mercy from the English king, and so it was in their interest to hold out as long as possible in the hope of relief or of simply outlasting the will of the besiegers.

The siege began on 6 October. Henry had done winter sieges before and was not unduly bothered by the lateness of the season. This time, though, the weather was against him. An unusually wet autumn and winter caused the river to flood, not only making it extremely difficult to maintain the siege, but also bringing about the same result as at Harfleur. Sickness once again spread through the camp of the besiegers.

It has been estimated that one in six of the English troops died at Meaux. Dysentery and rheumatic fever were the main causes, but the weather and a cut in rations due to supply problems would have made a contribution. Men died there that had survived Harfleur and Agincourt. Nor was sickness the only factor. While Henry daily bombarded the walls of the town, those inside fired back using some of the latest and best artillery pieces. The seventeen-year-old son of Sir John Cornwaille was beheaded by a gunstone while standing beside his father – who soon afterwards renounced all war and departed for home.

Morale was low. Even Cornwaille is reputed to have said they should have been satisfied with Normandy instead of grasping at France. Henry, however, was determined to see it through. Then in December came news that must have cheered them. On the sixth of that month, Queen Katherine had been safely delivered of a son at Windsor Castle. Christened Henry, his godparents were the king's brother John, Bishop Henry Beaufort and Jacqueline of Hainault. It seemed the Lancastrian succession was secured for another generation.

As the siege dragged on towards the New Year, Henry sent ambassadors to his brother-in-law the Duke of Bavaria and to the Emperor Sigismund dropping heavy hints that he could do with more men to help bring the siege and the war itself to an end. There is little doubt that he felt Sigismund had not lived up to his obligations under the Treaty of Canterbury – but likely the Emperor felt the same about him.

In the end it was the Duke of Burgundy who provided reinforcements. The town of Meaux fell in March and the Marché a few weeks later on 10 May. The siege has been called Henry's finest military achievement and his greatest display of leadership but its consequences were to be far-reaching.

Initially things seemed set fair to improve. The impact of the surrender of Meaux was such that another Dauphinist stronghold, Compiègne, surrendered at the same time, and a number of the French nobility changed allegiance and accepted the Treaty of Troyes. The terms imposed on Meaux were harsher than usual. Four men were hanged, including the Bastard of Vaurus and, with uncharacteristic vindictiveness, a trumpeter who had blared defiance at the king from the walls of the town. Large numbers of prisoners were taken, to be spread around castles all over England and north Wales while awaiting their ransoms. There was also, apparently, great wealth deposited in the town which was appropriated by the victors as some recompense for their labours.

This time, however, the king had not escaped unscathed from the dangers of the long siege. The king was ill. Though some have suggested the illness might date back as far as the siege of Melun the previous year, the first indication that something was wrong had come in late December 1421 when a doctor was sent from England to minister to him. Henry had been lodged quite comfortably away from the siege camp, but he would have visited regularly if not daily to conduct operations. It is most likely that the illness that struck him was the same as was carrying off men by the hundred in that unhealthy situation. Dysentery, most likely amoebic dysentery, is the usual diagnosis, and in the aftermath of the siege it was clear the king was struggling to regain his normal robust health.

On 26 May Queen Katherine came over from England, though leaving the baby prince behind in the care of his nurses. This was not a mercy dash to the bed of a sick man but a planned visit, accompanied by John of Bedford who was changing places with his brother Humphrey. At the time, in fact, Henry seemed to be improving and the expectation was that the summer weather would help restore him to full fitness. In the meantime, as well as welcoming his wife he was busy meeting with Philippe of Burgundy and his loyal commanders and making plans for the future.

The king and queen spent Whitsun together in Paris before their court and the French king's court moved together to Senlis. By July, though, it was clear there was no improvement in Henry's health, rather the reverse. Descriptions of the king at the time say he was emaciated and unable to eat or sleep properly. Some put this down to simple exhaustion after so many years of hard campaigning, but the problem was deeper than that.

In that same month the Dauphin, his army stiffened not only by French but by doughty Scottish fighters, was emboldened to make an attack on the town of Cosne on the edges of the duchy of Burgundy. Once again it seemed it might be possible to face him in the field for one decisive battle and Henry immediately set about assembling an army of his own, boosted by the thousand or so men Bedford had brought with him.

Of course Henry, their talisman, was to lead them, but when it came to the time he failed to set off with them. Instead he sent them ahead to Melun, promising to join them in a few days and indeed made a valiant attempt to do so. He was unable to sit a horse, however, and soon was being carried in a litter as far as Corbeil where it became obvious he could go no further. Bedford and Warwick were dispatched to Cosne in his place, and the king, after resting for some while, was transported down the Seine by boat as far as Charenton near Paris, and then carried to the nearby castle of Vincennes, his favourite residence in France.

Over the next three weeks the life slowly drained away from the king, though he seems to have been clear-headed to the end. He is last recorded as having taken part in government on 6 August, but on the 26th he was able to review and add a codicil to his will, clarifying certain points and particularly providing for his infant son who had not been born at the time the will was drawn up. Bedford, Exeter and Warwick were recalled from the operations in the south to attend the dying king's bedside, but there is no record of his wife being present and nor was she given any particular role under the terms of his will.

On 31 August it seemed the king was slipping away. Prayers were said and psalms sung around his bed, and once he roused himself to say that it had been his intention, when he had achieved his ambition in France, to travel to Jerusalem and reclaim the holy places for Christianity.

Then, according to one account, 'when he laboured in his last moments he cried out, "Thou liest! Thou liest! My portion is with the Lord Jesus Christ!" as if he spoke boldly to an evil spirit'. If true it might be the first evidence of self-doubt ever shown publicly by the king. After this, clasping the crucifix between his hands, he prayed, 'Into thy hands, Lord ...' and passed away, 'perfectly and devoutly ... in the tenth year of his reign'.

12

LEGACY

The king was dead. Henry the Conqueror as the French called him was dead. As the news spread across two kingdoms the initial feeling must have been one of shock. Against all probability the strong, energetic English king had predeceased his fifty-three-year-old incapable father-in-law – and his heir, now King of England and regent and heir of France, was a baby not yet nine months old. Though the death had not been abrupt and there had been time for both Henry and his followers to contemplate the future and make arrangements for what was to follow, still the outcome was never likely to be completely satisfactory.

It took some time for the body to be returned to England and the journey was slow and stately, planned in detail by John of Bedford so that all on the way might be impressed at the passing of the king. Despite some stories that suggest the corpse was dismembered and boiled, as if it had died on a remote battlefield, it is generally accepted that it was embalmed and sealed in a lead-lined coffin. There was plenty of time for such a procedure and all the materials necessary would have been to hand. In general the entrails would be removed and buried separately and there was some excitement in 1978 when it was thought that a pot dug up in a nearby church might contain these remains of the king. In fact it proved otherwise, and indeed one account has suggested that the body was so utterly emaciated at death that this stage in the process might not have been necessary.

A life-sized effigy of the king was made, dressed in royal robes and laid above the coffin, with a crown on its head and sceptre and orb in its hands. Then finally, a fortnight after the death, the funeral cortège set out from Vincennes. Accompanied by the dukes of Bedford and Exeter, King James of Scotland and Philippe of Burgundy, it bypassed Paris and arrived first in Saint-Denis (the resting place of the kings of France) where a service for the dead was held.

Travelling on by river, it reached Rouen on 19 September to be greeted by the tolling of bells and a great procession of clergy, citizens and Englishmen, all in black, all bearing torches and intoning dirges. The coffin rested overnight in the cathedral and then was taken to the castle where soon after Queen Katherine arrived, escorted by the Duke of Bedford and accompanied by a large number of carts containing the effects of the late king.

For some days the coffin remained at Rouen, presumably to allow time for all those in the area to pay their respects. Many of these, including Bedford himself, had responsibilities that would not allow them to accompany their king home to England.

On 5 October the cortège set out again, and travelled by slow stages through Abbeville, Hesdin and close to Agincourt before reaching Calais, where it was met by a fleet of ships assembled for the purpose, and carried across the Channel to land at Dover at the end of October. From here the sad procession made its way to Canterbury, Rochester and Dartford on its way to London, services being held in each place.

This time the crossing of London Bridge was not the triumphal celebration of earlier days. Accompanied by mayor and aldermen, bishops and abbots, and escorted by representatives of all the guilds of London, the coffin was taken through streets cleaned for the purpose to St Paul's Cathedral. Here another service was held and again the coffin remained overnight.

On Friday 6 November there was one last journey, from St Paul's along sombre thoroughfares, where no doubt every citizen crowded to get a view, to Westminster. On a black funeral carriage bearing banners and devices representing the Trinity, the Virgin, St George, St Edmund and St Edward, the coffin and effigy were laid, draped in black velvet and other costly cloths. It was accompanied by a great multitude of clergy, members of the chapel royal, lords, knights and members of the late king's household. Prominent among them were close friends and doughty fighters such as Richard, Earl of Warwick, who had been with the king since the early days of campaigning in Wales, and many others who had served him for a dozen years or more.

At Westminster Abbey the coffin was received into the church and laid before the high altar, close now to its final resting place. A short service was held and then a vigil kept overnight by monks from the abbey. Next day a solemn Requiem Mass was celebrated, and amid much ceremony the king was finally laid to rest, behind the high altar, close to the tomb of Edward the Confessor, and close, too, to the tomb of Richard II where he himself had overseen the burial of that unhappy king.

One part of the ritual, described as customary, would seem very strange to modern eyes. At some point in the ceremony a fully armed knight bearing the king's coat of arms and with a crown on his head rode up to the altar on a warhorse and was symbolically stripped of weapons and armour. The meaning would have been clear to the onlookers. An anointed king, a sacred person, was a knight for Christ on earth. Now, however, his fight was over and he must go into eternity without these trappings of knighthood and royalty.

And when at last the ceremony was over and the body of the king sealed up in its final resting place, it must have been with some trepidation that those who were left turned away to take up the roles allotted to them in the new order. Henry had made a will on each occasion when he had departed for France, adding his last thoughts in a codicil when close to death. The contents are revealing not only of the king's mind, but also of his assessment of the qualities of the people to whom he was entrusting his son and his kingdoms.

The two surviving Lancaster brothers, John, Duke of Bedford, and Humphrey, Duke of Gloucester, were the two most entitled to assume responsibility for both, but they were very different in character and in capacity. John, capable, loyal and dependable, had been acting the role of trustworthy lieutenant since his early teens. Perhaps if Henry had had only one kingdom to think of, things might have turned out differently. He had, however, the expectation of two, and in fact Charles VI had died on 21 October while Henry's funeral cortège was winding its way slowly up through France.

Of the two kingdoms it seemed likely that France would be by far the most troublesome, particularly as Henry had made it clear that he wanted the struggle to continue until all of that land recognised the Treaty of Troyes. John, therefore, was given the task of subduing France, and was appointed regent of France, on behalf, now, of his baby nephew, and specifically Governor of Normandy. There is a suggestion that Henry might at the last have recognised that obtaining all of France was a step too far. Further instructions given to his brother stipulated that he should make no treaty with the Dauphin that involved giving up Normandy.

Similarly he was told that the Burgundian alliance must be preserved at all costs. He even suggested that Philippe of Burgundy should become regent of France if he showed he wanted the job. (He didn't.) True to this and to the requirements of the Treaty of Troyes, John duly married Anne, Philippe's sister, the following year. Though this sounds rather like a shotgun marriage, records tell us that John and Anne had a very happy, though childless, marriage until she died of the plague in 1432.

It is interesting that the only Lancaster brother not given early responsibility was the one who would turn out to be the least reliable. His loyalty was never in doubt and he had shown himself capable enough in military matters at the siege of Cherbourg, with a particular interest in the new artillery weapons. Selfish and wilful, however, are some of the kinder adjectives that have been applied to Humphrey of Gloucester. These character flaws would appear to have been well known to his older brother, but with John having his hands full in France it was necessary that Humphrey should have responsibility for England. No doubt Henry felt that the solid administration he had left behind in the hands of long-serving, capable councillors would cause few problems. His qualms show through, however, in the rather ambiguous proviso that Humphrey should always be subject to John – a proviso that allowed the council to consistently refuse to give him the title of regent that he so craved.

With the care of his son, too, Henry seems to have shown some reservations. Though Humphrey was given the role of protecting and guarding the new king, his upbringing and education were to be the responsibility of Thomas Beaufort, Duke of Exeter, with parts to be played by a whole range of friends and servants of the late king including Bishop Henry Beaufort, the Earl of Warwick and Sir Walter Hungerford. Sadly, though the greatest care was taken in educating the king, instilling into him all the virtues and skills required of a Christian prince, the outcome was probably not at all what his father would have intended.

The executors of Henry's will – Bishop Henry, Humphrey of Gloucester, Thomas of Exeter and the chancellor, Thomas Langley – were charged with a number of other tasks. The king directed that his debts should be paid and it was Bishop Henry Beaufort who became responsible for this, possibly in the hope or expectation that he might recover some of the money he had, over the years, lent to the Lancastrian cause. It was an onerous task, some debts going back as far as the reign of Henry IV, while much was still outstanding from the Agincourt campaign. Some twenty years passed before all the liabilities were untangled and satisfied, and some of the royal jewels and precious ships that Henry had intended to leave to his son had to be sold in order to do so.

It was Bishop Henry again who took responsibility for the construction of the chantry chapel that the king had requested to surround his tomb. The tomb itself, paid for by Queen Katherine, was of Purbeck marble, on top of which on a bed of wood was laid an effigy of the king. Mostly wooden and plated in silver gilt, the head, sceptre and orb were originally solid silver. This was stolen in 1546 and the head is now a modern replacement made of resin. Around this tomb was built the chapel, with an altar and statuary reflecting the king's devotion to the Virgin and to the English saints who had been his predecessors in wearing the crown, St Edmund and St Edward. Carved around the outside are scenes from the king's life including his coronation and a representation of a knight in battle. For many years the saddle, shield and great helm belonging to Henry were displayed above the tomb, and these are still preserved, together with a sword which may be his, at Westminster Abbey.

The size of this chapel would have been impressive at the time when it was completed around 1450, though now it is dwarfed by the Tudor extensions beyond at the eastern end of the building. The fragility of the nearby tomb of the Confessor makes visiting difficult, and in fact, despite all the efforts of his family and friends to make a fitting monument, the casual visitor might miss the chapel entirely, the only view of the king now presented to the general public being that of the soles of his feet.

As one might expect, the will contained many legacies to religious bodies and for Masses to be said for his soul, and there were gifts of horses, books, jewels and other effects for family members and others close to him. Provision was made for his widow's dower from the Duchy of Lancaster and from estates in France. Money was left for gifts to the poor, some in particular to be distributed each year on the anniversary of his death when prayers should be said for him. It seems that this practice was continued for over a hundred years until the time of the Reformation.

Finally in the will Henry pardoned his enemies and in turn asked forgiveness of those he had wronged, directing that, where possible, restitution should be made to them. Chief among these ranked his stepmother, Joan of Brittany, who had a few years earlier been accused of practising witchcraft against her husband,

Henry's father. By some accounts it was her chaplain who accused her, though others say it was Henry himself who had her arrested and held in captivity while he seized her dower and other revenue to help finance his campaigns. If the latter is true he was certainly in need of her forgiveness, and she was immediately set free and had her revenues restored to her.

Such magnanimity did not extend to the high-ranking prisoners still in the keeping of the king. It would be another eighteen months before King James of Scotland would be returned by negotiation to the homeland he had not seen since he was a boy of eleven. He took with him then as his wife Joan Beaufort, niece of Bishop Henry and the Duke of Exeter, and immediately set about trying to impose on his own kingdom the 'good governance' and sound administration he had witnessed in practice in England.

As for Charles of Orleans, the will directed that under no circumstances was he to be returned to France until Henry's own son came of age and was able with good advice to make the decision himself. In fact he was finally freed amid great controversy in 1440, having spent the interim languishing in fairly comfortable captivity, composing poetry and love letters to his wife, one of which is recognised by some as the earliest example of a valentine.

The early and untimely death of Henry V gives us one of the great 'What ifs' of history. What if Henry had lived even a little longer – time enough to outlive his father-in-law and be crowned and anointed King of France? Would that have led to the total collapse of the already demoralised Dauphinist party? If not, in a little longer still could he really have achieved the total conquest of France? It seems even Henry himself might have begun to doubt that possibility at the end of his life, though that might have been as a result of the debilitating nature of his illness. Henry in full strength and vitality generally believed that anything he wanted to do was possible.

What if he had lived long enough to have a hand in the upbringing of his own son, maybe to have further sons, and to instil in them his own sense of discipline and single-mindedness? How would he have reacted to the events that unfolded in France in the late 1420s? We don't know. We can never know, but the possibilities are intriguing.

What is clear is that he was held in such esteem by those he left behind that they spent the rest of their lives trying to carry out his wishes. In another time or place there would have been no chance of a nine-month-old baby being acknowledged as king. Now with no whisper of dissent everyone set out to do what he could to secure the child's inheritance, and 'What would Henry have done?' became a guiding principle. Unfortunately without Henry's strong hand there to guide them it quickly became obvious that they could not at all agree about what it was he would have wanted them to do.

The supreme skill of Henry V as a leader of men is shown in the way he had managed over a long period of time to blend a disparate group of strong personalities into a harmonious team. Without him the cracks began to show almost immediately. At the very first parliament, sitting only two days after his funeral, the division between Bishop Henry and Humphrey of Gloucester became apparent, a split that would only grow wider over time. On the one hand the council and the nobility did not know and trust Humphrey as they had his brother. On the other he felt he was not being given the rights and powers due to him as a royal prince and guardian of the new king.

In France the death of Charles VI may in fact have tipped the balance away from rather than towards the English cause. The Treaty of Troyes was by and large accepted in the northern parts where John of Bedford immediately had Henry VI declared king, but south of the Loire loyalties remained with the Dauphin. Even in the north there was some feeling that it was more natural for the son rather than the grandson to inherit, especially when the latter was an unseen, unknown babe in arms. If nationalist feeling had grown in England in the last half-dozen years, at least the seeds of it were also present in French soil.

Initially, however, things in France seemed to be going well. Bedford acted with his usual efficiency to see that the policies set in motion by his brother were carried through as smoothly as possible. It has been suggested that many of the French actually preferred him to Henry who was seen as remote and aloof. The return of the Scottish King James to his kingdom, along with his Beaufort wife, in general took from the stage the many Scots who had been reinforcing the French, and there was even an extension to the territory ruled by the English in the next few years. After the victories at Crévant and Verneuil it seemed that the Dauphin might be doomed to be forever 'King of Bourges' (as he was contemptuously called after the place where he held his court) rather than King of France.

The Burgundian alliance was badly shaken, however, by the activities of Humphrey of Gloucester. In March 1423 he secretly married Jacqueline of Hainault, who had by now obtained a decree annulling her previous marriage from the no-longer-recognised Pope Benedict. As if this did not cause enough shock and scandal in Burgundy, he then set about raising an army to invade and recover control of her hereditary lands in Holland and Hainault, which were still under the control of her former husband, the cousin of Philippe of Burgundy. Although John of Bedford managed to patch things up with the Burgundians the alliance was never as strong again.

The greatest challenge to the English, however, came not from Humphrey of Gloucester or from the Dauphin, but from a peasant girl, Joan of Arc, who now appeared at the court of the Dauphin in 1429. By this time Bedford and his commanders, having achieved some notable successes, were besieging the great city of Orleans, while Dauphin Charles seemed to have lost all confidence in himself, and even in his claim to be the rightful heir. Within a few months, however, Joan of Arc, inspired as she claimed by messages from God, had restored his confidence, taken an army to relieve the siege of Orleans and even had him crowned King Charles VII in the cathedral of Rheims on 17 July 1429. Hurriedly a coronation was arranged in England for Henry VI one month before his eighth birthday, but events in France were deemed too volatile for him to be crowned King of France in Paris at the time.

The star of Joan of Arc shone very brightly but briefly. Persuaded to continue beyond her original inspiration, she took an army to the very gates of Paris before her first setback, and only then, when it had retreated and disbanded, was the young Henry VI rushed over to Paris to be belatedly crowned King of France. The coronation was an almost entirely English affair, the crowning being carried out by Henry Beaufort, now finally a cardinal, and the state banquet that followed seems to have been something of a shambles.

The jealousy of the former advisers of Charles VII soon led to the betrayal of Joan of Arc, who was captured by the Burgundians in 1430, sold to the English and put on trial for witchcraft. The French court declared her to be 'excommunicate and heretic' and 'infected with the leprosy of heresy' and she was burnt at the stake in Rouen in May 1431. Characteristically Charles VII made no move to save her.

If John of Bedford had thought that would end the problem he was mistaken. Once again the nationalist spirit in France had been stimulated. In England, too, there were further problems between Humphrey of Gloucester and the Beauforts. It seemed that whenever Bedford was in France there were troubles in England, and whenever he was in England there were troubles in France. The English parliament begged him to remain and take charge of the council, but when he did so raids and rebellions sprang up like a rash over the territories of northern France.

In 1433, following the death of his wife Anne, Bedford married again, once more hoping to shore up the weakening Burgundian alliance by taking as a bride Jacquetta of Luxembourg, niece of Philippe of Burgundy's chief captain. In fact this had the opposite effect, Philippe claiming to be outraged that his sister's death had been so briefly mourned and that he had not been consulted on the match. From about this time Philippe began making contact with the French, eventually engaging to bring the English to negotiate for peace. The negotiations took place at Arras in 1435 but came to nothing, the English being only prepared to offer a truce until the young king came of age in some nine years' time. The outcome, however, was the loss of the Burgundian alliance, with Philippe now finally accepting Charles VII as his rightful king.

The end of English power in France was not immediate but it was now inevitable. There were still some victories to come but the tide was running strongly against them. It was said that France, which had been given away by a woman (Isabeau), was won back by a maid (Joan of Arc). The death of John of Bedford in 1435 was a serious blow, as was that four years later of Richard, Earl of Warwick, who died at Rouen while acting as lieutenant of France and Normandy. The Earl of Salisbury had been killed at Orleans in 1428 and a whole generation of strong military leaders was coming to an end. Their replacements were not of the same calibre.

In England a peace party led by Cardinal Beaufort and William de la Pole, Earl of Suffolk, was in the ascendency, despite the fierce opposition of Humphrey of Gloucester whose power was waning fast. In 1440, despite Gloucester's vehement denunciations, Charles of Orleans was at last set free, and soon after Suffolk was proposing a marriage between Henry VI and a French princess as a further step towards peace. Margaret of Anjou was selected as close enough but not too close to the French throne. She was the daughter of Renée, younger brother of the Duke of Anjou and second son of the redoubtable Yolande of Aragon, and she had been largely brought up and trained by her grandmother.

Sadly, by the time of his marriage in 1445 it was apparent that the twenty-three-year-old Henry VI had none of the strong mental qualities of his father. Amiable and eager to please, he was happy to do whatever was advised by the counsellor who had his ear for the time being. Either as part of the marriage arrangements or certainly soon afterwards it appeared that the territories of Maine and Anjou were to be handed back to the French, and Henry seemed quite willing to do this without any thought of the future consequences of such an act. Had the long-sighted Cardinal Beaufort still been attending the council this might not have happened, but he had by now retired to Winchester to live out his days in peace.

With both Suffolk and now the queen favouring peace with France, though without being able to produce a satisfactory treaty, the removal of Humphrey of Gloucester, probably at the instigation of Suffolk, seems timely. Arrested in February 1447 on a charge of treason, he allegedly suffered a stroke and died a few days later, though some have claimed foul play on the part of Suffolk and his supporters as the real cause of death.

Having sold the idea of peace, however, Suffolk proved totally unable to achieve it. In 1449, a foolish raid by uncontrolled English troops provoked the Duke of Brittany to invade Normandy where he was soon backed up by Charles VII. The Duke of Somerset, showing none of the fire and resolve of his Beaufort uncles, put up a feeble defence and by July 1450 the whole duchy was lost.

Even before this Suffolk had paid for his failures with his life. In January of that year Parliament had insisted he be impeached and put on trial for his mismanagement. In an attempt to save his friend and counsellor, Henry decided he should instead be banished for five years, but the ship on which he set sail was intercepted and the duke summarily beheaded, his body then being left on the beach at Dover.

Less than thirty years after his death, therefore, all the lands won by Henry V had been lost again. Nor was this the end, for in the next three years Gascony, too, was attacked and retaken by the French, leaving the small district around Calais as the sole English possession.

The shock of this last loss may have been the trigger for the first mental collapse of Henry VI. In an attack frighteningly reminiscent of his French grandfather he spent more than a year in a kind of waking coma, not speaking or moving, being fed with a spoon and not even acknowledging the presence of other people. Even the appearance of his baby son in October 1453 did not rouse him. After six childless years of marriage there were rumours that the child was not Henry's, but in the absence of any sign from the king the boy was christened Edward and duly acknowledged as heir to the throne.

The first descent into madness was the spark that set alight the conflict that has come down to us as the Wars of the Roses – imaginatively named by a nineteenth-century historian with more than a dash of romance about him. Following the death of the Earl of March in 1425 the heir presumptive to the throne had been a strong and capable military leader, Richard, Duke of York. He was descended on both sides of his family from Edward III, on his mother's side through Edward's second son, Lionel, and on his father's side through the fourth son, Edmund, Duke of York. Although acknowledged as heir he had not been favoured by King Henry VI, and the queen, influenced first by Suffolk and then Somerset, was convinced he was trying to steal the throne. He had therefore taken no role in government and had been sidelined, first in France and then in Ireland, watching with increasing fury as the incompetent lords who had the king's favour frittered away the legacy of Henry V.

Somerset, despite his role in the loss of Normandy, had been welcomed back as chief advisor by the king, and there had even been talk of altering the law so the succession fell on him. He was, after all, the grandson of John of Gaunt, and therefore also a great-grandson of Edward III. All that stood in the way was the Act of Parliament passed in 1407 barring the Beauforts and their descendants from the throne. The birth of Henry's son, and also the king's sudden affliction, changed all that. Though Richard of York fully accepted the rights of the new baby he would not stomach Somerset depriving him of his own rights, as senior prince of the blood, to act as regent for the ailing king.

And so the events in England mirrored almost exactly those in France of fifty years before, as the nobles divided into rival parties fighting for the control of a feeble and incapable king. It needed no invasion now, however, to clear out a generation of the nobility. They did a good enough job themselves, even to the extent of, 'Your father killed my father, so now I will kill you.' There is a strange irony, however, about those who became 'last man standing' and claimed the crowns as king and queen.

Katherine of France, widow of Henry V, was of course required to remain in England to care for her infant son but was given no role in his upbringing. Her sole duty seemed to be to take him on her lap through the streets of London when he was still a baby and present him to Parliament. (Even here the story goes that he screamed so much that he had to be taken away. One can only speculate what might have passed through the minds of Henry V's noble warriors on bowing the knee to a bawling baby.) Soon there were rumours that the queen was falling for Edmund Beaufort (later to become Duke of Somerset) and a law was quickly passed to say that she could not marry without the king's consent and any man that did marry her without that consent would forfeit his lands for life. Since the king was still a six-year-old child at the time and the Act declared he could only give consent once he had attained his majority it was obvious that his consent would be a long time coming and Beaufort beat a hasty retreat. Sometime between 1428 and 1432, however, the queen may have married a bolder man, Owen Tudor, who at the time was probably the Keeper of the Queen's Wardrobe, a kind of superior steward. The marriage was never definitely proved but they certainly had at least two children (and probably more) together, Jasper and Edmund Tudor. The latter of these married Margaret Beaufort, great-granddaughter of

John of Gaunt through his eldest Beaufort son, John. The child of this marriage was Henry Tudor, whose slenderest of rights to the throne came through his mother, but only then if the Act of 1407 barring the Beauforts is disregarded.

Even more bizarre is the descent of his wife. Jacquetta of Luxembourg, the widow of John of Bedford, had travelled to England after his death in the company of his chamberlain, Sir Richard Woodville. Once again love blossomed and they were married in secret some time before March 1437. Their eldest daughter, Elizabeth, was widowed at the Second Battle of St Albans in 1461 and subsequently (some say by her mother's use of the dark arts) succeeded in enchanting the Yorkist king, Edward IV, to such an extent that he risked his throne to marry her. At first the marriage was secret (something of a family tradition) but later Elizabeth was acknowledged and crowned as queen, and it was their daughter Elizabeth of York who became the wife of Henry Tudor in 1486. It seems a very odd coincidence that the Tudor dynasty trace their origins on both sides back to women who were married to the two most capable Lancaster brothers, Henry and John.

Writing in 1908 in her *Groundwork of English History*, M. E. Carter declares of Henry V that 'his wars had won him great glory but they conferred no permanent benefit upon England and they brought many troubles in their train'. The first part is certainly true. He was in his time renowned throughout Europe for his military prowess though the cynical might suggest that his early death meant he had departed the stage before his house of cards came tumbling down. Comparing his reign with the troubled times before and the near anarchy that followed, however, it is easy to see why it was viewed as a beacon of order and achievement, at least by the accepted standards of the day. To modern sensibilities, of course, the invasion of another country, the sieges and the bloodshed are easy to condemn, but they were the common currency of life and death in the times in which he lived.

Harder to swallow for some late Victorian historians was his claim that in doing this he was carrying out God's will to punish a wicked nation and impose on them good governance. In considering what he calls Henry's 'double-faced and shifty diplomacy', Oman comments rather sniffily, 'The selected tool of Providence should not indulge in such tricks.'

Another result of his early death was that many of his contemporaries – friends, military commanders, household and advisers – outlived him in some cases by decades and all were determined to keep his memory alive. There were already accounts of his exploits written in his own lifetime but these were soon added to and perhaps embroidered by those left behind. Providing an example for his son to follow is one reason for this, but another is the use of his story to influence political decision making. Humphrey of Gloucester, for example, commissioned an Italian writer, Tito Livio, to produce a life of his brother in the late 1430s when he felt the peace party was moving too far from the policies Henry had recommended. Later the loss of Normandy and other French possessions was a spur to further writing, some containing new anecdotes and details, presumably gleaned from those still alive who had known the king. French and Burgundian writers, too, admiring of Henry's qualities if not always of his achievements, produced further accounts, in some cases claiming to be scrupulously neutral and in others clearly representing a national viewpoint.

In the next century the Tudors, with their peripheral links to the Lancastrian cause, were also keen to promote the memory of a time of glory for an English king. Henry VIII in particular saw comparisons between himself and his predecessor that went beyond just the name. He was, after all, in a similar position to Henry, the second in a line of kings that had acquired the throne in a less than conventional way, and was similarly anxious to promote a national identity and national unity. He also saw himself as following in Henry's footsteps in aspiring to recover English possessions in France. He used the title 'King of France' and actually invaded and fought one small engagement, the Battle of the Spurs, though at the request of the Pope rather than for national purposes.

This stimulated further accounts of the life and achievements of Henry V, culminating at the end of the century in the three plays of Shakespeare to feature that king. Although Shakespeare clearly made full use of the sources available to him his Henry is necessarily a character in a drama, and some would say that, although it guaranteed his immortality, it is unfortunate that the real king should have attained it by this process. For many if not most people, Shakespeare's Henry *is* the king.

It is true as well that troubled times did follow the king's death though not immediately, and it is not at all clear how far he can be asked to shoulder the blame for what happened later. For some the whole adventure in France is to blame and Henry 'made a grievous mistake in choosing his life's work'. For others it was the failings of the next generation who did not possess the qualities displayed by their parents that led to the catastrophe that followed. Shakespeare is quite clear that it was those who acted for the infant king that should be condemned: 'Whose state so many had the managing that they lost France and made his England bleed.'

No doubt Henry would have preferred not to die young with his projects half achieved and left to others. No doubt he would have preferred his heir to be older and more substantial. It seems, however, a little harsh to account these facts as failures on his part. Even those who accuse him of using his will to tie the hands of his successors, for example in directing that the war should continue, overlook the fact that the council was later quite choosy about which of his directions they would follow and which they would ignore. In the matter of Humphrey's regency, for instance, they firmly declared that the king could not dispose of government matters after his death. Perhaps at most we can say that his reign established a potential for later trouble, and without his firm hand and single-minded vision trouble duly followed.

When, however, we look for permanent benefits arising from Henry's actions we are on firmer ground. If his policies in France were ultimately counted a failure, such was the energy and capability of the king that there is hardly an area that his hand touched domestically that was not in some way improved. His overhaul of royal finances and the administration of government enabled a long-running war and a regularly absent king to be accommodated with very little fuss. While many would say that this was in large measure due to the quality of the men who served him, it must still be acknowledged that there is a skill required in finding the right man for the right job and then trusting him to do it. Henry demonstrated this skill throughout his reign, and we might note that it was something that seemed to be quite beyond the powers of both his predecessors.

Henry's formal indenture system and regular pay for his armies was also a substantial improvement on what had gone before, as was his control over those who served in his forces. The lack of looting, the purchasing of provisions and the discipline of his troops were all commented on even by his enemies. If, as some claimed, this was maintained purely by fear of his harsh reprisals, still it was more than most could manage at the time. Similarly his care for his men and his ability to keep a standing army in the field for long periods, including overwintering, was unprecedented.

The navy, too, benefitted from his care. Henry VIII is traditionally seen as the founder of the modern navy, but as Rodger comments, 'Until 1525 Henry VIII had done nothing by land or sea which Henry V had not done a great deal better.' He was the first to recognise the importance of controlling the seas, particularly between England and the Continent. It is from the time of his earliest intervention in government that the permanent office of Admiral of England dates. He set up the first regular patrols of the Channel by royal ships, issuing detailed orders to their commanders, and contributed substantially to both ships and shipbuilding, in particular establishing an embryonic naval dockyard on the south coast.

Henry was perhaps the first king to recognise the value of asking rather than demanding. His relations with Parliament were consistently harmonious and smooth, again in sharp contrast to those of his predecessors. For that he had to thank not only his own character and reputation, but also the skills of his long-time chancellor Bishop Henry Beaufort. Nevertheless, during Henry's reign Parliament itself was accorded a status it had rarely previously enjoyed. Generally stable and with a recognised role in government, it was becoming the natural place for the rising middle classes – the minor gentry of the countryside and merchants and lawyers of the towns – to express themselves and to expect to be heard.

One of the hardest questions to answer about Henry V is, 'What was he really like?' So many people have written about him, most with a particular view in mind, so many have borrowed his image to promote some ambition of their own, it is as hard to see the real face of the king as to see that of a model airbrushed to perfection on the cover of a modern magazine. All we can do is to try and draw a general trend from the variety of different descriptions.

That he was a military strategist and commander of genius seems undisputed. From his time to our own, military men who should know about such things have been unanimous in their praise. Equally unanimous is the acclaim given to his energy, hard work and sheer attention to detail. Meticulous planning is evident in everything, from the provisioning of the army gathered in Southampton in 1415 to the building of huts for his men for the winter siege of Rouen. He was apparently one of those people who needed little sleep, using the night hours to visit and encourage or to check that orders given had been carried out.

One virtue that endeared him to the Victorians was his impeccable clean living. Despite tales of his wild youth, no mistress has ever been identified and no bastard acknowledged, something almost unheard of for a prince of his day. Even those who relate such tales can find no speck against him after he became king. He was frugal, courteous but plain-speaking, careful of his religious observance, and if his humility in victory was a show it was a consistent one and well maintained in public and in private. Similarly if he had any secret vices they were so secret they have not yet come to light.

All the accounts, even those penned by his enemies, acknowledge his commitment to good order and to justice, for the least as well as for the greatest in the land. His care for the common people is not only well documented but evident from his regular actions.

Though Shakespeare put words into his mouth, his night-time visits to troops and encouragement of those on the march to Calais are recorded by witnesses and seemed to inspire rather than terrify, suggesting a common humanity rather than a controlling tyranny. Nor did this stop at caring for his own people. Many a town that could have been sacked was spared on his orders, and his tight control of his soldiers had some complaining about the lack of loot to be won on his campaigns.

It was not only for profit, however, that men followed him. Success and charisma are equally attractive but he was clearly a natural leader able to fire others with his own vision. Where some have claimed that he was merely lucky, the comment of the famous golfer comes to mind, that the more he practised the luckier he got. Perhaps it was Henry's meticulous planning and ability to seize an opportunity that made it seem that the dice rolled his way so often.

All these positives, however, are countered by others who see his single-mindedness as ruthlessness and cruelty, and his humility and religious practice as so much hypocrisy. Oman points out that, when piety and magnanimity threatened to get in the way of his ambition, it was ambition that won every time. There is no doubt he was a driven man, though whether it was pure ambition or something else that drove him is open to question. If his claim to the throne of France was hypocrisy, it was an hypocrisy maintained to the very end. With almost his dying breath he declared he believed his cause was just and that it should be pursued. Maybe had he lived he would have shown more flexibility in the matter. He was in general a realist about what could be achieved, though he often aimed higher than his contemporaries.

He has also been accused of being a religious fanatic, with the persecution of the Lollards in particular being laid at his door.

His views and practices were narrow and rigid, we are told, and the burning of Bradbury is singled out as a personal black mark. There is a danger here, and with the previous point, of viewing fifteenth-century actions with twenty-first-century eyes. In his own time his beliefs would have been entirely orthodox and his actions praiseworthy. Nor does it seem the act of a fanatic to spend so much time with his friend Sir John Oldcastle trying to persuade him back to what he saw as the true Church. In general it seemed the role of others to persecute and the role of Henry to attempt to reconcile. Perhaps a better target for rebuke might be his willingness to cut short the reforming work of the Council of Constance, which might have spared the Church he loved a great deal of anguish in the future.

Many have professed to find Henry hard and unlovable, though, apart from French comments about his cold reserve, that does not seem to have been the case for those who actually knew him. We know he loved music and books, which suggests he was more than just a man of action, but if there is an absence of a softer side to his nature the cause would not be difficult to find. Whatever female influences there were in his life were gone well before he entered his teens. His household at Chester was that of a prince not a child, and if from that time he was expected to play the part of a man in a man's world that must surely have left some mark on his developing character.

Possibly the greatest characteristic of Henry, though, and his most lasting legacy to his country, was his sheer Englishness. At a time when the idea of nation states was in its infancy he did more than most to forge a national identity. His determined championing of the use of the English language, and its adoption not just by the king but by his chancery and officials too, led to a rapid development and standardisation of literally 'the King's English'. In only a handful of generations the native tongue had progressed from the Wycliffite 'And sche bare hir first borun sone and wlappidde hym in clothis and leide hym in a cratche' to the King James 'And she brought forth her firstborn son and wrapped him in swaddling clothes and laid him in a manger'. The developments since are tiny in comparison.

It was not only in language, though, that Henry encouraged a feeling of national identity. He saw himself as king of all his people, not just the nobility, and after the divisions that had gone before set himself to draw all his subjects together in a common cause. An overseas war is always useful in such a case, and maybe that was also part of his thinking in reviving memories of Edward III and his claim to the throne of France.

More than that, his armies were by and large English armies, drawn from all parts of the country and all levels of society, many of them directly contracted to the king himself. His appeals for finance involved a huge range of people, from the bishop lending thousands of pounds down to townsmen contributing their tuppence. The war therefore became an English war with everyone in the country involved in one way or another.

Even the Church, important though it was, had to know its place in this England of Henry's. Bishop Henry Beaufort was prevented from accepting his cardinal's hat during Henry's lifetime, and there was the traditional tussle about whether king or pope would have the power to appoint bishops, settled with the usual English compromise.

It has been suggested that Henry consciously shaped himself into what he thought a king should be. The Arthurian legends were popular at the time and offer an obvious role model. Once again we need to be careful to separate the reality from the propaganda, but the accounts of Henry that have come down to us suggest that, in that as in many other things, he largely achieved what he set out to do.

It is that image too, of the hero of Agincourt, that has come down to us today, making Henry himself into a role model. When we want to be inspired by a national hero he is more accessible than Alfred the Great, more English than Richard the Lionheart, more stirring than Lord Nelson. It was not a coincidence that in the dark days of the Second World War Churchill demanded that a film be made of Shakespeare's *Henry V*, and that film itself was dedicated to those who were at the time fighting in Normandy in the very places where Henry himself had fought.

No doubt flawed and human as we all are, and more complex by far than the stage character, still it seems that Shakespeare's summary might be allowed to stand. 'Small time, but in that small most greatly lived this star of England.'

MAPS & GENEALOGICAL TABLES

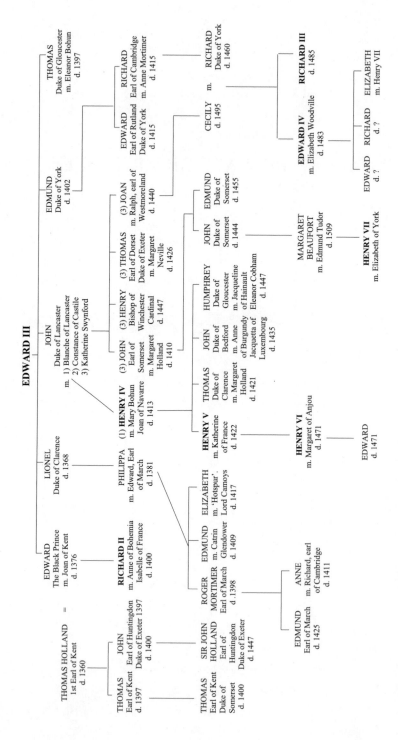

Family connections of selected descendants of Edward III.

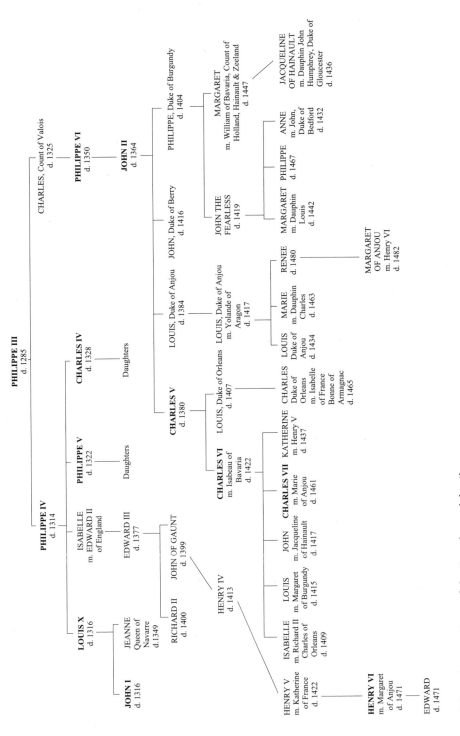

Selected connections of the French royal family.

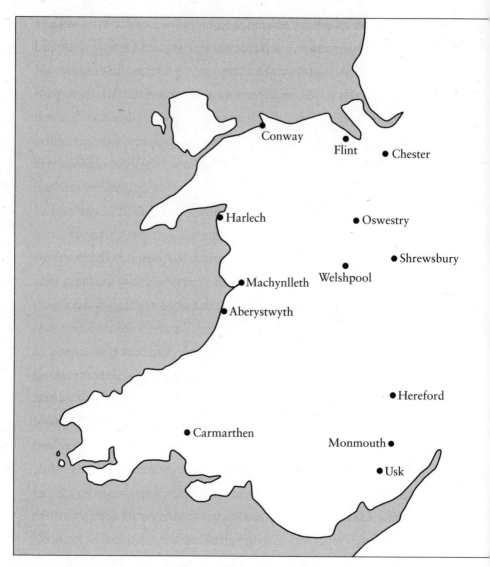

Wales in the time of Henry V.

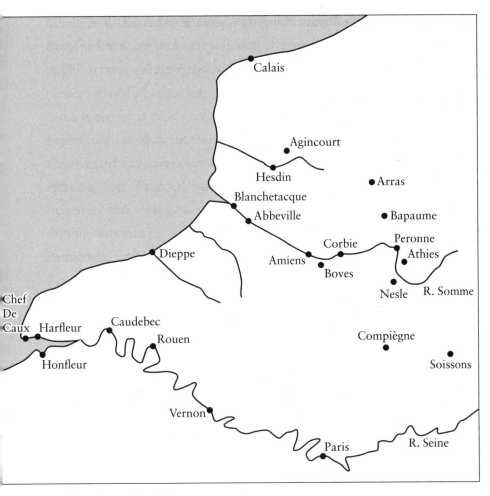

Key locations of the Agincourt campaign.

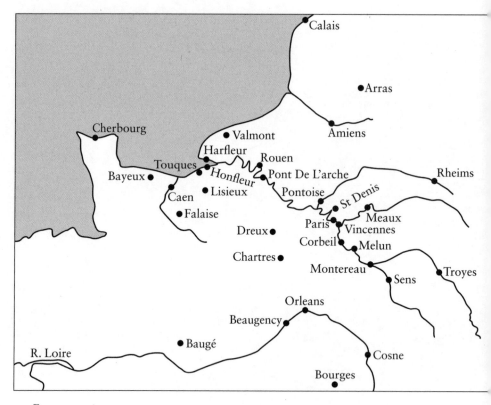

France, 1415–1422.

Appendix I

WHO'S WHO & WHAT HAPPENED AFTER AGINCOURT

The following information may help those who wish to know more of the extended family of Henry V, their rival claims to the throne, and also the further stories of many of the characters appearing in this book.

Descendants of Edward III

Edward (b. 1330, d. 1376), the eldest son, was later referred to as the Black Prince though the origin of the name is not clear. Famous (or infamous) for his exploits in France, including the battles of Crécy and Poitiers, he married relatively late. His wife, Joan of Kent, was his father's cousin. They had been brought up in the same household but Joan was married twice before she married Edward (see below) and a papal dispensation was needed before the marriage (which was apparently a love match) could take place. This was in October 1361, although there are some who claim they had been married in secret before this. Edward and

Joan had two sons: Edward, who died young, and Richard, who became Richard II.

Richard II (b. 1367, d. 1400) was born in Bordeaux and reigned from 1376 to 1399. He married Anne of Bohemia in 1382. Following her death in 1394 he married Isabelle of France, the seven-year-old daughter of Charles VI of France as part of a peace settlement. Richard had no children. One of Richard's lasting achievements was the extensive rebuilding of Westminster Hall together with the magnificent hammerbeam roof.

Joan of Kent (b. 1328, d. 1385) was the daughter of the Earl of Kent, but was brought up in the household of Edward III's queen, Philippa of Hainault. Aged twelve she secretly married Thomas Holland without seeking royal permission. The following year, when her family arranged for her to marry William de Montacute, heir of the Earl of Salisbury, she didn't mention the earlier marriage fearing her husband, who was overseas at the time, would get into trouble. For several years she lived with William until Thomas Holland returned, having earned a position in society by military prowess. After proof of the first marriage the second was annulled by the Pope and she returned to her first husband until his death in 1360. She is the ancestress of the Holland family and their close connection to royalty, and it was through her that her husband became 1st Earl of Kent in 1352. Her sons, Thomas and John, were the half-brothers of Richard II.

Joan's eldest son Thomas (b. 1350, d. 1397) became 2nd Earl of Kent. His son, also called Thomas, became 3rd Earl of Kent on his father's death in 1397 and was appointed Duke of Surrey later that year by Richard II. He was deprived of this dukedom by Henry IV in 1399, took part in the January plot against the king in 1400 and was beheaded by a mob in Cirencester. His sister Margaret married

John of Gaunt's son, John Beaufort (see below) and after his death in 1410 married Henry V's brother Thomas (see below). Another sister, Eleanor, married Roger Mortimer, 4th Earl of March (see below) and after his death married Thomas, earl of Salisbury (see below) one of Henry V's most important commanders in France.

Joan's second son John Holland (b. 1352, d. 1400) was Earl of Huntingdon. He married Elizabeth of Lancaster, sister of Henry IV. He became Duke of Exeter in 1397, was deprived of the dukedom by Henry IV in 1399, took part in the same plot as his nephew Thomas in 1400 and came to the same end, being beheaded in Pleshey Castle, Essex.

Joan's grandson, the son of the Earl of Huntingdon, was Sir John Holland (b. 1395, d. 1447), who by faithful service to Henry V regained the title and estates of his father in 1416. He served at Harfleur and Agincourt in 1415, led sea patrols of the English Channel in 1417 and later fought again in France. He was captured at the Battle of Baugé and only released four years later in 1425. Afterwards he was Admiral of England from 1435 and regained the title Duke of Exeter in 1439. After the death of Edmund, Earl of March, in 1425 (see below) he married his widow, Anne.

Lionel (b. 1338, d. 1368) was Edward III's second son and became Duke of Clarence in 1362. He had no sons so the title became extinct on his death until bestowed again by Henry IV (see below). Lionel's daughter Philippa (b. 1355, d. 1382) married Edmund Mortimer, 3rd Earl of March. She is the ancestress of the Mortimer family and the source of their claim to the throne.

Philippa's eldest son, Roger Mortimer (b. 1374, d. 1398) became Earl of March in 1381 following the death of his father. He was the nephew and heir presumptive of Richard II. He spent much of his time in Ireland as the king's lieutenant, and was killed there in a skirmish at Kells in 1398, his death provoking Richard's expedition to Ireland the following year.

Philippa's second son, Edmund Mortimer, fought against Owen Glendower in Wales. In 1402 he was captured at the Battle of Bryn Glas, and when Henry IV refused to allow his family to ransom him he switched allegiance to Glendower and married his daughter, usually named as Catrin. Edmund died at the siege of Harlech in 1409 and his surviving wife and daughters died soon after in London.

Philippa's daughter, Elizabeth, married Sir Henry Percy ('Hotspur' see below).

Roger Mortimer's son Edmund (b. 1391, d. 1425) became Earl of March at the age of six and again was heir presumptive until the usurpation of the throne by Henry IV. He was then held in custody at Windsor by Henry and at first was brought up with the king's younger children. After a plot to abduct him and make him king in 1405 he was moved to a more secure custody at Pevensey Castle until 1409 when he was given into the care of the Prince of Wales. When Henry V became king, Edmund was immediately freed and restored to his title and estates. He then served Henry faithfully, refusing to be drawn into the Southampton plot of his brother-in-law. He fought at Harfleur and was invalided home, but took part in the later campaigns in France. After Henry's death he was part of the regency council until sent as king's lieutenant to Ireland, where he died of the plague at Trim Castle in 1425. He had no sons and was the last Earl of March from his family.

Edmund's sister Anne married Richard, Earl of Cambridge, who was the son of Edmund, Duke of York (see below).

John of Gaunt (b. 1340, d. 1399) was Edward's third surviving son. He saw military action in France, Aquitaine and Spain, though with less success than his father and elder brother. He became Duke of Lancaster in 1362. John married three times, his first wife being Blanche of Lancaster. Their son Henry of Bolingbroke became Henry IV (see below). Their eldest daughter, Philippa, married John I of Portugal, while the second, Elizabeth, married as her second husband Richard II's half-brother John Holland (see above). She was the mother of Sir John Holland (see above) and later married Sir John Cornwaille.

John's second wife, Constance of Castile, brought him a disputed claim to the throne of the Spanish kingdom which he failed to turn into reality. In 1388 he renounced his and his wife's claim in a treaty which provided for the daughter of their marriage, Catherine, to marry Henry, the heir to the Castilian throne. In 1390 she became Queen of Castile and Léon.

John's third wife was Katherine Swynford. She entered his household as governess for his younger children, Philippa and Elizabeth, while his first wife was still alive. She was already married and had three children, her younger daughter being named Blanche after the duchess, who had her brought up with her own children. After the death of the duchess in 1369 Katherine became the mistress of John of Gaunt, her own husband dying some two years later. This relationship continued for more than a quarter of a century, producing four children who were given the surname Beaufort. In 1396, both their former spouses being dead, Richard II gave permission for them to marry and the children were later legitimated, though with a bar to them inheriting the crown. Katherine's son Thomas, from her first marriage, was the constable of Pontefract Castle when Richard II was imprisoned there and is accused of deliberately starving the king to death. Katherine's sister Philippa married the poet Geoffrey Chaucer. The Beaufort children were therefore the nephews and niece of the poet, and the cousins of his son Thomas Chaucer who was Speaker of the Commons on several occasions and later served Henry V in France, including at the Battle of Agincourt.

The eldest Beaufort son was John Beaufort (b. *c.* 1371, d. 1410). He became 1st Earl of Somerset in February 1397 and later that year Marquis of Somerset and Marquis of Dorset. In 1397 he married Margaret Holland, daughter of the Earl of Kent. Following the usurpation of his half-brother Henry IV the marquisates were revoked and he became again Earl of Somerset. Nevertheless he did not join in the rebellion of the other disgruntled nobles (including his father-in-law) who had had honours revoked, instead remaining loyal to the new king. He was given the confiscated estates of Owen Glendower, and served Henry in various ways, including being Admiral of England in 1407. Following his death in 1410, his widow Margaret married Henry V's brother Thomas.

John Beaufort had a number of children who made their mark on the history of the times. The eldest son, Henry, became Earl of Somerset in 1410 but died without issue in 1418. His brother John (b. *c.* 1403, d. 1444) then became 3rd Earl of Somerset. He fought in France in 1419 and later accompanied the Duke of Clarence on campaign. He was captured at the Battle of Baugé aged around eighteen years and spent seventeen years as a prisoner before being ransomed in 1438. He was created Duke of Somerset in 1443.

Edmund Beaufort (b. 1406, d. 1455) became 4th Earl of Somerset on the death of his brother John, but did not inherit the title Duke of Somerset. He was lieutenant of France from 1444 to

1449 and was created Duke of Somerset in 1448. Taking over from the Duke of York as military commander in 1449, his failures led to the loss of Normandy and then to the loss of the rest of English possessions in France with the exception of Calais. Despite this Henry VI favoured him as adviser over the Duke of York and the bitter division between these men led ultimately to the Wars of the Roses. Edmund was killed at the First Battle of St Albans in 1455.

Edmund's sister Joan Beaufort married King James of Scotland and accompanied him when he was finally returned to his kingdom.

Henry Beaufort (b. 1374, d. 1447) was the second son of John of Gaunt and Katherine Swynford and was educated for a career in the Church. He became Bishop of Lincoln in 1398 and Lord Chancellor of England for the first time in 1403. He resigned the chancellorship in November of the following year, when he became Bishop of Winchester. He was a long-time friend and advisor to Henry V, first serving him in the royal council when he was Prince of Wales, and as chancellor from 1413 to 1417. He was instrumental in the election of Pope Martin V but was not allowed to accept appointment as cardinal and papal legate in 1418. He eventually became cardinal in 1426. Following the death of Henry V he was an executor of his will and served as chancellor again from 1424 to 1426, clashing with Humphrey of Gloucester. In 1427 he supported a crusade against the Hussites in Bohemia, though without success. Later he raised troops which were used against Joan of Arc in France and was involved in her trial. In 1430 he accompanied Henry VI to Paris and crowned him King of France, but thereafter he pursued the aim of peace with France, being consistently opposed by the Duke of Gloucester.

The third Beaufort son was Thomas Beaufort (b. *c.* 1377, d. 1426) who made a major military contribution to the wars of his nephew Henry V. He was made a Knight of the Garter in 1399, probably fought at the Battle of Shrewsbury and commanded forces in 1405 against the rebellion of Archbishop Scrope, taking part in the irregular commission which condemned the leaders of that rebellion to death. In 1408 he became Admiral of England, having already proved his ability in patrolling the seas around the south and east coast. He was Lord Chancellor of England from 1410 to 1412, accompanied Clarence's expedition to France and in the same year became Earl of Dorset. On the accession of Henry V he was appointed lieutenant of Aquitaine, though the following year he was gathering forces in preparation for the first campaign in France. Taking part in the siege of Harfleur he was afterwards appointed captain of that town and held it in the face of French blockade and opposition until relieved in the summer of 1416. He was then created Duke of Exeter. In 1417 he was in England and took part in the repulse of the Foul Raid in the north. Next year taking reinforcements to France he received the keys of Rouen following the surrender of that town and then conducted operations in Normandy, including the long and successful siege of Chateau Gaillard. He took part in the negotiations for the Treaty of Troyes and was left as Governor of Paris when Henry V returned to England with his wife. He was at the bedside of the dying king and was appointed executor of his will, being given a share in the education of the young Henry VI. He married Margaret Neville in 1397 but their only son, Henry, died young.

Joan Beaufort (b. *c.* 1379, d. 1440) was the fourth child and only daughter of John of Gaunt and Katherine Swynford. Her second marriage in 1397, at the age of eighteen, was to Ralph de Neville, 1st Earl of Westmoreland. Their daughter Eleanor married Hotspur's son, Henry Percy, 2nd Earl of Northumberland (see below). Their first son (the tenth child of Ralph) was Richard Neville, who married Alice Montacute and through her became 5th Earl of Salisbury. Another daughter, Cecily, born at Raby Castle, was so beautiful she was called the 'Rose of Raby', though allegedly she had pride and a temper to match. She married Richard, 3rd Duke of York (see below), and was the mother of Edward IV and Richard III.

Edmund (b. 1341, d. 1402) was the fourth surviving son of Edward III. He was created Earl of Cambridge in 1362 and Duke of York in 1385. He was left in charge of the kingdom when Richard II left England to campaign in Ireland in 1399, but when Henry Bolingbroke returned from exile swiftly surrendered to him at Berkeley Castle.

His eldest son was Edward (b. *c.* 1373, d. 1415) who became Earl of Rutland in 1390 and held various posts under Richard II. He assisted in the removal of the Duke of Gloucester in 1397, received a large grant of his lands and was created Duke of Aumale in the same year. He was also given lands confiscated from Henry Bolingbroke on the death of John of Gaunt. He accompanied Richard II to Ireland in 1399 and some have claimed it was his advice that led Richard to divide his army on his return to Wales. After hearing of his father's surrender he quickly joined Bolingbroke. After the usurpation he was briefly imprisoned at Windsor and lost the dukedom but retained his other titles. He was implicated in the plot of January 1400 but revealed it to his father and to the king. In 1402 he inherited the title Duke of York. He was again implicated in a plot to abduct Edmund, Earl of March, and make him king in 1405 and was imprisoned in Pevensey Castle for seventeen weeks but quickly forgiven. He accompanied

Clarence on his expedition to France in 1412 and took part in the negotiations between England and France between 1413 and 1415. He accompanied Henry V to France in 1415 and took part in the siege of Harfleur. Commanding the vanguard of the army on the march to Calais, he also commanded the right wing at the Battle of Agincourt, where he was killed in the thickest of the fighting.

Edmund's second son was Richard (b. 1375, d. 1415) who received no inheritance from his father, raising a suggestion that he might have been illegitimate. He served in Wales in the early 1400s and became acquainted with the Mortimer family. Despite having no money of his own he secretly married Ann Mortimer, sister of Edmund, earl of March, in 1408. This marriage which was subsequently approved brought him no financial gain so we must suppose it was a love match. Richard was created Earl of Cambridge in 1414 but was 'the poorest of the earls'. While preparing to accompany Henry V to France in 1415 he was secretly plotting to overthrow him in favour of his brother-in-law the Earl of March. The plot was betrayed by the earl who refused to take any part in it. Richard was found guilty of treason and beheaded at Southampton in August 1415.

Richard's son, also called Richard (b. 1411, d. 1460), was descended through both father and mother from Edward III, his mother's claim possibly being stronger than that of the Lancastrian kings. His mother died when he was born and he was four when his father was beheaded. He became the ward of Ralph, 1st Earl of Westmoreland, and at the age of thirteen was betrothed to Neville's nine-year-old daughter Cecily. On the death of Edward, Duke of York, at Agincourt Richard inherited his estates and title, and in 1425 when Edmund, Earl of March, died he inherited the Mortimer estates as well. He succeeded John, Duke of Bedford, as lieutenant in France in 1436 and had some success before being replaced by Somerset (above) in 1443. He was an opponent of the peace party led by Suffolk and Somerset and out of favour with Henry VI, whose wife disliked and distrusted him. He became Protector of the Realm during Henry's bout of madness and was the leader of the Yorkist faction in the Wars of the Roses. Though he was killed at the Battle of Wakefield in 1460, his son was proclaimed King Edward IV soon after. His younger son, Richard, became King Richard III after the children of Edward IV were declared illegitimate.

Thomas (b. 1355, d. 1397) was the fifth surviving son of Edward III. He became Earl of Buckingham in 1377 and Duke of Aumale and Duke of Gloucester in 1385. He married Eleanor Bohun, elder sister of the wife of Henry Bolingbroke. He is chiefly famous for his persistent opposition to Richard II. Along with Richard, Earl of Arundel, he was leader of the Lords Appellant in 1388. He was arrested by the king personally in 1397 and imprisoned at Calais awaiting trial for treason. Probably on the king's orders he was murdered there, by or with the connivance of Thomas Mowbray, Earl of Norfolk, who was Captain of Calais at the time and who was shortly after created Duke of Norfolk.

Descendants of Henry IV

Henry Bolingbroke married Mary Bohun, probably in 1381, and had four sons and two daughters. Following her death and his accession as Henry IV he married Joan of Navarre, widow of the Duke of Brittany, in 1403. They had no children.

Henry V (b. 1386, d. 1422) was the eldest son of Henry IV. He married Katherine of Valois in 1420. They had one child, Henry.

Henry VI (b. 1421, d.1471) inherited the crown of England at the age of eight months on his father's death in August 1422. Two months later, under the terms of the Treaty of Troyes, he inherited the crown of France. A number of guardians and educators were appointed for him under his father's will. He was crowned King of England by Henry Chichele, Archbishop of Canterbury, on 6 November 1429, and crowned King of France by Cardinal Henry Beaufort in Paris on 16 December 1431. Declared of age in 1437, his marriage was arranged with Margaret of Anjou as part of a peace settlement with France. They married in 1445. His first bout of madness lasted from August 1453 to December 1454 and thereafter he suffered repeated bouts of this illness. Henry was deposed and imprisoned by Edward IV in 1461, but Margaret and Prince Edward (b. 1453, d. 1471) fled to Scotland to keep the war going. When Edward IV fell out with his major supporter the Earl of Warwick, a marriage was arranged between Warwick's daughter Anne and Prince Edward. Edward IV was briefly overthrown in 1470 and Henry VI returned to the throne. The following year Edward IV returned and won a decisive victory at the Battle of Tewkesbury and Prince Edward was killed. Within a month Henry VI died (probably murdered) in the Wakefield Tower at the Tower of London, ending the direct line of Lancastrian kings.

Thomas of Lancaster (b. 1387, d. 1421) was the second son of Henry IV and possibly his father's favourite. He was appointed Governor of Ireland in 1401 though he does not appear to have lived there all the time. He sided with his father in the division of 1410 and was created Duke of Clarence in 1412, leading a fruitless expedition to France in that year. Accompanying Henry V to France in 1415, he guarded the opposite side of Harfleur to his brother during the siege, and it was to him that the burgesses notified their intent to surrender on the morning of the final assault. He missed Agincourt but fought in later campaigns. He was killed after a rash cavalry charge at the Battle of Baugé in 1421. In 1411 he had married Margaret Holland, the widow of John Beaufort, but had no legitimate issue. His illegitimate son John, called the Bastard of Clarence, fought with him in France and brought his father's body home for burial in Canterbury Cathedral.

John of Lancaster (b. 1389, d. 1435) was the third surviving son of Henry IV. Knighted at his father's coronation, he was appointed in 1403 as Warden of the East March on the Scottish borders, a post he held until 1414. He was created Duke of Bedford by his brother in that year. In 1415 he was appointed lieutenant of England when Henry V departed on his first campaign in France, an appointment repeated in 1417. In between he took part in the visit of Sigismund and commanded the fleet at the Battle of the Seine which relieved the blockade of Harfleur. Joining the king in France in 1420, he was present at the signing of the Treaty of Troyes and at his brother's marriage. Returning to England, he was also present at Queen Katherine's coronation. He was briefly heir to the throne following the death of his brother Thomas in 1421, was present at Henry's deathbed and arranged the funeral cortège that returned the king's body to England. Appointed regent of France for Henry VI, he spent the rest of his life trying to carry out the policies of Henry V in France while keeping the peace between the rival factions in England. He arranged, but took no part in, the trial of Joan of Arc, and arranged the coronation of Henry VI in Paris in 1431. He was a notable patron of the arts and some of his illuminated manuscripts are preserved in the British Library. He married Anne of Burgundy in 1423, and following her death married Jacquetta of Luxembourg in 1434. He died at Rouen in September 1435 and left no children.

Humphrey of Lancaster (b. 1390, d. 1447) was the youngest son of Henry IV and instead of being given military responsibilities was brought up as a scholar. He was created Duke of Gloucester in 1414 by Henry V, to whom he was closely attached. He accompanied him to France in 1415 and fought and was wounded at Agincourt. In 1416 he was held as a hostage for the safe return of John the Fearless during the meeting at Calais. Following the death of Henry V he was appointed Lord Protector of Henry VI but the council would not give him the title of regent even after the death of his brother John. He was popular with the people but carried on a bitter feud with Cardinal Henry Beaufort. In 1422 his marriage to Jacqueline of Hainault threatened the Burgundian alliance. He tried and failed to recover her lands and then abandoned her. The marriage was annulled in 1428. He then married his mistress Eleanor Cobham, who was convicted of witchcraft in 1441 and forced to do public penance before being imprisoned for life. Following this Humphrey retreated from public life. He was arrested on a charge of treason in 1447 and died a few days later. Many of his collection of manuscripts were donated to Oxford University, where his name lives on in Duke Humphrey Library, in the Bodleian. He left no children.

Henry IV had two daughters, **Blanche** (b. 1392, d. 1409) and **Philippa** (b. 1394, d. 1430) and each was used to forge useful alliances. Blanche married Louis of Bavaria in 1402 at the age of ten and died seven years later while pregnant with her second child. Philippa married Eric of Denmark in 1406 when aged twelve. Her husband was ruler of Denmark, Sweden and Norway. Philippa lived mostly in Sweden and acted as regent on many occasions when her husband was absent. She had no living children.

The Warriors

Arundel – Thomas FitzAlan (b. 1381, d. 1415) was the son of the Earl of Arundel executed by Richard II. He was sixteen at the time of his father's death and was made a ward of John Holland, 1st Duke of Exeter (see above), who, it is claimed, treated him badly. Escaping to the Continent, the boy joined his fellow exiles, his uncle Thomas Arundel, former Archbishop of Canterbury, and Henry Bolingbroke. He returned to England with Henry and shortly afterwards was restored to his estates and titles, becoming Earl of Arundel and Earl of Surrey. Following the January 1400 rebellion he was present when the Duke of Exeter was apprehended at Pleshey Castle in Essex and it is claimed he got his revenge by demanding his execution. Having estates in the Welsh Marches, he fought in the Welsh campaigns against Glendower, coming to know the Prince of Wales, whom he later supported in the royal council. He was a commander in Henry's army in 1415, fell ill at the siege of Harfleur, returned to England and died soon after, leaving no legitimate children.

Warwick – Richard de Beauchamp (b. 1382, d. 1439) was the son of Thomas, Earl of Warwick, who had appeared as a Lord Appellant against Richard II and was later charged with treason.

Thomas was first imprisoned on the Isle of Man and then in the Tower of London (in the Beauchamp Tower) before being released by Henry Bolingbroke on his return to England and restored to his estates and titles. On his death in 1401, the nineteen-year-old Richard became 13th Earl of Warwick, and he was to become the closest friend and most reliable military commander of Henry V. He fought at the Battle of Shrewsbury and in Wales against Glendower. In 1408 he went on pilgrimage to the Holy Land, making a long tour of Europe in the course of his travels. Returning in 1410, he was again indentured to serve in Wales and in 1413 he was a steward at the coronation of Henry V. In 1414 he was appointed Captain of Calais and also sent as a representative to the Council of Constance. Some accounts suggest he was with Henry at Harfleur but he was certainly back in Calais to welcome him after the Battle of Agincourt. There he also received the Emperor Sigismund before and after his visit to England, and he escorted John the Fearless to the tripartite meeting there in 1416. From 1417 on he was one of the chief commanders of Henry's army in France and also took part in the negotiations leading to the Treaty of Troyes. Sent with the army to Cosne, in 1422 he was recalled to the dying king's side and accompanied his body back to England. In Henry's will he was given special responsibility for the education of Henry VI and spent the next fifteen years travelling between England and France to discharge his duties in each country. In 1437, when the king was deemed to be of age, Warwick was appointed Lieutenant of France and Normandy where he remained until his death in 1439.

Salisbury – Thomas Montacute (b. 1388, d. 1428) was the son of John, 3rd Earl of Salisbury, who was a staunch supporter of

Richard II. John was imprisoned when Henry IV came to the throne and when released joined in the plot of January 1400 and was beheaded by a mob in Cirencester. Although titles and lands were lost, Thomas was being referred to as Earl of Salisbury as early as 1409, and his marriage to Eleanor Holland restored his fortunes. He was one of the seven peers to try Richard of Cambridge for treason after the Southampton plot was uncovered. He spent most of his life as a soldier, serving as a commander at Harfleur and Agincourt and in the later campaigns. He led the reinforcements at the Battle of Baugé and recovered the body of Clarence. After the death of Henry V he became Bedford's chief lieutenant in France. He was killed by a cannonball at the siege of Orleans in 1428 leaving an only daughter, Alice. She was married to Richard Neville, son of Ralph Neville and Joan Beaufort (above), and he claimed the title Earl of Salisbury through her. He fought for his brother-in-law Richard, Duke of York, in the Wars of the Roses and was beheaded after the Battle of Wakefield in 1460.

The French

Charles VI (b. 1368, d. 1422) inherited the throne of France in 1380 at the age of eleven. A regency council was appointed to rule in his name until he took power personally in 1388. Before then he had married Isabeau of Bavaria, apparently falling in love with her at first sight. His first bout of madness took place in 1392 and it would recur regularly from then until his death in October 1422, changing his title from Charles the Good to Charles the Mad. He and Isabeau had twelve children. Among them were:

Isabelle (b. 1389, d. 1409), who married Richard II in 1396. Following his death she was allowed to return to France and married Charles of Orleans in 1406. She died in childbirth in 1409, leaving one daughter.

Louis (b. 1397, d. 1415), who became Dauphin in 1401. He married Margaret of Burgundy, daughter of John the Fearless, in 1412 and is credited with sending a gift of tennis balls to Henry V, a story which might be purely propaganda. He did not go to Agincourt but died, possibly from dysentery, shortly after.

John (b. 1398, d. 1417), who was Dauphin from 1415 to 1417. He was married to Jacqueline of Hainault in 1406 when he was eight and she was five, and was then brought up in Hainault. Following his death Jacqueline married (as her third husband) Humphrey, Duke of Gloucester (see above).

Katherine (b. 1401, d. 1437), who married Henry V in 1420. She was the mother of Henry VI and after the death of her husband married Owen Tudor. She was the mother of Edmund and Jasper Tudor and the grandmother of Henry VII.

Charles (b. 1403, d. 1461) became Dauphin in 1417. He had been betrothed for many years to Marie of Anjou and brought up in the household of Louis of Anjou and his wife Yolande. He was present at the death of John the Fearless but may not have planned it. Afterwards disinherited by the Treaty of Troyes, he was supported by the House of Anjou, in particular by Yolande. Proclaimed King Charles VII in some parts of France in 1422, he was eventually crowned at Rheims in 1429 after the intervention of Joan of Arc. In 1435 Philippe of Burgundy gave him his support and he gradually recovered all of France except Calais.

Charles of Orleans (b. 1394, d. 1465) was the son of Louis of Orleans, and therefore the nephew of Charles VI. He was thirteen years old when his father was assassinated by John the Fearless. He had married Isabelle of Valois in 1406 (see above) and following her death married Bonne, daughter of Bernard of Armagnac, in 1410. His father-in-law took up his cause as leader of the Armagnacs. Charles was captured at Agincourt and spent the next twenty-four years as a prisoner in England, during which time his wife died. Following his release in 1440 he retired to his estates with his third wife, Marie of Cleeves, and continued with the writing and reading he had pursued while a prisoner. He was a notable patron of the arts.

Louis of Anjou (b. 1377, d. 1417) was a cousin of Charles VI and became Duke of Anjou in 1384. He married Yolande of Aragon in 1400. Their son Louis was betrothed to the daughter of John the Fearless but the engagement was called off when they changed allegiance to the Armagnacs following mob violence in Paris instigated by John. Their daughter Marie married Charles of Valois, who became Dauphin in 1417 and later King Charles VII. Their son Renée was the father of Margaret of Anjou, who married Henry VI (see above). Louis of Anjou was not at Agincourt, apparently due to illness. Afterwards he returned to Anjou and died there in 1417.

John, Duke of Berry (b. 1340, d. 1416), was an uncle of Charles VI. He was present at the Battle of Poitiers and saw his father taken prisoner by the English. He served on the regency council of Charles VI and later tried to act as a peacemaker between the different factions. He prevented the king and Dauphin from attending the Battle of Agincourt and died the following year.

Charles d'Albret (b. *c.* 1369, d. 1415) was born into a Gascon family and spent most of his life in the service of France. He became Constable of France in 1402, a post he held until his death, with the exception of the time of the Burgundian occupation from 1411 to 1413. In the early 1400s he campaigned in Aquitaine with Louis of Orleans and Bernard of Armagnac, and later strongly supported them against the Burgundians. He was part of the group negotiating with Henry V prior to his invasion of France. In 1415 he was appointed the king's lieutenant for the defence of France, but was unable to prevent the royal princes insisting on a battle with the forces of Henry V. He was accused of treason by some for not preventing the landing of Henry and for not relieving Harfleur. He fought and was killed in the vanguard at Agincourt, and despite this some again suggested he had deserted the French cause. He was buried before the grand altar in a church in Hesdin near Agincourt.

Marshal Boucicaut (b. 1366, d. 1421) was originally Jean Le Maigre. He began as a page in the court of Charles VI, was knighted at the age of sixteen and travelled and fought all over Europe including in Prussia and Spain. He fought the Ottoman Turks at the Battle of Nicopolis and was taken prisoner, eventually being ransomed. He was named Marshal of France in 1391 and later became Governor of Genoa when that was subject to French rule. In 1415 he was named captain-general of the French forces, fought in the vanguard at Agincourt and was taken prisoner. Never ransomed, he died in 1421 in Yorkshire.

Bernard of Armagnac (b. 1360, d. 1418) became Count of Armagnac on the death of his elder brother in 1391. He married

Bonne, daughter of the Duke of Berry, and their daughter, also Bonne, married Charles, Duke of Orleans, whose cause he then took up against John of Burgundy. He became Constable of France and head of the Dauphin's government in 1415 and held the post until he was killed during the Burgundian insurrection in Paris in 1418.

Raoul de Gaucort (b. 1371, d. 1462) was a long-time servant of the French Crown whose family came originally from Picardy. Much of his early fighting was done in the company of Marshal Boucicaut, including at Nicopolis where he was knighted, and where he was also captured and ransomed. Both held strong chivalric ideas. He was sent to the defence of Harfleur and became a prisoner of the English when it surrendered. He took Henry's challenge to the Dauphin, and then surrendered himself in Calais and was transported to England. His ransom was set to include not only money but the recovery of jewels belonging to Henry which had been lost at Agincourt and the freedom of certain English prisoners. De Gaucort himself was sent to obtain these, and though he thought he had fulfilled the demands, Henry disagreed. On his deathbed Henry instructed that de Gaucort should not be freed until Henry VI came of age, but he finally gained his liberty in 1425 as part of a deal to secure the release of John Holland, Earl of Huntingdon, who had been captured at Baugé. On returning to France de Gaucort immediately took up arms again against the English and fought in every campaign to drive them from France. He was Captain of Orleans during the siege in 1428, championed Joan of Arc and was present to see Charles VII crowned in Rheims in 1429. By the time of his death all that was left to the English in France was Calais.

Rebels and Traitors

The Percys were major landowners and magnates in the north-east of England whose ancestors had come over with William the Conqueror.

The 1st Earl of Northumberland was Henry Percy (b. 1341, d. 1408). He had been a follower of Edward III, particularly active in keeping the Scottish border, and was a long-time Warden of the Scottish Marches. He was created earl in 1377 at the coronation of Richard II. Ten years later his brother Thomas was created Earl of Worcester.

Henry's son, also Henry Percy (b. 1364, d. 1403) was one of the most famous figures of his day. Nicknamed 'Hotspur' by the Scots for his speed in rushing to battle, he fought for Richard II in Scotland and France. At the Battle of Otterburn in Scotland in 1388 he had been taken prisoner and ransomed, and had then undertaken further diplomatic and military missions for the Crown, including acting as deputy to John of Gaunt in Aquitaine.

Both Percys supported Henry Bolingbroke when he landed in 1399 supposedly to claim his inheritance. Both had further supported his claim to the throne and served him for a number of years in Wales and on the Scottish borders. By 1403, however, both father and son had a long list of grievances against him, not least of which was his failure to pay wages due for defending the Scottish borders.

At the Battle of Shrewsbury in 1403 Hotspur was killed and his uncle the Earl of Worcester beheaded. The Earl of Northumberland, who had not taken part in the battle, was pardoned for his share in the rebellion, but then joined in Scrope's rebellion in 1405. When that failed he fled to Scotland, taking with him Hotspur's son, also

Henry Percy (b. 1393, d. 1455). The Percy lands and castles in the north-east were confiscated and distributed between the Earl of Westmoreland and Henry IV's son, John of Lancaster, who also took over as Warden of the East March on the Scottish border.

The Earl of Northumberland finally lost his life at the Battle of Bramham Moor in 1408, a further attack on Henry IV. Hotspur's widow married Lord Camoys, who commanded with great distinction the rearguard of the English forces at Agincourt and was afterwards made a Knight of the Garter.

Young Henry Percy was released as part of a prisoner swap with Scotland in 1416. As part of that deal he was required to marry Eleanor Neville, daughter of the Earl of Westmoreland. With estates restored, and created 2nd Earl of Northumberland, he then supported the Lancastrian kings until his death in the First Battle of St Albans in 1455.

Owen Glendower (b. *c.* 1350, d. probably 1415) was a descendant of the Welsh princes of Wales. Very well educated, he studied law in London in his youth, and married the daughter of a judge of the King's Bench. He returned to Wales in 1383 as a landowner with estates at Sycarth and Glyndyfrdwy in the north. He gave military service to Richard II and was knighted by him. At different times he served under John of Gaunt and the Earl of Arundel, and it is claimed he was present as squire to Henry Bolingbroke at the Battle of Radcot Bridge. The 1390s saw the beginning of the land dispute that escalated into a full-scale Welsh rebellion. On 16 September 1400 he declared himself Prince of Wales and thereafter, aided by his cousins the Tudors of Anglesey, used guerrilla tactics to spread the revolt and avoid confrontation with the forces of Henry IV. His diplomatic efforts involved both France and the Pope. In 1404 he called a Welsh parliament at Machynlleth, was crowned as Prince of Wales and issued a manifesto of policies for an independent Wales. The coastal fortresses of Harlech and Aberystwyth were taken, and early the following year the 'Tripartite Indenture' was apparently agreed with his fellow rebels, Mortimer and Northumberland. This was the summit of his success, followed by a slow but steady decline. The end came with the fall of Harlech in 1409. Though Glendower and at least one of his sons escaped and rewards were offered for his capture, no one betrayed him. He was rarely seen in public again and never after 1412. A story which may be merely legend claims he spent some years in the household of one of his surviving daughters, passed off as a Franciscan friar acting as tutor to the family. According to one chronicle he died in 1415 and was buried on the estate of another daughter, though the whereabouts of his grave has never been definitively established. One son, Maredudd, accepted a pardon from Henry V in 1421.

Sir John Oldcastle (b. *c.* 1370, d. 1417) came from an old Herefordshire family. He held various positions in the Welsh campaigns of the 1400s, including as captain of Builth Castle and then Hay Castle. In 1408 he was at the siege of Aberystwyth. It was in this way that he first became acquainted with Henry, Prince of Wales. In 1404 he entered Parliament as a knight representing Herefordshire, but his status advanced on his marriage to Joan, the heiress to Baron Cobham. As Lord Cobham he inherited not only land and money but also a seat among the lords in Parliament. It is suggested he had been a confirmed Lollard for some time and his hand is seen behind attempts in 1410 to reduce the effect of the statute *De Heretico Comburendo*. He is known to have been writing to followers of Jan Hus in Bohemia about this time too.

He held a command on the expedition sent by Prince Henry to aid the Burgundians in 1411 and was still firmly in favour when denounced as a heretic on the basis of a book of his found at a booksellers in London in 1413. Condemned in 1413, Oldcastle escaped from the Tower to lead a rebellion against Henry V and, when this failed, he returned to hide out in his home territory on the Welsh borders. He has been linked to the Southampton plot of 1415 and some stirrings of Lollardy in 1416 before finally being captured in a violent encounter in 1417. Brought back to London, he was condemned again as a traitor and heretic and executed on 14 December 1417.

In the Shakespeare play, *Henry IV, Part 1*, the character Sir John Falstaff was originally called Sir John Oldcastle, though there seems no similarity between the two except that both are friends of Henry when Prince of Wales. When the play was published in 1598 the name was changed at the insistence of a descendant of the Cobham family, one of whose members had recently been Lord Chamberlain to Elizabeth I. In *Henry IV, Part 2* an epilogue specifically declares, 'For Oldcastle died a martyr, and this is not the man.'

Appendix II

NOTE ON SOURCES

The life and times of Henry V are unusually well chronicled, with both English and French sources giving eyewitness accounts of some of the major events. These need to be used with care, however. Both the king and his chancellor were adept at presenting a positive image to the country as a whole, and while it would probably be unfair to label Bishop Henry as a spin doctor, he could be powerfully persuasive in producing the correct response to events as they unfolded. Patriotism too played a part, the 'hateful swarms of Frenchmen' in one account being mirrored by the 'proud, pompous, deceitful' English in another. Bearing this in mind, however, we have a rich stream of chronology, anecdote and detail from which to produce a history of Henry V.

Adam of Usk was a canon lawyer who worked for both Henry IV and Archbishop Arundel. He helped establish the legal grounds for ousting Richard II and saw him a prisoner in the Tower of London. Later he worked in France and Flanders while his suspected sympathies for Glendower kept him out of England. His writings cover the period 1397 to 1419, being particularly good on the time around the turn of the century. While initially he is very supportive of Henry V, by the end he is complaining of high taxes and is full of foreboding for the future.

Another English chronicle of the time was compiled at St Albans Abbey, an important stopping place on the road to and from London, and which had a reputation for its historical writing. One major chronicle covered the three reigns of Richard II, Henry IV and Henry V, ending at 1420, while a shorter version had an additional section extending to 1422. Much of this has been attributed to a monk at the abbey called Thomas Walsingham, who for many years was head of the scriptorium. Certainly by him is another piece chronicling the history of Normandy, including the conquest by Henry V, which was written between 1419 and 1422. These works are very detailed, very contemporary and seem to be well informed, no doubt gleaning facts from all the important people who would have stayed at the abbey. As might be expected they are also pro-Lancastrian, anti-Lollard and anti-French, while the history of Normandy, which was dedicated to Henry, unsurprisingly invests him with every Christian virtue, describing him in glowing terms as 'everywhere and always victorious'.

Among eyewitness accounts we have two lives of Henry written during or very soon after his lifetime. The earliest, the *Gesta Henrici Quinti* (Deeds of Henry V) was anonymous, but various clues in the text establish that it was probably written by an English priest attached to the royal chapel, who was familiar with diplomacy, had access to the texts of treaties and probably was closer to Archbishop Arundel than to his successor. He is in fact our royal chaplain, who sat in the rear at Agincourt and recorded what he saw. His story gives outstanding details not just of the whole Agincourt campaign, but also other events he witnessed such as the Lollard uprising in 1413 where he seems to have been present with the king at St Giles's Fields.

A second account, the *Liber Metricus*, appeared a few years later. The author of this, Thomas Elmham, was a monk who became prior of the Cluniac monastery in Lenton, Nottinghamshire. Since he claims this is a shorter version of his earlier prose history of Henry, some have thought he might be the author of the *Gesta* but this is now discredited. Much information is the same as in the *Gesta*, though Elmham claimed he wrote only what he had witnessed himself or got from other eyewitnesses. He is the first to mention the tennis balls story, and to claim that St George was seen fighting for the English at Agincourt.

John Strecche, a canon at Kenilworth (one of Henry's favourite residences), seems to give us the news and gossip as it was current there. His short account of Henry V is rich in anecdotes. In one he gives us an account of Henry's response to the gift of tennis balls in words that must have inspired Shakespeare: 'Within a few months I will play with such balls in the Frenchmen's own streets that they will stop their joking, and for their mocking game win nothing but grief.'

Other contemporary English sources include the archives of the Exchequer, giving us details of the financing of campaigns; the archives of Parliament, which particularly detail the 'keynote speeches' of the chancellor at the beginning of a session; and some of Henry's own letters, showing his championing of the use of the English language for his own correspondence. Poems and ballads are also useful, such as the Agincourt Carol and the verse account of the siege of Rouen by John Page.

A little later but still drawing on the memories of those who were there, further accounts of the life of Henry were written. One, the *Vita Henrici Quinti* (Life of Henry V) was commissioned specifically by Humphrey of Gloucester in the late 1430s. Humphrey, a noted patron of the arts, had a number of scholars in his household, and an Italian, Tito Livio, was directed to produce this work. Its aim is clear. Directed to the young Henry VI, it tells him, 'You should resolve to imitate that divine king your father in all things ... by using the same methods and martial valour as he used to subdue your common enemies.' Needless to say, the work emphasises the military achievements of Henry and also the part played by Humphrey in these.

Around ten years later, another life history was commissioned, this time by Sir Walter Hungerford, who had played a major part in Henry's campaigns and been steward of his household. This, the *Vita et Gesta Henrici Quinti*, was written anonymously though a mistaken attribution to Thomas Elmham causes it to be known as Pseudo-Elmham. It contains stories of Henry's wild youth and his visit to the recluse on the night of his accession. Although the early years seem derived from other accounts, from 1420 it appears to draw on original sources, probably Hungerford himself and also possibly the French chronicles.

The French equivalent of the St Albans chronicle is that of the monastery of St Denis near Paris. This was a semi-official work that had been carried on anonymously by the monks there for some centuries. They clearly took their job seriously. Writing on Agincourt, the chronicler declares, 'I will acquit myself of my duties as an historian however painful it is to me.' They also took trouble to provide a detailed, well-informed and above all balanced account of events. While other writers in Paris and Normandy spoke of Henry as tyrannical, cruel and feared by all, the St Denis chronicler tells us that, having questioned prisoners of the English king, he found that though he seemed cold and proud this was not so and that he treated such prisoners with kindness and respect. Similarly he found from envoys to the king that he made it a point of honour to treat everyone courteously and affably whatever their rank. This, he says, would of course be different during a siege, when Henry's ruthlessness was well known.

In general, while French writers saw Henry's claims to the throne as utterly spurious, they were more concerned to apportion the blame for the conquest among the French factions. Jean-Juvenal des Ursines, present in Paris in 1415 and giving much detail on Agincourt, was strongly Armagnac, blaming Burgundians for the Treaty of Troyes, while Robert Blondel on the Burgundian side put the blame squarely on the Armagnacs.

The best-known French accounts, however, were written for the Burgundian court some time after the events they recorded. Enguerrand de Monstrelet, writing in the 1440s, had campaigned with Philippe of Burgundy and served in his court, and though claiming to be neutral his Burgundian sympathies do show through. He also claimed to be painstaking in collecting and sifting his evidence. His account is long and detailed, showing some admiration for the English king but condemning his treatment of Charles VI after the Treaty of Troyes. He also claimed that Henry ruled by fear and tyranny and that no one dared to look him in the face.

Similarly George Chastellain had both military and political experience when he became official chronicler to Philippe of Burgundy in 1455. His account covers the later years of Henry's reign and its aftermath. Again strongly critical of Henry, he nonetheless called him a valiant prince and a prince of justice, and it is a feature of all the French writers, however anti-English they may be, that they all refer to the king's personal courage and to his strong sense of justice and order.

SELECT BIBLIOGRAPHY

Primary Printed Sources

Book of London English 1384–1425, ed. R. W. Chambers and M. Daunt (Oxford: Clarendon Press, 1967)

Brut, or The Chronicles of England, ed. F. W. D. Brie, ii (London: Early English Text Society, 1908)

Chartier Alain, *Le Quadrilogue Invectif*, ed. and trans. F. Bouchet (Paris: Honoré Champion, 2002)

Chartier, Alain, *The Poetical Works of Alain Chartier*, ed. J. C. Laidlaw (Cambridge: Cambridge University Press, 1974)

Chastellain, Georges de, *Oeuvres. I. Chronique, 1419–1422*, ed. K. de Lettenhove (Brussels: 1863)

Chronicle of Adam of Usk 1377–1421, ed. and trans. C. Given-Wilson (Oxford: Clarendon Press, 1997)

'Chronicle of John Streeche for the Reign of Henry V (1414–1422)', ed. F. Taylor (Bulletin of the John Rylands Library xvi, 1932)

Chronicles of London, ed. C. L. Kingsford (Oxford: Clarendon Press, 1905)

Chronique d'Enguerran de Monstrelet, ed. L. Douët d'Arcq, ii, iii (Paris: Societé d'Histoire de France, 1876)

Chronique du Religieux de Saint-Denys, ed. L. Bellaguet, ii (Paris: 1840)

Elmham, Thomae de, Vita et Gesta Henrici Quinti Anglorum Regis, ed. T. Hearn (Oxford: 1727)

Elmham, Thomas, 'Liber Metricus de Henrico Quinto', *Memorials of Henry the Fifth, King of England*, ed. C. A. Cole (London: Longman & Co., 1858)

English Historical Documents IV 1327–1485, ed. A. R. Myers (London: Eyre & Spottiswoode, 1969)

Froissart, Jean, *Chronicles*, ed. and trans. G. Brereton (London: Penguin, 1968)

Gesta Henrici Quinti, The Deeds of Henry the fifth, ed. and trans. F. Taylor and J. S. Roskell (Oxford: Clarendon Press, 1975)

Historical Collections of a Citizen of London in the Fifteenth Century, ed. J. Gairdner (Westminster: Camden Society, 1876)

Parisian Journal 1405–1449, trans. J. Shirley (Oxford, 1968)

St Alban Chronicle 1406–1420, ed. V. H. Galbraith (Oxford: Clarendon Press, 1937)

Titi Livii Foro-Juliensis, Vita Henrici Quinti regis Angliae, ed. T. Hearne (Oxford: 1716)

Ursins, Jean-Juvénal des, *Histoire de Charles VI*, ed. J. A. C. Buchon (Paris: Choix de Chroniques et Mémoires sur l'Histoire de France, iv, 1836)

Walsingham, Thomas, *Historia Anglicana, ii, 1381–1422*, ed. H. T. Riley (London: Rolls Series, 1864)

Waurin, Jean de, *Recueil des Croniques et Anchiennes Istoires de la Grant Bretaigne, A present Nomme Engleterre*, ed. W. Hardy (London: Rolls Series, 1868)

Secondary Sources

Allmand, C., *Henry V* (New Haven and London: Yale University Press, 1997)

Barker, J., *Agincourt: The King, the Campaign, the Battle* (London: Little Brown, 2005)

Bennett, M., Bradbury, J., DeVries, K., Dickie, I., Jestice, P. G., *Fighting Techniques of the Medieval World AD 500–AD 1500: Equipment, Combat Skills and Tactics* (Staplehurst: Spellmount, 2005)

Carter, M. E., *The Groundwork of English History* (London: University Tutorial Press, 1908)

Curry, A., *Agincourt: A New History* (Stroud: Tempus, 2005)

Dockray, K., *Warrior King: The Life of Henry V* (Stroud: The History Press, 2006)

Earle, P., *The Life and Times of Henry V* (London: Book Club Associates, 1972)

Hibbert, C., *Agincourt* (London: Batsford, 1964)

Jacob, E. F., *The Fifteenth Century 1399–1485* (Oxford: Clarendon Press, 1961)

Maurois, A., *A History of France* (London: Jonathan Cape, 1949)

McKisack, M., *The Fourteenth Century 1307–1399* (Oxford: Clarendon Press, 1959)

Oman, C., *The History of England: From the Accession of Richard II to the Death of Richard III 1377–1485* (London: Longmans, Green & Co., 1906)

Ramsay, J. H., *Lancaster and York: A Century of English History AD1399–1485 Volume 1* (Oxford: Clarendon Press, 1892)

Rodger, N. A. M., *The Safeguard of the Sea: A Naval History of Britain 660–1649* (London: Penguin, 2004)

Soar, H. D. H., *The Crooked Stick: A History of the Longbow* (Yardley: Westholme, 2004)

LIST OF ILLUSTRATIONS

I gratefully acknowledge the help of Heathcliff Heroics with the illustrations.

1. Monmouth Castle. The Tower where Henry V was born. (Teresa Cole)
2. Monmouth castle ruins. (Teresa Cole)
3. Coronation of Queen Joan, second wife of Henry IV. (Jonathan Reeve JR1724b90fp8 14001500)
4. Battle of Shrewsbury 1403. (JR1817b90fp5c 14001500)
5. Battlefield of Shrewsbury today. (Teresa Cole)
6. Kenilworth Castle. (Teresa Cole)
7. English forces fighting Owen Glendower. (JR1819b90fp13c 14001500)
8. Westminster Abbey. (Teresa Cole)
9. Later extensions to Westminster Abbey. (Teresa Cole)
10. The Earl of Warwick being appointed as Captain of Calais. (JR1837fb90fp49c 14001500)
11. Henry V appoints ambassadors for the Council of Constance. (JR1844fb90fp64c 14001500)
12. English longbowmen. (JR1851b90fp80Lc 14001500)
13. Henry V sending letters to the French king. (JR1727b90fp81 14001500)
14. King Charles of France receives Henry's letters. (JR1840fb90fp56 14001500)
15. Emperor Sigismund. (JR1847fb90fp69c 14001500)
16. A battle at sea, circa 1415. (JR1848fb90fp72c 14001500)

INDEX

More Kings & Queens of England from Amberley Publishing

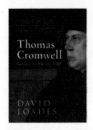

THOMAS CROMWELL
David Loades

'Fresh, fair, lucid and a pleasure to read'
HILARY MANTEL

£25.99   978-1-4456-1538-7   352 pages HB 27 illus, 20 col

INSIDE THE TUDOR COURT
Lauren Mackay

'A superb, sound, engagingly written & much needed study...
highly recommended '
ALISON WEIR

£20.00   978-1-4456-0957-7   288 pages HB

ALFRED THE GREAT
David Horspool

'If you have time to read just one book about the great man, you
should make it this one'
THE DAILY TELEGRAPH

£9.99   978-1-4456-3936-9   272 pages PB 40 illus, 30

THE PRINCES IN THE TOWER
Josephine Wilkinson

'Wilkinson investigates the prime suspects, asks wether they might ha
survived and presents her own theory about what really happened to
ALL ABOUT HISTORY

£18.99   978-1-4456-1974-3   192 pages HB

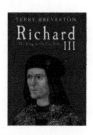

QUEEN VICTORIA & THE STALKER
Jan Bondeson

'The amazing story of the first celebrity stalker' **THE SUN**

£12.99   978-1-4456-0697-2   224 pages PB 47 illus

RICHARD III
Terry Breverton

£16.99   978-1-4456-2105-0   200 pages HB 20 col illus

CATHERINE HOWARD
Lacey Baldwin Smith

'Beautifully written'
SUZANNAH LIPSCOMB, BBC HISTORY MAGAZIN

£9.99   978-1-84868-521-5   288 pages PB 25 col illu

JANE SEYMOUR
David Loades

£20.00   978-1-4456-1157-0   192 pages HB 40 illus, 2

RICHARD III
Amy Licence

£9.99 978-1-4456-2175-3
96 pages PB 75 col illus

THE KINGS AND QUEENS OF ENGLAND
Robert J. Parker

£9.99 978-1-4456-1497-7
128 pages PB 80 illus

ANNE OF CLEVES
Elizabeth Norton

£9.99 978-1-4456-0183-0
224 pages PB 57 illus, 27 col

RICHARD III
Peter Rex

£12.99 978-1-4456-047(
256 pages PB 30 col ill

Also available as ebooks
Available from all good bookshops or to order direct
Please call **01453-847-800 www.amberleybooks.com**